Peter Kavanagh

THE STORY OF THE ABBEY THEATRE

"The Story of The

Abbey Theatre "

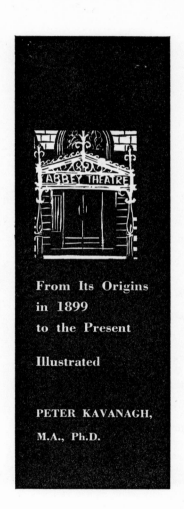

From Its Origins
in 1899
to the Present

Illustrated

PETER KAVANAGH,
M.A., Ph.D.

THE DEVIN-ADAIR COMPANY • NEW YORK • 1950

By the same author

THE IRISH THEATRE

*Being a History of the Drama in
Ireland From the Earliest Period
up to the Present Day*

For Miriam

CONTENTS

ACKNOWLEDGMENTS

I received help from many sources in the preparation of this book. My first thanks are to Dr. Hayes, Director of the National Library of Ireland, and to his staff, for the many courtesies and the exceptional help they extended to me. They gave me every library privilege and allowed me to search through much uncatalogued manuscript material. Of particular importance was their permission to use the very valuable *The Diary of a Dublin Playgoer* by Joseph Holloway. Mr. L. Carbery, also of the National Library of Ireland, is thanked for his care and efficiency in microfilming many important documents for me.

Thanks are also due to the following libraries and institutions: to Mr. Hanna and the staff of Trinity College Library, Dublin; to the Public Record Office, Dublin, for giving me permission to copy the original Patent granted to the Abbey Theatre; to the Office of the Prime Minister for letting me copy the Patent under which the Abbey Theater presently functions; to the Public libraries of the city of Dublin; to the

Office of the Registry of Companies and Business Names, Dublin Castle; to His Majesty's Home Office, London; to the Office of the Lord Chamberlain, London; to the British Museum; to the New York Public Library; to the Newberry Library, Chicago; to the library of the University of Chicago, and to the Columbia University Library, New York.

The Irish and British publishers from whose books, magazines, and newspapers I have quoted are also thanked and my indebtedness to them is hereby recorded.

I extend my thanks to the following American publishers for permission to quote from books published by them: Appleton-Century-Crofts, Inc., for quotations from George Moore's *Hail and Farewell;* G. P. Putnam's Sons for quotations from Lady Gregory's *Our Irish Theatre;* Alfred A. Knopf, Inc., for quotations from Wilfred Scawen Blunt's *My Diaries;* The Macmillan Company for permission to use quotations from the following books published by them: *Reveries Over Childhood and Youth, The Cutting of an Agate, Dramatis Personae, Four Plays for Dancers, Wheels and Butterflies,* and *Last Poems and Plays,* all by William Butler Yeats; J. M. Hone's *W. B. Yeats,* and *Lady Gregory's Journals,* edited by Lennox Robinson.

I wish to give my special thanks to Mr. T. O'Conor Sloane III for the care with which he edited the manuscript for publication.

Peter Kavanagh

AUTHOR'S NOTE

My reason for writing this book is to vindicate the ideals of the original founders of the Abbey Theatre, to tell of their struggles and successes and their perpetual battle against degrading influences.

From its beginnings in 1899 up to the death of Yeats in 1939, the Abbey was a theatre of the highest integrity. It was dedicated to a poetic ideal. From 1930 on I attended all of its productions—new plays and revivals—and I received the highest excitement from them. Even discussing the plays in the foyer during intermission was stimulating and memorable. For the Abbey was the center of Dublin literary life and one of the few places where the imaginative genius of Ireland found expression.

The Story of the Abbey Theatre is intended as a serious and positive exposition of Yeats's ideal and the ultimate decline of this ideal. As far as possible I have kept my own opinions out of the story so that the evidence might speak for itself.   P. K.

THE STORY OF THE ABBEY THEATRE

Introduction

The Abbey Theatre's contribution to dramatic literature during the twentieth century has been so great that the story of its extraordinary achievement is deserving of attention. Many of the small theatres that came into existence during the same period are remembered because they helped in the development of a single dramatist of genius: the Moscow Art Theatre (1898) produced Chekhov; the Théâtre Libre in Paris (1887) helped Ibsen; the Avenue Theatre in London (1894) produced Shaw's first play. The Abbey Theatre in Dublin, however, produced a whole school of dramatists, many of whom were of the first rank. Immediately the names of Yeats, Synge, O'Casey, Lady Gregory, Colum, Robinson, and Murray come to mind. To explain this phenomenon as an accident would be neither honest nor adequate.

The birth of William Butler Yeats at a period of great national energy was doubtlessly a fortunate accident, but the existence of the others cannot be attributed to the workings of chance. The story of the Abbey Theatre shows that the existence of so many fine dramatists in Ireland at this time was the result of a well-defined artistic policy on the part of Yeats. Yeats was more than a major poet: he was an inspiration, a flame from which men could light their torch. In addition, he was an organizer and a diplomat of the highest order.

Yeats succeeded in making the Abbey Theatre the model for all literary theatres, because his poetic imagination and intellectual courage kept him from condescending to tawdry ideas or to dishonest factions. Artistic and poetic integrity was everything, and though by its nature the drama must appeal to the crowd, Yeats would never cater to anything less than the poetic mind. Rather than woo his audience he attacked them, was contemptuous of their demands, and frequently drove them out of the theatre. Once, when he entered his theatre and discovered that it was more than half full, he turned to Lady Gregory and said: "Who are all these people, Lady Gregory? What can we do to drive them away?" Such was his attitude. If the audience disliked a play, he would take this as a compliment to the play and would certainly run it a second week.

Yeats would never lower his standard. He was content to perform his plays to a small, understanding group. For the mob, he had a savage hate. In an introduction to his last play, *The Death of Cuchulain,* he is explicit on this point:

I wanted an audience of fifty or a hundred, and if there are more, I beg them not to shuffle their feet or talk when the actors are speaking. I am sure that as I am producing a play for people I like it is not probable, in this vile age, that they will be more in number than those who listened to the first performance of Milton's *Comus.* . . . If there are more than a hundred I won't be able to escape people who are educating themselves out of the Book Societies and the like, sciolists all, pickpockets and opinionated bitches.

This attitude would annoy any audience, and it is not to be wondered at that it infuriated the Irish audience, particularly when his views ran counter to popular national sentiment. This was the basis for many of the fights in the theatre, which add so much interest to the story. Yeats had faith in his genius and in his judgment; never would he stoop to catch the applause of the mob nor alter his views to please the pettishness of an actor. He cared as little for the actor as he did for the audience, and whenever he entered the Green Room of the Abbey Theatre every actor and actress stood up. If the actors rebelled, as they did on many occasions, he dismissed them immediately at the risk of ruining the theatre. His view was that the author, not the actor nor producer, was the person who counted.

Ibsen is generally regarded as the prophet of the modern theatre, but Yeats took nothing from him and, in fact, disliked his plays. That Ibsen revolted from the commercial theatre was not sufficient reason to deserve the praise of Yeats. He did not revolt for the right reasons. The problem play, with which Ibsen replaced the conventional boy-meets-girl theme of the commercial theatre, was distasteful to Yeats. The place for debate or for propaganda was the newspaper or the pulpit. Yeats would have his plays create something new, express something of the depths of man's soul.

While it is true that Yeats, in founding the Abbey Theatre, copied from no one, it is possible that he was influenced by the Théâtre d'Art of Paul Fort in Paris. This theatre revolted from the naturalistic school of Brieux and Ibsen. Instead, it staged Maeterlinck, Marlowe, Shelley, and, most important of all, *Axël* by Villiers de l'Isle Adam, the father of symbolism in poetry and in drama. *Axël* excited Yeats, and he saw in its poetic quality something at which he aimed. The production of Shelley's *The Cenci* also interested him. It was under the influence of this symbolist movement that he wrote his second play, *The Land of Heart's Desire*.

When in 1899 Yeats laid the foundations for the Abbey Theatre, he was introducing no novelty to the Dublin audience. Ireland had had behind it a long tradition of support for the drama. A theatre had been built in Dublin in 1637, and James Shirley, the Elizabethan poet, had come from England to write plays for it. All down the years Dublin had had many theatres and was famous for its playwrights and actors. Playwrights of Irish birth were Southerne, Farquhar, Goldsmith, Sheridan, and Wilde. Actors were Barry Sullivan, Macklin, and Peg Woffington. In the nineteenth century, Dublin, no less than London, sank into the slough of accepting cheap, conventional, and spectacular plays. Irish drama before the twentieth century was a vigorous part of British drama. Little in it was distinctly Irish. Now and then a national sentiment would be expressed, but this was external to the play. The Abbey Theatre was a new thing: it was the first theatre to establish a drama in Ireland which would be distinctly Irish and of the highest standard. It would express the real spirit of Ireland, which had been suppressed for centuries by the British, and it would counteract the vulgar, journalistic plays imported from England.

It was not Yeats's intention that the new drama should descend to doling out nationalistic propaganda for Ireland. He took a higher stand. He felt that he and his associates were genuinely Irish and in sympathy with all Ireland's desires, that they stood on the high slopes of Parnassus above all politicians and wrote sincerely out of themselves. They knew that, because of their fundamental sympathy with Ireland, their plays, however remote from the problems of modern Ireland, were bound to express, subconsciously at least, the Irish spirit.

The public naturally supposed that a self-styled national theatre should propagandize for Ireland; because the Abbey Theatre did not do what was expected of it, many of its members were accused of being anti-Irish. This view was furthered by the fact that Yeats and all his associates in the new theatre belonged to the hated landlord class and were, with one exception, non-Catholics. The suspicion was always present that the Abbey Theatre was one more of the subtle weapons of British propaganda concealed beneath an Irish cloak.

The question was often asked how a theatre founded mainly by non-Catholics could be Irish. In this also, Yeats showed himself a man of great perspicacity. Just as the Abbey Theatre was not to be a vehicle of positive Irish propaganda, neither would it be one for Roman Catholicism. It was to be a "Celtic" theatre. Its inspiration would come from pre-Christian Ireland—a period rich in mythical heroes and romantic tales. This was the Ireland beloved by the tellers of folk tales. There is a richness, a romanticism, and a spirituality about the pre-Christian sagas which is absent from the heroic tales of Beowulf in England or of Wotan in

Scandinavia. Queen Maedbh, Connar Mac Nessa, Cuchulain, Deirdre of the Sorrows, Diarmuid, Grainne, Finn Mac Coul, and Oisin were popular, almost human, figures, beloved by every peasant. Around these characters Yeats would build his theatre.

The author has made use, for the first time, of the unique *Diary* of Joseph Holloway, which is now in the National Library of Ireland. Holloway was present at every Abbey Theatre performance, and his impressions total approximately fifteen million words in a script which is almost illegible.

HISTORICAL NOTE

Since about 1169, the year the British invaded Ireland, the population of Ireland has been divided into two classes: those who speak English and those who speak only Gaelic. The English speakers became the ruling class and are referred to as Anglo-Irish. England was generally regarded by the Anglo-Irish as the mother country, and English literature was to them the only literature. To this class belonged Berkeley, Goldsmith, Burke, Sheridan.

The Gaelic speakers, though a majority, always were treated as mere peasants. Although they had produced a considerable literature in their own tongue, it remained completely unknown to the Anglo-Irish down to the nineteenth century. Toward the middle of that century a few curious professors discovered Gaelic literature and undertook to translate many of the Gaelic sagas as a kind of scholarly exercise.

Thomas Davis, Gavan Duffy, John Mitchel, and a few other nationalistic politicians and journalists saw in the discovery something they could use to further their cause, and they wrote about it in their newspapers and preached it from their platforms. The Anglo-Irish did not care to listen, for they associated the discovery with nationalist propaganda. In 1878 Standish O'Grady, a brilliant Anglo-Irish writer and historian, made a special study of Gaelic literature and history and published his *History of Ireland,* which gave authenticity to the claims of Irish nationalistic journalists. He also translated into English, in popular style, many of the Irish sagas.

It happened that Victorian literature was running its course, was becoming barren, and Anglo-Irish writers were shocked but at the same time delighted to find a completely new field of inspiration opened to them.

At this precise moment, Yeats was born. Yeats belonged to the Anglo-Irish class and consequently did not understand the Gaelic language. But his imagination was fired by the O'Grady translations, and on many occasions he was to acknowledge his indebtedness to him. George Russell (AE), in an introduction to the works of O'Grady, spoke not only for himself but for all the writers of the Irish dramatic renaissance when he wrote:

When I close my eyes and brood in memory over the books which most profoundly affected me I find none excited my imagination more than Standish O'Grady's epical narrative of Cuchulain. . . . With reference to Ireland, I was at the time I read, like many others who were bereaved of the history of their race. I was a man who through some accident, had lost his memory of his past, who could recall no more than a few months of new life, and could not say to what songs his cradle had been rocked and what mother had nursed him, who were the playmates of childhood or by what woods and streams he had wandered. When I read O'Grady I was as such a man who suddenly feels ancient memories rushing at him, and who knows he was born in a royal house, that he had mixed with the mighty of heaven and earth and had the very noblest for his companions. It was the memory of race which rose up within me as I read, and I felt exalted as one who learns he is among the children of kings. That is what O'Grady did for me and for many others who were my contemporaries. . . . In O'Grady's writings the submerged river of national culture rose up again a shining torrent, and I realized as I bathed in that stream that the greatest spiritual evil one nation could inflict on another was to cut off from it the story of the national soul.

Anglo-Irish writers, having learned what they had been missing, were fired with interest in Irish literature and in the spirit which pervaded it. They looked for guidance as to how they might make the best use of their discovery. Yeats was there to direct the form it should take. He perceived that Gaelic-speaking Ireland rarely read anything, but it was always willing to listen—whether it be to a political speech or to a sermon. From Yeats's awareness of this fact rose the idea of founding a theatre which would be truly representative of the real Ireland so ignored by his class. From this the Abbey Theatre was born.

The Irish Literary Theatre

At the close of the nineteenth century the idea of founding a poetic theatre in Dublin seemed fantastic and even impossible. Ireland, it was said, was unprepared. But Yeats knew the country well, and he followed a higher logic. Living in poetic poverty in a London garret, he started planning the actual establishment of his idealistic and noncommercial theatre. He had no money, no company of actors, no plays except two he had written himself. Most embarrassing of all, perhaps, he had no audience explicitly demanding a theatre— at least such a theatre as Yeats contemplated. He had only a dream and the desire to realize it.

He would rent a small theatre, preferably in Dublin, but as a last resort even in the suburbs of London. There he would produce his own play *The Countess Cathleen*. For this he would need money: there was no hope that his play would pay its way. He was so enthusiastic over his project that he seriously considered making money by taking a job. He thought this matter over for one day and rejected it. When his father, John Butler Yeats, the noted portrait painter, heard of this decision he exclaimed, "Willie, you have taken a weight off my mind."

Yeats then decided on the artist's conventional method of getting money: he would find a patron. Wealthy patrons usually demand a measure of compromise for their help, but on the other hand compromise is less distasteful to the artist than giving himself over to hack writing, the final compromise.

The names of his wealthy acquaintances floated through Yeats's mind. There was no hope in London, since his acquaintances there were themselves artists, most of whom were also seeking patrons. Ireland offered greater hope. He knew Lady Gregory, a widowed landowner who had been giving him occasional small loans. Then there was Edward Martyn, a neighbor and friend of Lady Gregory, and a landlord also. Martyn had all the qualities of the patron Yeats was looking for: he was wealthy, he was a bachelor and likely to remain one, he was an extreme nationalist, and he even was interested in the modern drama, having written a play or two after the manner of Ibsen. Unfortunately he was a very narrow-minded Catholic and basically a philistine, despite his interest in art. But Yeats did not hesitate: he realized he had found the right man and felt confident he could handle him. He would touch up one of Martyn's plays, if need be, and produce it along with his own.

Yeats crossed over to Ireland at once, visited Martyn in his Gothic castle, and explained his plan. Martyn was enthusiastic when he saw the prospect of having his play *The Heather Field* produced. He stipulated that Dublin, not London, must be the centre of the dramatic revival.

Lady Gregory, learning that Yeats was in the neighborhood, with feminine casualness dropped in on the discussion. Her practical mind at once turned to the important question of how the costs of producing the plays were to be met. Yeats, of course, had been careful not to ask Martyn directly to meet the expenses, lest it convey the impression that he considered him only a moneylender and not an artist. When Lady Gregory proposed rather a wild scheme for raising money, Martyn quickly assented. The scheme was that they send a letter to their friends explaining what they intended to do and asking for guarantees to a £300 fund. Part of the letter read:

We propose to have performed in Dublin in the spring of every year certain Celtic and Irish plays, which whatever be their degree of excellence will be written with a high ambition, and so to build up a Celtic and Irish school of dramatic literature. We hope to find in Ireland an uncorrupted and imaginative audience trained to listen by its passion for oratory, and believe that our desire to bring upon the stage the deeper thoughts and emotions of Ireland will ensure for us a tolerant welcome, and that freedom to experiment which is not found in theatres of England, and without which no new movement in art or literature can succeed. We will show that Ireland is not the home of buffoonery and of easy sentiment, as it has been represented, but the home of an ancient idealism. We are confident of the support of all Irish people, who are weary of misrepresentation, in carrying out a work that is outside all the political questions that divide us.[1]

Many favorable replies came in. Even a glance at the list is sufficient to distinguish those who replied out of genuine interest in the movement from those who replied merely because they were friends of Lady Gregory. Douglas Hyde, T. M. Healy, John O'Leary, Jane Barlow were all supporters of Yeats; while the Duchess of St. Albans, the Viceroy of India, the Lord Chancellor of Ireland, and Lord Dufferin were obviously friends of Lady Gregory. The amount guaranteed was, of course, inadequate. This fact did not worry Yeats, for he knew that Martyn would gladly pay if a situation could be created whereby he could do so without implying he was merely the money man of the organization. The opportunity came in January, 1899, at a meeting of the National Literary Society called to consider the question of the society's sponsorship of the Irish Literary Theatre, as Yeats had named it. After a long debate centring mostly on financial liability, Martyn offered to defray all the expenses and had the following guarantee inserted in the minutes of the meeting:

Gentlemen,
I hereby undertake to hold you harmless and free from any liability in connection with the promotion of the Irish Literary Theatre.

[Signed] Edward Martyn

Now that financial worries were solved, a Dublin hall, The Antient Concert Rooms, was rented for the week beginning May 8, 1899, and Martyn and Yeats set off for London in an enthusiastic mood to engage a company of actors. A theatrical agency quickly provided the actors, but the difficult problem was to find someone with experience who could produce these unusual plays. The commercial producer would be useless, and neither Martyn nor Yeats could put into practical effect his own elaborate theories on production. Martyn remembered his friend George Moore, the novelist, who had once written a successful unconventional play, *The Strike at Arlingford*, which had received much comment in the press. Moore consented to desert his eternal proof reading to take on the job of producer. Having made Yeats agree not to insist on his own theories of production, Moore reorganized the group of actors, dismissed some, hired others, and put the plays into rehearsal.

Yeats now found himself in strange, almost dangerous, company. On one side he had Martyn, a narrow pietist, and on the other, Moore, a blasphemer—"ungovernable and preposterous." Only the most skillful diplomacy could save the theatre project from dying at birth. Trouble began at once. Martyn discovered a theological heresy in *The Countess Cathleen* and on the advice of his confessor withdrew his support. Yeats then submitted his play to two priests, one a Jesuit, and Martyn agreed to accept their verdict. In the meantime, a pamphlet, *Souls for Gold*, issued by an anonymous enemy of Yeats, attacked the play on theological grounds. It is a heresy, the pamphlet said, to hold up to admiration a woman who would sell her soul to save a nation.

The newspapers took up the controversy, and Cardinal Logue, to whom a reporter had shown extracts from the play, condemned it. This was enough for Martyn; he dashed up to Yeats's hotel in Dublin, his pudgy body shaking with emotion, big beads of perspiration on his face, and announced to Yeats, "I withdraw again." [2] The cardinal's condemnation was annoying enough, but to make matters worse George Moore had written Martyn a wicked letter in which he attacked Martyn's "most valued friend, Archbishop Healy" in a manner most disgusting.

Yeats, a dialectician of the first order, was able to persuade Martyn that the cardinal's condemnation, based on extracts only, had no validity. The tension was broken when reports were received from the theologians. Both agreed that the play should be produced. In a letter to Yeats, Father Barry reported:

Your play, *The Countess Cathleen,* is beautiful and touching. I hope you will not be kept back from giving it by foolish talk. . . . You have given us what is really an *Auto* in the manner of Calderon, with the old Irish folklore as a perceptive; and to measure it by the iron rule of experts and schoolmen would be most unfair to it.[3]

Martyn accepted the decision, opened his purse strings once more, and this time issued a broadsheet, *Beltaine,* which was to be the official organ of the Irish Literary Theatre. In its first issue Yeats explained the real purpose of *The Countess Cathleen*: "The play is not historic but symbolic and has little to do with any definite place and time as an *Auto* by Calderon. One should look for the Countess Cathleen and the peasants and the demons not in history . . . but in one's own heart." In the same publication, Lionel Johnson pointed out that the real theme of the play is the triumph of innocence over the malicious cunning of evil.

The theological controversy was only a skirmish; the real battle —for the establishing of an Irish National Theatre—was about to begin. The same elements who downed Parnell tried to strangle the Irish Literary Theatre in its cradle. They claimed to be Irish nationalists. In reality they were merely members of the worldwide army of the philistines fighting its never-ending battle with the artist.

One might describe the opponents of the Irish Literary Theatre as "sentimental nationalists." They lived in the past, not far enough back to be interested merely in antiquity, nor close enough to the present day to be out-and-out nationalists. Their hero was Patrick Sarsfield, an Irish soldier who took flight from Ireland a half century after the departure of the Wild Geese in the seventeenth century. They resembled most closely those who today take part in St. Patrick's Day parades in American cities—who imagine Ireland to be as green and level as a lawn, where the girls go around with eyes cast down, green garlands in their hair, and Rosaries at their girdles, while the men, armed only with shillelaghs, beat heavily armed battalions of British soldiers. For them, Boucicault's *The Colleen Bawn* represents the highest form of drama. Indeed, it was the American counterpart of these Irish elements who later threw cabbages and potatoes at the Abbey Players when they came to America.

The views of these sentimental nationalists found expression in *The Daily Nation*. A leading article in the issue of May 6, 1899, stated of *The Countess Cathleen*:

> We wish to protest in the name of morality and religion and Irish nationality against the performance [of *The Countess Cathleen*]. . . . The audience should hoot the impersonators of such grotesque impiety from the Irish stage. . . . Is our ideal of Catholic and Celtic Ireland in its golden or any age, a famine stricken island with brutalising inhabitants outdistancing each other in their eagerness to sell their souls for food without manliness, religion or morality? Does it offer us anything more than a blasphemous perversion of our people's historical attitude towards the Faith and a hideous caricature of our people's mental and moral character?

A correspondent writes in the next issue:

> Thanks to the Great God that there is at least one editor of a Dublin Journal whose ardent faith, national instinct, independent spirit and brave heart urges him to protest against the performance of *The Countess Cathleen* here in the capital of the most truly Catholic country in the world. . . . The extracts you have given are brimful of iniquitous suggestion and they outrage the highest and holiest instincts of our religion and our race.

Yeats replied to this attitude in *Beltaine* (1899):

> Why should we thrust our works, which we have written with imaginative sincerity and filled with spiritual desire, before those excellent people who think that Rossetti's women are "guys," that Rodin's women are "ugly". . . . We must make a theatre for ourselves and our friends and for a few simple people who understand from sheer simplicity what we understand from scholarship and thought. We have planned the Irish Literary Theatre with this hospitable emotion, and that the right people may find out about us, we hope to act a play or two in the spring of every year, and that the right people may escape the stupefying memory of the theatre of commerce which clings even to them, our plays will be for the most part spiritual and ideal. . . . The theatre of Art must discover grave and decorative gestures, and grave and decorative scenery, that will be forgotten the

moment an actor has said "It is dawn" or "It is raining" or "The wind is shaking the trees"; and dresses of so little irrelevant magnificence that the mortal actors and actresses may change without much labour into the immortal people of romance. The theatre began in ritual and it cannot come to its greatness again without recalling words to their ancient sovereignty.

This dignified reply was lost on the enemy. On the day of the first performance of the Irish Literary Theatre (May 8, 1899) *The Daily Nation* called on its readers to attend the performance of *The Countess Cathleen* "to make emphatic judgment against these anti-Irish, anti-Catholic monstrosities." Yeats's reply to this challenge was to bring the hated British police into the hall to defend the players against violence. The mob immediately seized on this act of Yeats as the final proof that he was pro-British and anti-Irish.

The dilapidated hall which was the Antient Concert Rooms was fairly well filled for the opening performance. The scenery was poorly and hurriedly built; rudely painted wings were advanced and a drop curtain improvised. The performance opened with a prologue by Lionel Johnson. Part of it read as follows:

> Ah, yes; for sacrifice this night we bring
> The passion of a lost soul's triumphing;
> All rich with faery airs that, wandering long,
> Uncaught, here gather into Irish song;
> Sweet as the old remembering winds that wail,
> From hill to hill of gracious Inisfail;
> Sad as the unforgetting winds that pass
> Over her children in her holy grass
> At home, and sleeping well upon her breast,
> Where snowy Deirdre and her sorrows rest.
> Come, then, and keep with us an Irish feast,
> Wherein the Lord of Light and Song is priest;
> Now at this opening of the gentle May,
> Watch warring passions at their storm and play,
> Wrought with the flaming ecstasy of art,
> Sprung from the dreaming of an Irish heart.

Martyn's play *The Heather Field* was well received by the crowd but *The Countess Cathleen* was hooted by a small section of the audience. Joseph Holloway was present at the first night, and he records in his *Diary*:

About twenty brainless, beardless, idiotic-looking youths did all they knew to interfere with the progress of the play and frequently mentioned the name of Davis. The play, however, ended amidst thunders of applause and Yeats was called onto the stage to take a bow. When he came out on the stage he appeared embarrassed and did not know what to do until, prompted by Trevor Lowe, he took Miss Whittey's hand and shook it heartily and then did the same with Miss Farr.

All the literary personalities of Ireland were present: George Russell (AE), John Eglinton, T. W. Rolleston, Standish O'Grady, Douglas Hyde, and many others. George Moore, underestimating the importance of the performance, remained in England, but immediately on hearing of the riot he hurried over to Ireland. To his great disappointment the excitement had subsided when he arrived. He was in time, however, for a banquet given by T. P. Gill, editor of the Dublin *Daily Express*, in honor of the formation of the Irish Literary Theatre. What worried Moore most about the banquet was that there was not an opera hat to be seen. Speeches were made by Yeats and others. Of Hyde's speech in Gaelic, Moore writes in *Ave* (p. 139):

A torrent of dark, muddied stuff flowed from him like the porter which used to come up from Carnucan to be drunk by the peasants on midsummer nights when a bonfire was lighted.

Many of the London drama critics attended the first performance in the Antient Concert Rooms, and all of them wrote favorably of the plays. Max Beerbohm, critic for *The Saturday Review,* wrote: "I know not when I have found in a theatre more esthetic pleasure. . . . Despite the little cramped stage which was as tawdry as it should have been dim, I was from first to last conscious that a beautiful play was being enacted" (May 13, 1899).

The Dublin press was in general friendly, and this delighted Yeats. Shortly afterward he wrote: "Whatever the merit of these plays, and that must be left to the judgment of time, their success means, as I think, that the 'Celtic Movement' which has hitherto interested but a few cultivated people, is about to become part of the thought of Ireland." [4]

The sentimental nationalists continued to fight on, this time through the medium of *An Claidheamh Soluis,* propaganda sheet of the Gaelic League. Of *The Countless Cathleen* it stated on May 6, 1899:

Such a play in the hands of Mr. Yeats cannot fail to be "literary" but it is not "Irish" drama and Europe will laugh at our conception of an Irish theatre.

And on May 20 the same paper returned to the attack:

Our readers will be interested to learn that three of the Trinity College defamers of the national language are guarantors of the *Irish* Literary Theatre.

It was the argument of the Gaelic League that no theatre which used the English language could be truly Irish. Yeats partly agreed with this idea, but when he looked around for a play in Gaelic he found none to be had: Gaelic-speaking Ireland never adopted the drama as a means of expression. It was then decided that Douglas Hyde be asked to translate into Gaelic *The Land of Heart's Desire* and the translation be produced at the next series of productions of the Irish Literary Theatre. The play did not lend itself to translation, but the gesture of the Irish Literary Theatre brought it the support of the Gaelic League—at least for a short time.

Yeats was pleased with his success in getting the new dramatic movement under way in spite of all opposition. His next problem was to find plays for the second series of productions. A translation of Calderon's *The Purgatory of St. Patrick* was rejected because it could not be considered a contribution to Irish drama. Someone remembered that Alice Milligan, a minor poet of the movement, had written a short play, *The Last Feast of the Fianna.* It was agreed that the play was worthy of production by the Irish Literary Theatre.

One play was not sufficient, and Yeats reluctantly accepted the inevitable—two further plays by Martyn. One of Martyn's plays, *Maeve,* had already been printed, and the other, *The Tale of a Town,* was not finished.

As soon as Martyn learned that two of his plays were to be produced at the next performance of the Irish Literary Theatre, he went up to Dublin and rented for the third week in February, 1900, Dublin's largest and finest theatre, the Gaiety. He felt that his plays deserved to be performed in a respectable playhouse. He retired then to his castle in Galway to finish *The Tale of a Town.* He sent it to Yeats and Moore for their approval.

Both saw at a glance that the play was extremely bad, and Moore tells us in *Vale* (p. 297) that Yeats immediately went over to Martyn's castle and denounced the play, "acting like a monk of literature, an inquisitor, a Torquemada." Martyn was shocked. He was still more shocked when, after he had rewritten parts of the play according to their instructions, Moore and Yeats again rejected it. Huffed, he handed over his play to them to alter it or do what they wished with it. He would do anything, he said, to avoid breaking up the Irish Literary Theatre—he warned them, however, that he would not sign the altered version of the play.

Moore and Yeats stayed a few days with Martyn in his castle, and it gave Moore great pleasure to watch Martyn writhe as he listened to Moore and Yeats discuss the alterations they would make in his masterpiece. Moore rewrote the play and named it *The Bending of the Bough.* The three authors then moved back to London with Lady Gregory, collected a company, and put the plays into rehearsal. When all was ready, Martyn was detailed by his associates to act as baggageman for the company, to buy tickets for the actors, to see that everyone got on the train, and to accompany them to Ireland. Yeats, Moore, and Lady Gregory followed in comfort the next day.

The second series of the Irish Literary Theatre opened at the Gaiety February 19, 1900. The house was well filled and the audience was friendly, particularly to Moore's satire *The Bending of the Bough.* There was no opposition to the plays of this series.

One important aspect of the productions was the new method of acting. The performers were instructed to use the minimum of action, to be statuesque if possible, and to speak their words more to the audience than to each other. This was Yeats's idea, but it failed to impress Joseph Holloway. "The actors," he said,[5] "spoke to the audience instead of to each other, with their heads on the side as if they had boils on their necks."

The second series of performances was received well by the press. *The United Irishman,* edited by the nationalist Arthur Griffith, said:[6]

We want more of such plays and more people to see them than attended on Tuesday night and despite the fact that there may be inconsistencies . . . their influence would soon be felt in the public life of Ireland.

Finding plays for the third series of performances was no great problem. For some time Yeats and Moore had been collaborating on a play about the love of Diarmuid for Grainne. True, Moore was a difficult man to collaborate with; he could not agree with Yeats that the play should be written in dialect nor that Grainne should be portrayed as a peasant. But the play was finished eventually, and Elgar wrote music for some of the lyrics. At the same time Douglas Hyde was completing a short play in Gaelic, entitled *Casadh an t-Sugain,* or *The Twisting of the Rope,* which he built around a scenario written for him by Yeats. It was decided to produce this play on the same program with *Diarmuid and Grainne.*

When Martyn learned that none of his plays was to be performed on this occasion, he became very angry, withdrew his support from the movement, and told Yeats that in future he would pay for the production of nobody's plays except his own.[7] Yeats was not worried by Martyn's withdrawal, for he had served his purpose and was beginning to become a burden on the movement.

George Moore, disgusted at the treatment of the Boers by the British, turned Nationalist, packed his belongings, issued a series of maledictions on England, and set sail for Ireland. He took over publicity for the Irish Literary Theatre, frequently to the embarrassment of Yeats. He did not believe in understatement. Of the forthcoming production of *Diarmuid and Grainne,* he said that, even if it turned out to be the greatest play of all time on this subject, they were offering on the same occasion something even better—a play in the original language of the country, a play in Gaelic by Dr. Douglas Hyde.[8]

After long negotiations R. A. Benson, an Englishman who managed a troupe of actors, was persuaded to undertake production of the third series of plays for the Irish Literary Theatre. This began on October 21, 1901, once more at the Gaiety Theatre, Dublin. The seats were filled, mostly by members of the Gaelic League who had come to see the first production of a play in Gaelic in a regular theatre. Hyde's play, acted by amateurs from the League, gratified the audience. *Diarmuid and Grainne* was fairly well applauded, even though the actors were British. But the reduction of the heroic characters Diarmuid and Grainne to the scale of normal people was not appreciated by the extreme nationalist press. The notice in *The Leader* represents this attitude:

Mr. Yeats and Mr. Moore have twisted it [the Gaelic story] beyond recognition and have changed Diarmuid from a Fenian chief into a modern degenerate. . . . They turned Grainne into one of those kind of creatures that have been so prominent in the degenerate London drama against which the Irish Literary Theatre is supposed to be an antidote! . . . It was a heartless piece of vandalism . . . and will injure the cause of Irish Ireland.[9]

George Moore was delighted to find himself in the middle of a controversy; actually, he was interested in the dramatic movement only for the fun he could derive from it. It was becoming clear to Yeats that Moore's perverse attitude might wreck his hopes of founding a truly national theatre, and he decided to rid himself of Moore.

In an interview published in *The Freeman's Journal*,[10] Moore made the mischievous statement that what the Irish Literary Theatre needed was to bring the priests into the movement so they could impose upon it the censorship of the Church. "The intelligent censorship of the Church," he stated, "will free the stage from the unintelligent and ignorant censorship of the public, the censorship of those without personal convictions, and of those whose ideas are the conventions and the gossip of the little coterie they frequent."

Yeats replied to Moore's statement in the same paper two days later: "If any literary association I belong to asked for a clerical censorship, I would certainly cease to belong to it. I believe that literature is the principal voice of the conscience and that it is the duty of age after age to affirm its morality against the special moralities of clergymen and churches, and of kings and parliaments and peoples."

Shortly afterward Yeats quarreled with Moore and brought the Irish Literary Theatre to an end. It had served its purpose. It had proved the possibility of a permanent national theatre in Dublin.

It is a curious fact that at the final performance of the Irish Literary Theatre there were present the two men who were destined in the following years to take a large part in shaping the new Irish National Theatre—Frank Fay and John Millington Synge.

Ideals

The three years' existence of the experimental Irish Literary Theatre gave Yeats the opportunity to test his theories of what an Irish National Theatre should be. His aim was to establish a poetic drama, but for a moment he wavered; he suggested that the dramatic movement should be "a return to the people as in Russia" and that "we may have to deal with passing issues until we have re-created the imaginative traditions of Ireland, and filled the popular imagination again with saints and heroes." [1] One man, at least, in Ireland saw the heresy in that theory—James Joyce, then a young student at the university. He replied to Yeats in an essay, *The Day of the Rabblement*:[2]

No man can be a true lover of the good unless he abhors the multitude; and the artist, though he may employ the crowd, is very careful to isolate himself. . . . If the artist courts the favor of the multitude he cannot escape the contagion of its fetishism and deliberate self-deception, and if he joins in a popular movement he does so at his own risk. Therefore the Irish Literary Theatre by a surrender to the trolls cuts itself adrift from the line of advancement. Unless he has freed himself from the mean influences about him—sodden enthusiasms and clever insinuations, and every flattering influence of vanity and low ambition—no man is an artist at all.

Yeats was, of course, as conscious of the danger of condescending to the crowd as was Joyce. The problem was not an easy one. According to the democratic view, the drama by its nature must appeal to the crowd, and a national drama would be expected to appeal to the nation. But there can be no democracy in art, and Yeats realized that if he did not rule the multitude, the multitude would rule him.

If the drama was to remain vital, thought Yeats, it must move in either of two directions—upwards in ever-growing subtlety with Verhaeren, with Maeterlinck, with Mallarmé; or downwards, taking the soul with it until all is simplified. His national theatre would demand not a national audience but an audience "large enough to lose itself in the lump." [3] The theatre must be a place as sacred as a church, and those who attend it must come not to be preached at but to listen to a poet explain his vision. Above all, politics must be kept out of the theatre, for politics presupposes defense, argument. "A continual apology, whatever the cause, makes the mind barren because it kills intellectual innocence; that delight in what is unforeseen, and in the mere spectacle of the world, the mere drifting hither and thither that must come before all true thought and emotion." [4] The imagination and the spirit is everything, and one must not allow (as one necessarily does in politics) "the substitution of arguments and hesitations for the excitement at the first reading of the great poets, which should be a sort of violent imaginative puberty." [5] As he stated in *Samhain*,[6] beauty and truth are their own end; "they justify and have no need of justification."

This did not mean that Irish writers were to avoid nationalistic themes. "If in the sincere working out of their plot, they alight on a moral that is obviously and directly serviceable to the National cause, so much the better, but we must not force that moral upon them." [7] Yeats's own patriotic play, *Kathleen Ni Houlihan,* he explained, was written unconsciously, out of a dream; "but if some external necessity had forced me to write nothing but drama with an obvious patriotic intention, instead of letting my work shape itself under the casual impulses of dreams and daily thoughts, I would have lost, in a short time, the power to write movingly upon any theme." [8]

Yeats wanted plays that were literature or were written in the spirit of literature, plays that had style. Characterization was important only in comedy. Tragedy gets its form from motives and from the wandering of passion. "A poet creates tragedy from his own soul, that soul which is alike in all men. It has not joy as we understand that word, but ecstasy, which is from the contemplation of things vaster than the individual and imperfectly seen, perhaps, by all those that still live." [9]

Irish dramatists, Yeats insisted, may learn form from the masters of the "new" drama such as Ibsen, but they must realize that the drama is a method of artistic expression and not an instrument for discussing social problems.

Art delights in the exception [Yeats wrote],[10] for it delights in the soul expressing itself according to its own laws and arranging the world about it in its own pattern. . . . But the average man is average because he has not attained to freedom. Habit, routine, fear of public opinion, fear of punishment here or hereafter, a myriad of things that 'something other than human life,' something less than flame, work their will upon his soul and trundle his body here and there.

The characters in Ibsen's *Ghosts* are . . . little whimpering puppets. . . . What was it that weighed upon their souls perpetually? . . . Is it the mob that has robbed these persons of the energy of their souls? Will not our next art be rather of the country, of great open spaces, of the soul rejoicing in itself? What is there left for us . . . but to labor with a high heart, though it may be with weak hands, to rediscover an art of the theatre that shall be joyful, fantastic, extravagant, whimsical, beautiful, resonant and altogether reckless. . . . Has not the long decline of the arts been but the shadow of declining faith in an unseen reality?

If one must follow the pattern of social plays set by Ibsen, then it is important that this kind of play be pushed to a more complete realism, for that would be its honesty—it was for this reason the French initiated the "naturalistic" play—but this kind of play must not be considered art.

Comedy need not be excluded from the Irish National Theatre, but it would not be allowed too prominent a part. Its chief function would be to rest the ear of the audience should it occasionally weary of listening to poetic drama.

Yeats wanted a new language for his plays. Language, like a cloak, wears out, and the English language was threadbare from many years of usage and journalistic vulgarization. To use Gaelic would be little help, for all the writers had learned English as their native language, and it is difficult to write well in an acquired tongue.

There was one alternative: to use dialect. Dialect is the by-road of a language, and Yeats insisted that the by-roads were always beautiful, while the broad road of the journalist was vulgar. Yeats found what he was looking for in the peasant dialect of west Ireland. The people there thought in Gaelic but spoke in English, and the result was a fresh and unspoiled language with personality.

It is the only good English spoken by any large number of Irish people today, and one must found good literature on a living speech. English men of letters found themselves on the English Bible. . . . The translation used in Ireland has not the same literary beauty, and if we are to find anything to take its place we must find it in that idiom of the poor, which mingles so much of the same vocabulary with turns of phrase that have come out of Gaelic. . . . But when we go back to speech let us see that it is either the idiom of those who have rejected or of those who have never learned, the base idiom of the newspaper.[11]

Kathleen Ni Houlihan, by Yeats, was the first play to employ this dialect for a serious and artistic purpose. The dialect used by the Irish National Theatre is sometimes described as the Kiltartan dialect, Kiltartan being the parish in the west of Ireland where Lady Gregory lived. As found in the plays, it is not completely authentic, but it has a quaint, unreal, dreamy flavor.

26   *Ideals*

Yeats also developed fixed principles on acting. At all times the actor must subordinate himself entirely to the words of the play. Especially in tragedy the actor should come as little as possible between the audience and the passion expressed. The more immobile the actor, the better. On occasions it is best that he cover his face with a mask, "for it is always ourselves that we see upon the stage, and should it be a tragedy of love, we renew, it may be, some loyalty of our youth, and go from the theatre with our eyes dim for an old love's sake." [12]

So much importance did Yeats attach to this method that on one occasion he planned to rehearse a company of actors while they stood in barrels, so that they might forget gestures and have their minds free to think of speech.

We must get rid of everything that is restless, everything that draws the attention away from the sound of the voice, or from the few moments of intense expression, whether that expression is through the voice or through the hands; we must from time to time substitute for the movement that the eye sees the nobler movement that the heart sees, the rhythmical movements that seem to flow up into the imagination from some deeper life than that of the individual soul.[13]

Scenery should be simple and unobtrusive and, as a rule, the background should be but a single color, so that the attention of the audience might not be distracted from the speech and movement. Greek acting was great because it did everything with the voice, and modern acting may be great when it does everything with voice and movement.

Briefly, it might be said that Yeat's ideal of a theatre was a building consecrated to art, where the poet as high priest explained his visions to a small but holy audience. Of such a nature was the Irish National Theatre to be.

The Irish National Theatre Society

When the Irish Literary Theatre came to an end in 1901, many of those interested in drama concluded that Yeats had failed in his attempt to found an Irish theatre. *The United Irishman,* which had been friendly to the experiment, wrote what seemed then like an obituary notice:

The fault seems to have been that the whole scheme was far too ambitiously conceived. There is not a public here capable of supporting at such a level such a theatre and on such a scale as the experiments have indicated. . . . I would say that the Irish Literary Theatre has shown too strong a partiality for the mythical and the semisupernatural.[1]

Yeats had returned to his London garret not completely satisfied with his success. He no longer had the patronage of Martyn, and it seemed he was back where he started. He still was poor and was existing on the few royalties from the sale of his books and on the small loans which he received from Lady Gregory.

Yeats was not easily defeated. He had made some advance if only in the form of experience. Although he lived in London, he kept Ireland always in his mind and continued to plan ways of setting up an Irish National Theatre. He was confident that a situation soon would arise that would enable him to realize his dreams. In the meantime he lectured in London on the reform of the theatre and even considered setting up in London a theatre of beauty where his own plays and those of Masefield and Bridges would be performed. He had completed a short patriotic play, *Kathleen Ni Houlihan*, inspired by Maud Gonne.

Over in Ireland the young George Russell's long red beard and untidy appearance were contributing as much as was his mystical and poetic philosophy to impress his young literary acquaintances. AE had become friendly with Yeats when both were at the School of Art together. Like Yeats, he was interested in the occult and in the national Ireland. He felt that, apart from literature, Ireland's salvation lay in the cooperative movement, and he cycled around the country preaching the same doctrine that Bishop Grundtvig had spread in Denmark. He continued to produce poetry, and the Irish Literary Theatre gave him the urge to write a play. He wrote two scenes of a one-act play about Deirdre and had them published in *The All Ireland Review*, edited by Standish O'Grady. This unfinished play written by AE in one night turned out to be the spark which really set the Irish dramatic movement alight.

There were in Dublin two brothers, Willie and Frank Fay, who were interested in acting. Frank was a stenographer and typist, and Willie was a clerk in the Gas Works. During their spare time they produced English farces in local halls and kept well in touch with theatrical affairs on the continent. They knew about Ibsen and about the Théâtre Libre, and they believed that what Antoine was able to do without much money they could do also. They had watched the Irish Literary Theatre with interest but were too humble to think of even approaching its aristocratic promoters. George Moore had met the Fay brothers but had thought them

30   *The Irish National Theatre Society*

barnstormers. It never occurred to him they might be able to act in literary plays.

The Fays had read AE's play in *The All Ireland Review* and realized at once that this was their chance to rise to the dignity of artists if only AE could be persuaded to finish his play and let them produce it. They spoke to Seumas O'Cuisin, then a nationalistic civil servant but later a writer of plays, and he approached AE, who consented to meet the Fays.

The result of the meeting was that AE guaranteed to finish the play at once. The Fays did not delay; they put it into rehearsal in December, 1901. Here was the real beginning of the Irish National Theatre—Irish plays acted by Irish players in an Irish hall.

Yeats, though he was living in London, had a sharp eye and a keen ear for anything which might further his idea of an Irish theatre. He heard of the Fays and of their intention to produce AE's play. He consulted Lady Gregory at once as to what should be done and then decided to offer the Fays his *Kathleen Ni Houlihan* for production on the same program as *Deirdre* if it happened that AE's play was not long enough for an evening's entertainment. *Deirdre* was a short play, but even had it been otherwise the Fays would gladly have extended the program until midnight that they might have the honor of producing a second poetic play.

A company was collected with great effort. Yeats persuaded his friend Maud Gonne to play the part of Kathleen Ni Houlihan, and many of the performers were recruited from her nationalistic organization, Inginidhe na h-Eireann. The Fays had only ten pounds between them, but they were able to get free the use of St. Teresa's Temperance Hall in Clarendon Street, Dublin, for three nights—April 2, 3, and 4, 1902.

On the following page is the program for the performance. It was given under the auspices of Maud Gonne's Nationalist Society and it led directly to the Abbey Theatre.

The room in St. Teresa's Hall was hardly suitable for play production. Properly speaking, it was only half a room: a thin partition cut off the other half for use as a billiard salon.

When Joseph Holloway arrived, the hall was full and he had to stand at the back. He writes:

The Irish National Theatre Society   31

INGINIDHE NA h-EIREANN

On Wednesday, Thursday and Friday Evenings,
2nd, 3rd. and 4th. April, 1902
Mr. W. G. Fay's Irish National Dramatic Company
will produce at
The Hall of St. Teresa's Total Abstinence Association,
Clarendon Street,
for the first time on any stage,

DEIRDRE

a play in three acts by "AE"

and

KATHLEEN NI HOULIHAN

A play in one act by W. B. Yeats.

Scenery by "AE" and W. G. Fay.
Dresses made by Inginidhe na h-Eireann from designs by "AE".
Orchestra String Band of the Workmen's Club, 41 York Street.

DEIRDRE

DEIRDRE .... MAIRE T. QUINN.
LAVARCAM .... MAIRE NIC SHIUBHLAIGH.
FERGUS .... P. J. KELLY.
BUINNE ⎫ Sons of Fergus .... P. COLUM.
ILLAUN ⎭ .... C. CAULFIELD.
ARDAN ⎫ Sons of Usna .... H. SPROULE (J. COUSINS).
AINLE ⎭ .... J. DUDLEY DIGGES.
MESSENGER .... BRIAN CALLENDER.
CONCOBAR ARDRI OF ULLA .... F. J. FAY.

Act I. The Dun of Deirdre's Captivity at Emain Macha.
Act II. In Alba, Naise's Dun on the banks of Loch Ettive.
Act III. The House of the Red Branch at Emain Macha.

KATHLEEN NI HOULIHAN

KATHLEEN NI HOULIHAN .... MISS MAUD GONNE.
DELIA CAHEL .... MAIRE NIC SHIUBHLAIGH.
BRIDGET GILLAN .... MAIRE T. QUINN.
PATRICK GILLAN .... C. CAULFIELD.
MICHAEL GILLAN .... J. DUDLEY DIGGES.
PETER GILLAN .... W. G. FAY.

Scene: A Farmer's kitchen close to Killala in 1798.

Was present at the performance of Deirdre and Kathleen Ni Houlihan at St. Teresa's Hall and were it not for the unceasing distracting noises, such as snatches of popular songs, erratic step-dances and the continual sounds of billiard balls coming in contact with each other wafted from an adjoining room so that most of what the performers said was lost to me—but for all this I would have had a delightful evening.[2]

The plays were well received, and the presence of eminent English critics gave a sense of importance to the evening. One woman in the audience was not annoyed by the billiard balls, but she took exception to AE's chanting from the pit during the performance. She accused him of practicing black magic. Writing to Yeats about this, AE says with delight: "She saw blue-black waves of darkness rolling down over the stage and audience and it made her ill. . . . I feel filled with pride and wickedness, almost a demon. Isn't it a delightful audience we get in Dublin? If I write another play I'll work in more magic." [3]

The woman can hardly be blamed for mistaking AE's chanting for black magic: he had caught from Yeats the habit of chanting verse to the accompaniment of the psaltery. In the letters of AE to Yeats one reads passages on semitones and quarter tones, though neither Yeats nor AE was capable of singing the simplest ballad. No wonder Moore laughed.

AE was pleased with the success of *Deirdre* and planned to write another play on the Gaelic story, The Fate of the Sons of Tuireann. Opposition came from an unexpected quarter, and AE discontinued writing plays: Standish O'Grady protested against the introduction of the heroic legends of Ireland on the stage. In his *All Ireland Review* he wrote:

Last year we witnessed the degradation of Finn; this year of Concobhar MacNessa. I confess I stand amazed before such phenomena and hardly know what to say, yet know I ought to say a great deal, for I was the first to direct the attention of our students to these things. They are being brought down into the very streets now. . . . The Red Branch ought not to be staged. That literature ought not to be produced for popular consumption. . . . I say to you drop this thing at your peril. . . . You may succeed in degrading Irish ideals and banishing the soul of the land. Leave the heroic cycles alone and don't bring them down to the crowd.[4]

O'Grady seemed to imagine that these heroic legends belonged in some special way to him, since he was one of the first to introduce them to the literary public. AE replied privately to this hysterical outburst. In a letter he pointed out to O'Grady that "he [O'Grady] was not great enough to issue fiats to other literary men and accuse them of decadence in a muddle of confused and contradictory sentences." [5] O'Grady withdrew his support from the dramatic movement.

The Fays were flattered at the prospect of having the national dramatic movement centre on them. To consolidate their position they at once formed a society, the Irish National Dramatic Company, and elected AE president. AE would not take the position but suggested they make Yeats president. This was done; and Maud Gonne, Douglas Hyde, and AE became vice presidents. W. G. Fay was to be the stage manager and Fred Ryan the secretary. All the members contributed to a fund; Lady Gregory gave twenty-five pounds (though she was not even a member of the Society, being up to this time only a friend of Yeats); Yeats gave twenty pounds, and the other members contributed similarly.

The election of Yeats to the presidency gave him hope for a national theatre. He became enthusiastic over the acting of the Fays, discovering, says Moore,[6] that their art was of French origin and could be traced back to the middle of the seventeenth century in France. He proclaimed their merits in his most dictatorial vein until not only did they believe it themselves but the public believed it also.

The Fays needed plays in a hurry if they were to keep their company together. Frank Fay asked Seumas O'Cuisin, who had been acting with the company, if he could write them a verse play. O'Cuisin wrote them two plays instead of one; the verse play was *The Sleep of the King*, and the prose play *The Racing Lug*.

These two short plays kept the company working through the summer; rehearsals took place mostly on Sunday afternoons on the Dublin mountains. Fred Ryan, secretary of the company, also wrote a short play, *The Laying of the Foundations*, which dealt with the problem of municipal politics. Finally Yeats sent along a one-act farce, *A Pot of Broth*.

There was no shortage of plays now, and to try themselves out

34   *The Irish National Theatre Society*

the company decided to give all four plays in the Antient Concert Rooms under the auspices of Cumann na nGaedheal, a nationalistic organization. The performances took place on October 29, 30, and 31, 1902. The audience was small but distinguished, and after the performances Yeats came over to O'Cuisin, clapped him on the back and said, "Splendid, my boy, beautiful verse, beautifully spoken; just what is wanted."

Holloway was not enthusiastic. "The curtains were unruly," he said, "and the orchestra vile. But there were several lights present, including W. B. Yeats and his father, George Russell (AE), T. O'Neill Russell, Douglas Hyde, Lady Gregory, Sara Purser and many others."

The Fays felt they were making progress, yet they realized that what they needed most was a special hall where all performances could be given. Accordingly, they rented at forty pounds a year a derelict hall at 34 Lower Camden Street, where they built a stage and installed some rough seats. They opened on December 4, 1902, with the same plays they had performed a few months before, adding to them a play in Gaelic, *Eilís agus an Bhean Déirce,* by Peadar Mag Fhionnlaoic.

That there were only twenty-five in the audience the first night was not surprising, for the hall was almost inaccessible, it was dilapidated, and it was in an obscure section of the city. Few even in Camden Street knew there was a playhouse there. To enter the theatre from the street, patrons had to negotiate a passage obstructed on one side by a grocer's egg crates and on the other by a butcher's cow carcases.

The press attended the first night, but their reports were not favorable. No more performances were given at the Camden hall. It was retained as an official address and was used only for rehearsals. A pleasant little hall on Molesworth Street was found for future plays.

About this time Lady Gregory read to the company in the Nassau Hotel the script of a play, *In the Shadow of the Glen,* by John Millington Synge, the Irish genius whom Yeats had discovered in Paris. At Yeats's suggestion Synge had returned to Ireland. Though he came of Anglo-Irish stock, he knew a little Gaelic and was easily convinced by Yeats that his artistic future lay in Ireland among the Gaelic-speaking peasants rather than among the Paris bohemians. Synge first went to live in Wicklow, associating with gipsies and wanderers, then moved to the Aran Islands off the west coast of Ireland. This life suited his temperament, for he was of a lonely disposition and even while living in town was inclined to live in a garret away from other people. He was quiet, spoke only seldom, and rarely mixed with literary people. He preferred listening, to talking, and during his later life he took no active part in the Irish theatre other than to write plays for it and to tender advice. He was a sick man, and charges that he was a bohemian decadent were untrue.

At the reading of *In the Shadow of the Glen* some immediately saw its merit, but others, no doubt prejudiced by the fact that Synge had lived for a time in Paris, mistook its realism for decadence. Yeats managed to force it into rehearsal, and a more popular play, *Sold*, by O'Cuisin was put aside after four rehearsals. This procedure annoyed many members of the company who had been growing restive over what they considered to be dramatic dictatorship.

Just as it seemed the company was about to break up, AE was appealed to. He came to a meeting of the society and settled the dispute by reorganizing the company in accordance with democratic principles. The name of the society was changed to The Irish National Theatre Society, rules were drawn up and a prospectus issued which stated that the society was formed "to continue on a more permanent basis the work of the Irish Literary Theatre." In a letter to Yeats, who was staying in London, AE wrote:

About the Theatre Society—I have been so busy this last autumn and winter that I have only been twice at the room since the Antient Concert Rooms performance. I went down a few weeks ago because I heard the society was likely to split up unless some definite rules on a democratic principle were drawn up. There was a rebellion going on which is natural among voluntary workers, at the way in which plays were accepted or rejected without their consent, so I drew up and got them to pass the only rules which were possible under the circumstances. I think you got a copy of them. I know you would not like them but if they were not passed

I do not think there would be a Society. . . . Now you will get copies of plays and can write your own opinion before the company learn parts, and you will find it works much better. You might be able to arrange better if you were constantly here but the rules are the only alternative.[7]

Yeats was angry with AE for making such an arrangement. All his diplomacy had been directed toward gaining complete control of the Society, and now AE had upset his plans. But there was nothing he could do at the moment.

The production of Synge's play was delayed and two other plays were put into rehearsal: *The Hour Glass*, a morality play by Yeats, and *Twenty Five*, a first play by Lady Gregory which she had written with Yeats's help. Yeats came over from England for the performance of these plays at the Molesworth Hall on March 14, 1903. Both plays were very short, and Yeats delivered a lecture during the intermission, which was a restatement of his ideas of a national theatre.

Lecture and plays received the customary unsympathetic notices from the press, although the production was taken a little more seriously than usual, presumably because it took place in a respectable hall. Scawen Blunt was present at a later performance of *The Hour Glass*, on May 3, and recorded his impressions:

The first piece was a terrible infliction called "The Hour Glass," by Yeats —a stupid imitation of that dull old morality, "Everyman," which bored me so much last year. What Yeats can mean by putting such thin stuff on the stage I can't imagine. It was all very well acted, for Yeats had drilled his actors to imitate Irving and other English mediocrities. They talked pompous stage English and were not allowed their natural Irish accent. I felt inclined to get up and protest that we had not come to the Irish Literary Society for that. I was indignant too but it exhausted my little strength.[8]

Stephen Gwynn, secretary of the London Irish Literary Society, was in Ireland at this time, but unlike Blunt he was deeply impressed with the National Theatre Society and invited them to visit London in May. As the players were all amateurs, it was difficult for them to leave their jobs, if only for a day. Finally they arranged to go over Friday night, May 1, and return Sunday night. They gave a matinee and an evening performance at the Queen's Gate Hall, South Kensington, under their official title, The Irish National Theatre Society.

They produced *The Hour Glass, Twenty Five,* and *Kathleen Ni Houlihan* at the matinee; and *Laying the Foundations, A Pot of Broth,* and *Kathleen Ni Houlihan* in the evening. When the players returned to Dublin they were surprised to find they had been highly praised by all the leading critics of the London Press. William Archer and A. B. Walkley agreed that the performance of The Irish National Theatre Society marked an epoch in the history of the English-speaking theatre, if not indeed of the European theatre.

Far more important than the praise of the critics, the Society's work in London attracted the attention of Miss A. E. F. Horniman, a wealthy but none-too-attractive lady who had known Yeats casually for many years by way of parties and occult meetings. Unlike Lady Gregory, Miss Horniman had not recognized Yeats's genius at their first meeting. Nor did he appeal to her then as a personal or emotional need. In her eyes he differed little from other esthetes who wore bow ties and baggy trousers. She was a patron of the Avenue Theatre in London, and *The Land of Heart's Desire* had appeared there, but the play excited little favorable comment and Yeats seemed a dreamer rather than a man of action.

The success of the Irish players in London came as a surprise to Miss Horniman; it was clear at once that Yeats was succeeding in putting his theories into practice, and he was the recipient of high praise from the London critics. She became interested. She had a real love for the theatre, although she was herself without talent. Yet she had money, and Yeats needed money badly. She spoke to Yeats about the Irish plays and offered to design and supply costumes for a new play he had written for autumn production. Yeats quickly accepted, for he saw in Miss Horniman a patroness of the Irish theatre. He could have had no other interest in her: emotionally, he was hopelessly attached to Maud Gonne, and intellectually he was bound to Lady Gregory. Miss Horniman was aware of all this but did not seem unduly concerned. After all,

Lady Gregory was a middle-aged widow with a son, and Yeats was an idealist. There was hope, even if only for interesting companionship.

Lady Gregory gave no indication she resented the intrusion of another woman into her friendship with Yeats. She was sure of herself, she had intellectual and emotional repose, and she knew she could always hold Yeats's interest. Too, she perceived that Miss Horniman had no genius and very slight talent; and Yeats hated mediocrity.

Even if Lady Gregory had had some doubts, they soon were set at rest when Miss Horniman completed the costumes for Yeats's play. They were badly done. Lennox Robinson, who examined them some years later, described them as horrible. So far as Lady Gregory was concerned, any jealousy that might arise would be entirely on Miss Horniman's part.

It was decided to produce Synge's *In the Shadow of the Glen* on the same program with Yeats's new play *The King's Threshold,* and rehearsals were therefore resumed.

An interesting production of AE's *Deirdre* took place in the open air on Sunday, August 22, 1903, at Dundrum with the Dublin mountains as background. As usual in Ireland, showers interrupted the performance. The audience raised their umbrellas about midway in the second act, but the pattering of the rain blotted out the words of the actors and distracted attention. Holloway was present, and he describes the scene:

The spectators sat on rude benches, chairs, or in picturesque attitudes on the grass. When the rain came down heavily the audience turned over their seats and stormed the stage (got under the tree) for shelter. . . . After some twenty minutes the rain lightened and the play was proceeded with to the end. The evening was now closing in and a flight of crows had noisily cawed their homeward route. . . . Humor was not absent. The Druid in the person of AE after casting his most weirdly-expressed "spell" over Naoise, on returning to the "Green Room" (a two acre field) discovered the loss of something (his glasses I was afterwards informed) cast off his druidic robes hurriedly and stood revealed in his everyday attire and searched and searched all his pockets in vain; and then with the aid of many of the sons of Fergus and Usna sought for the missing article high and low through the grass, as I enjoyed the pantomime from where I stood. . . . The distant whistling and noise of passing trains rudely broke in frequently on listeners' ears.[9]

The King's Threshold and *In the Shadow of the Glen* were performed for the first time in the Molesworth Hall on October 1, 1903. *The King's Threshold* caused no comment and is memorable as the play which introduced Sara Allgood to the stage. It was far otherwise with Synge's play. Synge had taken Yeats's advice and had lived first in Wicklow and then in the wild Aran Islands, where the inhabitants spoke only Gaelic and made their living by fishing. As already noted, the production of Synge's play had caused some dissension among the actors. *The Irish Independent,* an influential daily newspaper, hearing the rumors that Synge's play was degenerate, violently attacked it in a leader the morning before the first performance. The paper appealed to those who were financing it and to the actors to withdraw their support. Even though the writer of the article had not seen the play, he felt qualified to condemn it. Mr. Yeats and his friends, the writer said, were perverting the aims of The Irish National Theatre Society. They will "never serve save on terms that never could and never should be conceded. . . . Mr. Yeats wants greater freedom. He declares that every dramatic writer should be encouraged to see life afresh 'even though he sees it with strange eyes'. . . . Sincerely we hope that no such tolerance will be extended to Mr. Yeats and his friends."

The Molesworth Hall was crowded. The Chief Secretary for Ireland, not a popular official in a national theatre, was there, and W. G. Fay unfortunately gave him a chair upholstered in red— England's cruel red, it was noted in the press. *The King's Threshold* was listened to with attention, despite the fact that the children playing on the street caused distraction. One could hear in the hall such phrases from outside as, "Hey, misther! Throw us that ball, misther," "I'll tell me father on ya," "Yeh, you'll get him in Mooney's snug."

After *The King's Threshold*, Yeats went up on the stage in response to the call for "Author." He made a speech replying to the attack of *The Irish Independent.* Holloway thought the speech "atrocious" and added, "He generally makes a mess of it when he orates. Kind friends should advise him to hold his tongue." [10]

An attack on the stage was expected when the curtain was drawn on Synge's play. Yeats was restless during the interval. He wandered around the hall, then would go backstage and pop his head out from behind the curtains. The next minute he would take a short spurt down the centre passage to the door on some urgent business. He could not be at rest. George Moore was present, J. B. Yeats, AE, and many other members of the literary world.

Synge's play was received without any protest.

The following day the press uniformly attacked *In the Shadow of the Glen* and condemned the Society itself. *The Irish Independent* pointed out that the play's only merit was its brevity. "It is nothing more or less than a farcical libel on the character of the average decently reared Irish peasant woman," said the critic.

The most damaging blow of all came from *The United Irishman*. Edited by Arthur Griffith, it had been consistently friendly to Yeats and his associates. Even in its issue previous to the production of *In the Shadow of the Glen* it allowed J. B. Yeats to praise Synge as the equal of Shakespeare. However, after seeing the play, the paper published a violent and bitter attack on Synge. "The play has an Irish name but is no more Irish than the Decameron. It is a staging of a corrupt version of that old-world libel on woman-kind—*The Widow of Ephesus*." [11]

Maud Gonne resigned from the vice presidency of the Society in protest. In a letter to *The United Irishman* [12] she scolded Yeats, alleging he had forgotten that the majority of the Irish people were at the time passionately engaged in a struggle for independence. This was a hurtful blow to Yeats.

Even in the face of the universal criticism, Douglas Hyde did not resign; he remained with the Society, at least nominally, until March, 1904. Being a poet himself, Hyde appreciated what Yeats was attempting to do, although he disagreed with Yeats's attitude. His choice of action was to drift away from Yeats rather than break with him abruptly. The dissension over Synge's play did have the effect, however, of clearing the Society of intransigent members, thus giving Yeats greater influence within it. More important, the dissension was a warning of more storms ahead.

On December 3 the Society introduced Padraic Colum's first play, *Broken Soil* (later changed to *Fiddler's House*). Colum had been acting with the company from the beginning. His play was done in the dialect of the peasant and aroused great enthusiasm among press and public.

Yeats's *The Shadowy Waters,* on which he had been working for seven years, was produced at the Molesworth Hall on January 14, 1904. It bored the audience, primarily because it seemed to have no sense. *The Leader,* in its usual cynical way, suggested that after all Yeats might be a comedian. A little play of no particular merit, Seumas MacManus's *Townland of Tammey,* also was presented on this occasion.

Synge had written another play, *Riders to the Sea.* He came to Dublin and read it to the Society in the Camden Hall. Moore claims to have been present when it was read, and he tells in *Vale* [13] how Yeats cried "Sophocles!" across the table immediately the reader had finished; then, "fearing that he was not impressive enough, he said: 'No, Aeschylus!' " The play was accepted at once and Synge stayed in Dublin, directing the rehearsal at the cold, draughty hall in Camden Street.

Riders to the Sea was presented February 25, and the audience was so moved by its beauty and tragedy they did not applaud it at the end. Few people were there; the reason, according to Holloway,[14] was that they feared it would be as depressing and tiresome as Yeats's *The Shadowy Waters.*

In March the company was invited to London once more. They played on March 26 at the Royalty Theatre. London critics praised Synge's plays and the way they were acted. This was to the good, but the nationalists in Ireland were convinced by the friendly reception in London that the Society was pro-British.

Beneath all the noise of battle, Yeats saw that his ideal of an Irish theatre could be achieved through The Irish National Theatre Society. Already a genius had arrived—John Millington Synge —and Colum and Lady Gregory gave indications of high talent. He saw too that circumstances had forced him into a delicate position—between two women, one of talent and the other of wealth. To lean too much toward one would alienate the other, and he needed both. Yeats showed he could handle women when he was not emotionally involved. He made a move of genius.

He had received an offer to go on a lecture tour of America in the winter of 1903-1904. This meant he could make some money easily. His borrowings from Lady Gregory had compromised his position slightly—he owed her £500—and he now decided to repay it. This state of affairs annoyed Lady Gregory somewhat, but it pleased Miss Horniman; she saw hope. Accordingly, Yeats went off to America, leaving Miss Horniman busily sewing. AE took over the job of directing the policy of the Society and, as before, he did not handle it to the satisfaction of Yeats.

An invitation was extended to the Society to take part in the International Exposition at St. Louis, Missouri. Some members wanted to go, others did not. AE objected to the idea of an Irish National Theatre Society's going on tour; their place was in Ireland, he said. The result was that many of the players quit, led by Dudley Digges. Yeats, who was in America at the time, was disturbed when he learned of this. Not that he objected to the Company's touring America—on the contrary, he favored it—but he felt they should go at the proper time and, of course, led by himself. He wrote to AE, expressing his views strongly. AE was irritated and replied:

You say that the only chance of the Company making money is by an American tour. If that is so, then I think the Company had better dissolve at once for I would lose all interest in it if it were only to live for America and by America. . . . I have quite as much interest in the Company as you have, and in my own way have worked quite as much as you have to preserve it here, settling to the best of my ability the rows which threatened its existence. . . . I hope having expressed myself you will not urge the matter further for I believe I would simply lose my temper.[15]

The mild AE did lose his temper and shortly afterward resigned from the Society. He wrote to Yeats:

I have written a letter to the Secretary of the Theatre Society resigning my position as Vice President for reasons which I explain. I write to you to say that I do this without the least ill-will, but I feel that as your views

The Irish National Theatre Society   43

and mine about the spirit in which the Society should work are so different, and as the future success of the Society must be to a great extent bound up with your future work, whereas I in all probability will never write again in the dramatic form, it would be unfitting that I should retain an official position in the Society with which your name is associated and which depends almost altogether on your work for its success. I know that you will be considerably relieved by my taking this step and that you have wished it for a long time. . . . You may of course rest assured that your work and that of the Society has all the goodwill from me which I have ever felt and that I will never be drawn in act or spirit in opposition to its work.[16]

Despite his protestations of everlasting friendship, AE became estranged from Yeats and correspondence was not resumed. Yeats was, indeed, happy over AE's resignation; from now on he could more or less dictate to the Society. He returned to Ireland in April, wearing a voluminous fur coat and with his pockets full of money. He paid his debts to Lady Gregory. Delighted with this gesture, Miss Horniman offered to buy him a theatre in Dublin. Success had at last dawned for him.

The Abbey Theatre

The offer of a theatre did not catch Yeats unprepared. For years he had been wandering around Dublin, examining every building and vacant lot for its possibility as a theatre site. When Miss Horniman made her offer, he was able at once to show her a good location. There was a small theatre popularly referred to as the "Mechanics" in Lower Abbey Street, and adjoining it was a disused building which had once been a city morgue. By taking over the "Mechanics" and buying the morgue, it would be possible to build a fine theatre.

Whether by luck or intrigue is not known, but just at this moment the "Mechanics" was forced to close down because it did not comply with the safety rules of the city fire department. Yeats and

Miss Horniman stepped in and leased both buildings. Joseph Holloway, besides being deeply interested in the theatre, was an architect. He was asked to survey the buildings and estimate the cost of alterations. One April morning he and Miss Horniman tried to get into the "Mechanics"; they were ordered away by the manager, Sean Glenville.

Yeats was sent for, and at 3:30 P.M. Holloway, Miss Horniman, and Yeats made a second attempt. This time they were more successful, but just as they reached the stage, Glenville appeared and, measuring them with a withering look, he shouted, "Get out, you bunch of land-grabbers! You have a cheek to come here. Get out, you bunch of foreign land-grabbers!" The three left as fast as they could, amid a volley of curses. As they were going out the door, Glenville shouted, "May you and your Morgue have luck." [1] However, the business acumen of Yeats was too much for the manager of the "Mechanics," who was quickly evicted. Building was begun almost immediately.

According to British and Irish law, a theatre must operate under a patent, which is granted by the King of England. It was therefore necessary for Miss Horniman and Yeats to apply to the courts for this patent. All the other theatres in the city objected in court to the application, because they thought the new theatre would be competing with them. Yeats's statement that the new theatre would be strictly noncommercial did not satisfy them. When they saw that the patent was likely to be granted, they agreed only on condition that a provision be inserted to the effect that the new theatre be permitted to produce only plays by Irish authors in the Irish or English language and all standard works in any language written not less than fifty years before the date of the patent. The court granted the patent for a period of six years. The opposing solicitor's final jab, "You could do a lot of damage in six years," turned out to have more point than he intended. [2]

The patent was granted not to Miss Horniman but to "Dame Isabella Augusta Gregory." The reason was that, according to law, the patentee must be a resident of Ireland; neither Miss Horniman nor Yeats was resident in Ireland, and Miss Horniman reluctantly agreed to allow the patent to be held in the name of "Dame" Gregory—the court being careful that she should not be taken as the daughter of a peer.[3]

Miss Horniman made it quite clear that she, and not Lady Gregory, owned the theatre, and when the Editors of *Dana* made the mistake of saying the theatre had been bought for Mr. W. G. Fay, she had them insert a correction: "The Abbey Theatre, we are informed, has not been 'bought' for Mr. Fay or for anyone else. It has been acquired by Miss Horniman, who has arranged to lend it on very generous conditions to the National Theatre Society for their performances, but she retains herself the entire proprietary interest in the Theatre." [4] Yeats was not interested in the minor point as to who owned the theatre; as far as he was concerned, the theatre was his. He knew that in a few years it would be an easy matter to obtain complete ownership.

It was believed the theatre would be ready by December, and rehearsals began. The theatre would open with four short plays: two revivals, *Kathleen Ni Houlihan* and *In the Shadow of the Glen;* and two new plays, *On Baile's Strand,* a one-act, blank-verse tragedy by Yeats, and *Spreading the News,* a farce by Lady Gregory. The first rehearsal at the Abbey Theatre was on October 31, 1904. The theatre was not completed at the time; only temporary lighting was installed, and the builders' tools still were in the theatre. Holloway was present on this, as on every occasion of importance, and he gives a vivid account of the scene:

Lady Gregory and Miss Quinn I found seated on the half finished front pit seats and W. B. Yeats wandering excitedly about among the planks and rubbish in momentary danger of coming a cropper. *On Baile's Strand* in rehearsal with W. B. Yeats at the helm. I can say without fear of contradiction that a more irritating play producer never directed a rehearsal. His ever flitting about and interrupting the players in the middle of their speeches, showing them by illustration how he wished it done, droningly reading the passage in a monotonous, dreary, sing-song; or climbing up a ladder onto the stage and pacing the boards as he would have the players do. (I thought he would come to grief on the rickety ladder several times.) Anon, he would rush on and erase, or add a line or two to the text but ever and always he was on the fidget and made each and all of the players pray backwards. Mr. George Russell and J. M. Synge dropped in during the rehearsal of this piece and Lady Gregory and Miss Quinn changed their places to an old carpenter's bench nearer the stage.

Despite Holloway's strictures on Yeats as a director, the plays were ready in good time. The designs for the costumes caused some worry, but Yeats settled this by saying, "Hang archaeology, it's effect we want on the stage." [5]

The Abbey Theatre opened for the first time on Saturday night, December 27, 1904. All seats—five hundred and sixty-two—were filled. Notabilities from the literary and political world were present: John Dillon, John Redmond, Stephen Gwynn, W. B. Yeats, AE, Edward Martyn, Hugh Lane, John Masefield (representing *The Manchester Guardian*), and many others. Neither Lady Gregory nor Miss Horniman was present; Lady Gregory claims to have been ill and Miss Horniman had "urgent" business in England. Immediately before the curtain went up, Yeats consulted the stars; he found them quiet and fairly favorable, he told Lady Gregory.[6] Had he consulted any ordinary Irishman, he might have received a more accurate prognostication.

The Dublin daily newspapers, impressed by the distinguished patrons of the Abbey, reported favorably. Even *The Irish Independent*, which had so violently attacked Synge's *In the Shadow of the Glen* a year before, now praised Yeats. It was otherwise with the weekly newspapers, which were mostly nationalistic. Arthur Griffith's *The United Irishman* returned to the attack, pointing out that Synge was as decadent as Petronious and that "the theatre which started so well, can now only alternate a decadent wail with a Calvinistic groan." [7]

One could not expect D. P. Moran, editor of *The Leader*, to be less antagonistic. All along, his dislike of Yeats and his associates had been so violent it blinded his judgment even to the merit of Synge's *Riders to the Sea;* he had described it as "a ghastly production" which "reminded me of a visit to a dissecting room." [8] However, his slightly cynical account of the Abbey Theatre opening is significant, because it represented the attitude of the masses at this time.

As he entered the Abbey, Moran tells us,[9] his first impression, after viewing the aristocratic, Anglo-Irish audience, was that he "had strayed by mistake into a prayer meeting of the foreign element in Ireland." He could not expect anything else, for the theatre had been built by an Englishwoman and was owned by her. She did not trust her Anglo-Irish friends enough to hand the theatre over to them, and the fact she retained full control made Moran suspicious that it might be one further attempt by the British Foreign Office to poison the Irish mind.

We fear that Mr. Yeats, shrewd man though he is, will never touch the Irish heart. If the movement as it has been developed by Mr. Yeats, rang true even to the hearts of the consciously "superior" class who are so evident these times on the edges of real Ireland surely some one or more of them would have backed this illustrated chanting movement with their money, and not have left it to a woman of the English to supply the Society with a theatre. . . . We note that the ha'penny *Independent* was "got at" by the melancholy twilight advertising ring on Saturday and a nicely posed head of W. B. was the centrepiece in an illustrated puff of the poor What-is-it to be boomed. . . . We fear that the National Theatre Society is not worth criticism in a widely-read paper. . . . These "National" people who flutter and twitter *outside* the land of the Irish people do not interest the people. On Saturday night, the first night, when the male and female social butterflies who like chatter and feigned excitement, flock to these places, the house was only very partially filled [this was not true]. . . . Some of the audience amused us. When our eyes glanced over the stalls, it warmed our Irish hearts to think that we have given so many of those present at one time or another, a well-deserved correction. The Celtic Christmas was incarnate between the acts. Melancholy Greys chattered to Rhythmic Twilights. For us the play was principally at the other side of the footlights. . . . An amusing feature of this grey and twilight race is that they are so grey that they are quite unconscious that people "have the weight" of them and are laughing at their posings and posturings. They are expert advertisers, however, and are entitled to credit for their excellence in that useful art. . . .

In fairness to Moran, it must be noted that on more than one occasion he suspended his attack, when asked to do so by Yeats, so that the theatre might be able to bring in an audience for a certain play.

When Yeats opened the Abbey Theatre, his bottomless contempt for public opinion was again apparent: he included Synge's *In the Shadow of the Glen* in the first program. Synge had written a new play, *The Well of the Saints,* and it had been in rehearsal since the previous June. It was a more controversial play than *In the Shadow of the Glen,* but Yeats played the latter because it was certain to displease, reserving *The Well of the Saints* for the second series of productions. Thanks to the novelty of having a new theatre, many people attended during the first week, and a profit of fifty pounds was made.

The Well of the Saints, performed on February 4, lost sixty pounds and emptied the theatre. This did not disturb Yeats; he was sure of the genius of Synge. "Irishmen," he told George Moore,[10] "had written well before Synge, but they had written well by casting off Ireland; but Synge was the first man that Ireland had inspired." Moore continued:

I asked if he were going to find his fortune in Ireland, his literary fortune, for *The Well of the Saints* had very nearly emptied the Abbey Theatre. We were twenty in the stalls: The Yeats family, Sarah Purser, William Bailey, John Eglinton, AE, Longworth, and dear Edward [Martyn], who supported the Abbey Theatre though he was averse from peasant plays. All this sneering at Catholic practices is utterly distasteful to me, he said to me. I can hear the whining voice of the proselytiser through it all. I never will go against my opinions, and when I hear the Sacred Name, I assure you—.

Having expressed his contempt for critics and public, Yeats was content to produce some noncontroversial plays, mostly comedies. *Kincora,* an historical play about Brian Boru written by Lady Gregory, appeared on March 25. It was well liked by the audience, and even *The United Irishman* praised it. On April 25 a first play by William Boyle, *The Building Fund,* also pleased, being partly of the commercial variety. *Land,* a peasant play by Padraic Colum, was performed in June. It was such a simple and innocent kind of play that critics of the Abbey agreed that Yeats and his associates had begun to see the light at last. But they were soon to be disillusioned.

These popular pieces were shown mainly because Yeats had not complete control of the selection of plays. AE's democratic method was still the rule. But Yeats was moving to have this changed. He accomplished this through the cooperation of Miss Horniman.

First he reorganized the company, turning it into a professional group. He argued that to do good work, actors would need to devote their full time to the job. Miss Horniman guaranteed £600 for salaries. Willie Fay was made manager of the theatre at a salary of 27 shillings per week, and to other members were given salaries of from 15 shillings to a pound. Only those who were really interested in the theatre would accept such negligible wages, and many of the original actors left. In return for her guarantee Miss Horniman asked that the Society assure her of its good faith by becoming a limited liability society, thereby protecting her against any serious financial loss. There was some opposition to this, because it meant appointing three directors who might develop into dictators on policy and play selection. Yeats had foreseen this objection and was prepared for it. He had submitted one of his own plays anonymously to the Society, and the selection committee rejected it.[11] Consequently, when the charge of dictatorship was made, he was able to argue that the dictatorship of the few who are of the highest intelligence is better than the democracy of the many. This rather shocking statement was difficult to reply to: it was answered by the secession of two thirds of the Society. This left only eight members: Yeats, Synge, Lady Gregory, Sara Allgood, Miss Esposito, Udolpho Wright, Frank Fay, and Willie Fay.

AE was disturbed when he heard of this. In a letter to Yeats he said: "You are committing the great mistake about Ireland, the 'twenty years of resolute government' theory. Irish people will only be held by their affections. . . . As a poet you could and would exercise an immense influence on your contemporaries, as a dramatist you lose influence." [12]   Holloway, always supporting the actor against the poet, expressed the attitude of the actors toward Yeats on this occasion:

What the society wants most is a person with business tact (having no connection with the theatre as actor or dramatist) to manage the commercial side of the theatre. The present people at the head of affairs are too stupidly egotistical to cater to the interests of the public at home and only look on Dublin as the training ground for London shows. . . . Yeats is an impossible man to have at the head of affairs. He lives in a dream-land Ireland of his own invention and understands not the real article when he comes across it in others' work. Synge, another writer puffed into existence by the log rolling of Yeats, sees Ireland through the glasses of non-moral Paris Bohemia.[13]

By the end of September, Yeats succeeded in turning the Society into The Irish National Theatre Society, Limited, under the *Industrial and Provident Societies Act of 1893*. He and Lady Gregory and Synge commandeered most of the shares, leaving the other members only one share each. Under this reorganization Yeats, Lady Gregory, and Synge became presidents of the Society, Willie Fay stage manager, and Frank Fay secretary.

Yeats had triumphed. The national theatre of which he had dreamed had become a reality, and he was master of its destiny.

Fighting the Audience

With Yeats in complete control of the theatre, it was only a matter of time when he would provoke the public to a riot. Even in 1905, when he had less power, he kept up a continuous attack on critics and public, charging them with being incapable of sound judgments. This so irritated the public that few attended the occasional performances, and plays rarely ran for more than three nights. The constant bickerings inside and outside the Society also helped to confuse the public and keep them away. When the Society opened its new season on October 2, 1905, there were fewer than fifty in the house, but what was lost in numbers was made up for in intellect: Edward Martyn, George Moore, W. B. Yeats, AE, Jack B. Yeats, Miss Horniman, Tom Kettle, D. J.

O'Donoghue, and Lord Monteagle. Holloway, of course, was there and he reported that the silence around made him feel as if he were in a church, where to speak would be a breach of decorum.

Another cause of the small audiences was the prices of admission. The prices of one, two, and three shillings, set by Miss Horniman, were too high for the ordinary Dubliner. She fixed on these rates because, intending to let the theatre to others for concerts and meetings when it was not needed by Yeats, she thought too-low admissions would attract a ruder crowd and so lower the theatre's letting value. The editor of *The Leader* did not fail to see the implications, and he so informed his readers:

We note that there are to be no sixpenny seats at the Abbey Theatre. The prices 3s. 2s. and 1s. may be raised, but they must not be lowered, whoever may rent the place; and the reason of this arrangement is "to prevent cheap entertainments from being given which would lower the letting value of the hall." Well, if the Abbey Theatre wants to fill its little self at these prices, it will have to import Little Titch or some "musical comedy"; illustrated chanting won't draw crowded houses to the diminutive theatre. . . . Art is art and literature is literature; they are both very well in their way; but "letting value" must not be depreciated, and so the sixpenny public must do without endowed art. . . . The fixing of the minimum prices at 3s. 2s. and 1s. places the Abbey Theatre practically outside the sphere of utility as far as the Gaelic League branches that have Irish plays to stage are concerned; perhaps the Gaelic League under any circumstances, would not improve the "letting value" of the new theatre. Might we suggest that "Upholding the Letting Value" would not be a bad title for a lively comedy.[1]

In his first year of absolute control of the theatre, Yeats adopted a policy of nonbelligerence toward the public. He even went so far as to produce two new farces by William Boyle, *The Eloquent Dempsey* (January 20, 1906) and *The Mineral Workers* (October 20, 1906). Neither of these two plays was of any artistic value, but they were very popular with the audience—especially *The Eloquent Dempsey,* a satire on the politician who wants to be on both sides at the same time.

The year was also notable for the performance of five new plays by Lady Gregory: *The White Cockade* (December 9, 1905), a play about the battle of the Boyne; *Hyacinth Halvey* (February 19, 1906), a short, amusing comedy; *The Doctor in Spite of Himself* (April 16), a translation into Anglo-Irish of the play by Molière; *The Gaol Gate* (October 20), a one-act tragedy, and *The Canavans,* a comedy.

The company also left Dublin five times to produce plays elsewhere: in November, 1905, they visited Oxford, Cambridge, and London; in February, 1906, Wexford; in March, Dundalk; in April, Liverpool, Manchester, and Leeds; in May, Cardiff, Aberdeen, Newcastle Upon Tyne, Edinburgh, and Hull. All their English tours, with the exception of the last named, were successful in every way. The Scottish tour was a financial failure—not through any lack of interest on the part of the audiences that actually attended, but because the weather was exceptionally fine and people wished to enjoy the sunshine while it lasted. The visits to the Irish provinces were an experiment: Yeats had always hoped the plays might reach the country people. It was a failure financially. Receipts on both occasions barely paid the expenses.

The shortage of good actors caused some embarrassment. Shaw's *John Bull's Other Island* was turned down ostensibly for this reason, namely, that there was no one skillful enough, it was said, to play Broadbent. It might be, however, that the real reason was different in this case: at this time Yeats and Synge did not feel that Shaw belonged to the real Irish tradition. His plays would thus have no place in the Irish theatre movement. *John Bull's Other Island* was a play *about* Ireland but not *of* it. Furthermore, Shaw's plays were mostly argument, and Yeats particularly detested this quality in dramatic writing.

There was indeed a shortage of good performers. Yeats had to bring over an English actress, Miss Darragh, to take the lead in his *Deirdre* (November 24, 1906). Miss Darragh's visit aroused discontent among the players: because she was a well-known actress, she had to be paid a high salary and be specially advertised. This represented almost a reversal of policy on the part of Yeats, but it soon was settled happily when Miss Darragh returned to England after playing in a revised form of Yeats's *The Shadowy Waters* (December 8).

A number of new actors joined the company in the fall, and the

Abbey had finally a brilliant group: Willie and Frank Fay, J. M. Kerrigan, Fred O'Donovan, Sydney Morgan, Sara Allgood, Maire O'Neill, Arthur Sinclair, and J. A. O'Rourke.

Another important addition to the theatre was the small orchestra, under G. R. Hillis. It had been obvious for some time that an orchestra was needed: plays were usually very short, and since four were often performed in one evening, there would be long delays while scenery was being changed. At first, Arthur Darley, a traditional violinist, was employed to play during the intervals, but the noise of the scene changers frequently drowned his music and he retired. Hillis, with his orchestra, then took over in the fall of 1906 and remained with the Abbey Theatre until fall, 1908, when he was replaced by John F. Larchet.

Yeats made a final peace gesture in October, 1906, when he set aside a section of the theatre for sixpenny seats.

All seemed serene. There was no shortage of good plays, the company was the best the Society had ever possessed, audiences were increasing—partly because of the commercial plays of Boyle, partly because of the skillful, soothing propaganda of the new manager, W. A. Henderson. By the end of 1906 the theatre even showed a profit of three pounds for the year.[2]

Just when it seemed to the public that Yeats had learned his lesson and was prepared to make concessions to public and nationalistic opinion, he struck again—this time more violently than ever. He put on a new play by Synge, *The Playboy of the Western World*.

Now, Synge was the most hated of all the Abbey dramatists. Lady Gregory and Yeats were disliked by the more sentimental nationalists, mainly because they were regarded as pro-British. But Synge was detested by nationalists of every shade and degree of political thought. To them, he was a Paris bohemian who went to the west of Ireland to write slanderous plays about the peasants. His first play, *In the Shadow of the Glen*, described an unhappily married Irish couple. There are no loveless marriages in Ireland, the nationalists cried. Such a thing cannot happen in Ireland; it is something Synge saw in Paris, and now he is imputing it to the Irish Catholic peasants. And *The Well of the Saints* was hardly less obnoxious.

Synge was naturally annoyed, and he told Willie Fay one night, "Very well, then; the next play I write I will make sure it will annoy them." [3] This was *The Playboy of the Western World*. The scene was laid in the west of Ireland. The story tells how Christie Mahon (the Playboy) arrives late at night at a peasant's cottage seeking shelter from the police because, as he says, he killed his Da with a blow of a loy (a heavy spade). The peasant takes him in at once, and Christie is left in the house with the daughter, Pegeen, while the peasant owner goes off to a wake. Pegeen falls in love with him because he is such a brave fellow to have the courage to kill his Da. In the end, it is discovered he did not really kill him. Pegeen savagely turns on the Playboy and burns his leg with a sod of turf because he has told her a lie. He is no longer a hero with the peasants and is thrown out of the house. Here, indeed, was a theme to antagonize the Irish audience. To make matters worse, the dialogue used in the play is a flamboyant dialect of English interspersed with numerous swearwords.

Yeats took exception to the public's antagonism toward Synge, whom he believed the equal of Aeschylus. He was therefore very glad to produce *The Playboy;* not only was it a good play, it was obviously one which would shock the public and teach them a lesson.

The curtain went up on *The Playboy of the Western World* for the first time on Saturday night, January 26, 1907, before a full house. Everyone in the Irish literary world was there except Yeats, who was away in Scotland, and George Moore, who was in Paris. Both quickly returned to Dublin when they heard of the reception given to the play.

The audience was somewhat puzzled at first as to how they should take the play; though they remembered the many sins of Synge in the past, they imagined he had reformed. Accordingly, the first act was applauded, then the second. However, in the middle of the third act, when the word "shift" was used, the audience was no longer in doubt. They booed, hissed, and shouted. They drowned the words of the players.

Synge was there, but his only comment on the row was, "I don't care a rap." People fought all over the house and many demanded that the play be withdrawn. The directors, of course, would not think of it, and the play continued all the next week. The papers reported the row and condemned the play as a slander on Ireland. Every night, starting Monday, groups of nationalists went to the theatre, some with tin trumpets, to prevent the play from being heard.

Yeats, home from Scotland, called in the police. This was the final insult. The British police, the symbol of oppression! Edward Martyn told George Moore it was unforgivable in an Irishman to seek the protection of the police.[4] Padraic Colum, whose father was arrested and convicted as a disturber at the theatre, wrote to *The Freeman's Journal:*

The management of the Abbey Theatre have made a tactical error in introducing police into the theatre. It was a mistake to associate a theatre whose effort it is to become a National Theatre with police protection. It was a risk to subject an audience to the ordeal of the police.

Even Joseph Holloway, who could not be called a nationalist, objected: "This was freedom of the theatre according to Yeats and his studies in blue ranged along the walls like Tussaud's waxworks."[5]

The protests continued all during the week, although the voices of the actors could rarely be heard above the noise. Yeats would not withdraw the play. He would act it in dumb show rather than take it off and so admit the public's right to dictate to him. His only concession was to hold a debate on the play in the Abbey Theatre on Monday night, February 4—after the play had run its scheduled course. An admission price of one shilling and sixpence was charged for the debate. Yeats opened the discussion. He said the attack on the play was not a reasonable expression of opinion but was an organized attempt on the part of a small group to prevent the play from being heard and judged. Defending the introduction of the police, he said:

When *The Countess Cathleen* was denounced with an equal violence they called in the police—that was in '99 when I was still President of the Wolf Tone Commemoration Committee of Great Britain (laughter and applause). I would indeed despise myself if for the sake of the popularity of a vague sentiment, I were to mar the task I had set my hand to, and to cast the precious things of the soul into the trodden mire. . . . Gentlemen of the little Clubs and Societies, do not mistake the meaning of our victory. It means something for us but more for you. When the curtain of *The Playboy* fell on Saturday night amidst thunders of applause, I am confident that I saw the rise in this country of a new thought, a new opinion, that we had long needed. . . . The generation of young men and girls who are now leaving colleges are weary of the tyranny of Clubs and Leagues. They wish again for individual sincerity, the eternal quest of truth, all that has been given up for so long that all might crouch upon the one roost and quack or cry in the one flock. We are beginning once again to ask what a man is and to be content to wait a little before we go on to that further question "What is a good Irishman?" Manhood is all, and the root of manhood is courage and courtesy.[6]

When the discussion was opened to the house, all the old charges were repeated. Synge was a decadent, his play was blasphemous and a slander on Ireland, and Yeats was a member of the British garrison in Ireland. J. B. Yeats, the poet's father, took part in the discussion. He said he believed the play gave a true and faithful picture of the western peasantry. The storm of hisses which greeted this statement was loud and long, and it was renewed with even greater force when he went on: "I have not forgotten that this is the Island of Saints—plaster saints. I myself have not a very great belief in saints, and therefore I enjoy the thought that it is an island of sinners."

The production of *The Playboy* was a great success financially. The house was packed every night, and seats were difficult to get. Holloway records that one man sought admission on the plea that "he did not hear a d—n word of the b—y show, the b—y night he sat the——show out." The girl refused to admit him. With a mighty oath against "the whole d—m play he and his companion left to visit the Empire Theatre." [7]

Yeats did not spare expense in advertising the play; fifty shillings a day was spent on having a group of men parade around the city with sandwich boards drawing attention to the play, and thirty pounds was spent on advertisements in the press.[8]

Even Synge, for all his detachment, was unnerved by the violence of the attack. Yeats actually was upset also, though he refused to show it. He walked the Dublin streets, his head in the air, his big fur coat with white astrakan collar hanging from his stooped shoulders.

One result of the antagonistic demonstration was the withdrawal by William Boyle of his plays from the theatre as a protest against *The Playboy*. Holloway's interpretation of this action is most illuminating: "This was the biggest blow the National Theatre Society received since it became a police-protected society. As an Irish theatre the Abbey's knell is rung. Boyle's retiring was the death-blow to the society." [9]

Even here, Yeats refused to be dictated to: he knew that Boyle's plays were of no artistic merit, but he wrote Boyle that the Society held the rights to the plays and would produce them when they wished. Boyle was very angry; he had signed an agreement giving the Abbey production rights on his plays for five years. He did not blame Yeats so much as he blamed Miss Horniman. "She is back of it all," Boyle wrote to a friend. "Her hatred of the Irish people almost amounts to lunacy. She would not allow a word of Irish patriotic sentiment to be brought out in what she calls her theatre. I know that Yeats has not as free a hand as he pretends. Every word I put in my plays of a soft or kindly nature was ruthlessly cut out." [10]

Boyle's accusation that Yeats had not complete freedom was correct; but it was not Miss Horniman who curtailed it; she was delighted with the publicity. Yeats's freedom was being challenged from another source.

Chastising the Actor

By the year 1907 everyone associated with the Abbey Theatre had been attacked. Synge was a decadent, Yeats a stupidly arrogant poet, Lady Gregory a proselytizer, Miss Horniman an English-woman. Only Frank and Willie Fay escaped censure. Even the bitterest enemies of the theatre were willing to admit that both the Fays were excellent actors. This gave the Fays a heightened notion of their importance, and they began to demand a greater control in the management of the theatre than they already had. They considered themselves the original founders of the Society, and they felt that Yeats and his associates were leading it to destruction. They even came to imagine that the Abbey Theatre building belonged to them.

This was a dangerous delusion on their part; Miss Horniman was always sensitive on this point, and she saw the challenge to her authority even before it came. She wrote Yeats that Synge and Lady Gregory were sacrificing his work by groveling at the feet of the Fays and making him an abject slave to them: "They only care to show themselves off to a small set in Dublin *at my expense*," she said. "Try to put yourself in the position of some decent person who cares for the drama and does not care a rap for a hole-and-corner Irish idea." [1]

Yeats had recognized the increasing presumption of the Fays, but he was not in a position then to do anything about it; he had enough trouble on his hands over the production of *The Playboy*. However, if Miss Horniman was willing to handle this problem, Yeats was willing to agree. Accordingly, Miss Horniman arranged for her friend Ben Iden Payne to go over to the Abbey as stage manager and thus try to oust the Fays. He arrived early in 1907 and took over as stage manager despite the protests of the brothers. Tension brought on by *The Playboy* had not died down, and Lady Gregory decided the best thing she could do was to take a holiday abroad. She stayed on for the production of three short new plays of her own, *The Jackdaw* (February 23), *The Rising of the Moon* (March 9), and *The Poorhouse* (April 3); then, inviting Yeats to accompany her, she departed for a tour of Italy.

While they were gone, Payne staged two unusual plays at the Abbey: Maeterlinck's *Interior* (March 16) and Scawen Blunt's *Fand* (April 27). The latter was a two-act poetic play founded on the legend of the fairy woman who enticed Cuchulain to fairyland. Receiving no cooperation from the Fays, however, his position was very difficult, and he went back to England.

As for Miss Horniman, she was dismayed by Yeats's sudden departure from the scene in the company of Lady Gregory, and she could see little inducement to fight his battles at home.

Lest it appear that his trip to Italy be construed as a sign of defeat, Yeats announced he was going to produce *The Playboy* in England. Once again cries of "traitors!" went up from the press. The editor of *The Freeman's Journal* wrote Lady Gregory a threatening letter, warning her against taking *The Playboy* to England. She could do nothing about it; Yeats had decided to assert again his contempt for public opinion, and she could not go against his will. In matters of policy, Yeats was always supreme.

Scawen Blunt dined with her at about this time, and in his diary for June 1, 1907, he says:

> Lady Gregory is in worse trouble than ever. The Editor of the "Freeman" has written threatening her with new displeasure if she persists with "The Playboy" in England and I fear her theatre will be altogether boycotted. I advise her to submit to Irish opinion, but though she admits that it was a mistake to produce the play, she says it is too late now to withdraw it. The worst of it is that she is already boycotted personally on account of it at Coole; the Local Council has forbidden the school-children to go to her house, or even to accept cakes or presents of any kind from her; it is the Sinn Fein that has done it.[2]

Yeats was obdurate. He took *The Playboy* to Oxford (June 5) and London. It delighted the London critics, and they could not understand why an Irish audience had attacked it. One phrase, incidentally, was deleted by order of the English censor; it was the reference to "khaki cutthroats," which meant the British soldiers.

When the company returned to Ireland, the press advised the public to avoid the Abbey Theatre. Yeats was unperturbed. He had in rehearsal a new play which he told his friends was so controversial it would take a troop of soldiers to keep the audience quiet.[3] It was *The Country Dressmaker*, a rural comedy on matchmaking, by George Fitzmaurice, a new dramatist. Yeats was to be disappointed. It was favorably received when it opened on October 3; there were no police in the theatre, and the audience was fashionable: Sara Purser, R. C. Orpen, William Orpen, Jack Yeats, Hugh Lane, W. B. Yeats, and other literary and artistic people.

Another new play by Lady Gregory appeared on October 31: *Dervorgilla*, based on the Norman invasion of Ireland. On November 21 Yeats's *The Unicorn From the Stars* opened. This was a rewritten version of his *Where There Is Nothing*. The theme of the play was Moore's, but Yeats had used it as his own, and the two had quarreled because of it.

Meanwhile, Lady Gregory was winning the battle for Yeats's

affections. It could hardly have been otherwise, for Yeats was impressed by her capacity for supplying the theatre with so many of its plays. Maud Gonne had been watching the struggle with interest, and in her memoirs she dates Miss Horniman's defeat from Yeats's Italian tour with Lady Gregory. In her book *A Servant of the Queen* she wrote:

. . . both were interested in Willie and both were interested in the Irish theatre. Miss Horniman had the money and was willing to spend it, but Lady Gregory had the brains. They should have been allies for both stood for art for art's sake and deprecated the intrusion of politics, which meant Irish Freedom; instead they were rivals; they both liked Willie too well. Lady Gregory won the battle. Miss Horniman's money converted the old city morgue into the Abbey Theatre, but it was Lady Gregory's plays that were acted there. Miss Horniman brought back Italian plaques to decorate it but Lady Gregory carried off Willie to visit the Italian towns where they were made. . . .[4]

When Miss Horniman saw Yeats, back from Italy, with his hair cut and himself dressed like a prosperous theatre manager, she saw the end. She made one last desperate effort before she retired from the struggle. Miss Horniman was establishing the Manchester Repertory Theatre, and she asked Yeats to write poetic plays for it. She said she would find the best verse speakers to play in them.

Yeats refused. He would not desert Ireland. He realized the Abbey Theatre was moving away from the poetic drama he had so desired: the peasant plays of Colum, Fitzmaurice, and even Lady Gregory were dominating the boards, and poets were not arising so quickly as he had expected. But he would continue to hope. He knew that the ear of the pit was being trained gradually by the language in the plays of Synge. And Mrs. Patrick Campbell, a good speaker of verse, had come from England and played in Yeats's verse play *Deirdre.* "I understand my own race," he wrote Miss Horniman, "and in all my work lyric or dramatic I have thought of it. If the theatre fails I may or may not write plays, there is always lyric poetry to return to, but I shall write for my own people, whether in love or hate matters little. . . ."[5]

Miss Horniman now knew definitely she had lost Yeats, and her reply is full of violent jealousy.

But what are my words against the wooing of the vampire Kathleen Ni Houlihan! That Mrs. Patrick Campbell has made such an offer . . . and that you are most naturally delighted with it are merely details. I believe she admires your poetical powers and very likely she has taken a fancy to you too although you are much too old for a woman of forty who might well go in for someone young. The root of the matter is whether Willie Fay will let the Directors and the Company consent to allow an Englishwoman to play at the Abbey. . . . This is the whole gist of it all, but you will only be angry with me for putting it so clearly. But I will not see the rest of your life wasted without raising my voice even if it be useless. You *must* know that Fay would not permit a second company of actors at the Abbey. . . . I will not waste the rest of my life on a Lost Cause.[6]

Yeats understood the justice of Miss Horniman's criticism of the Fays, and he decided they must go. They were becoming altogether too presumptuous. First they demanded complete control of the actors, then they complained they had no voice in selecting plays. They blamed Yeats for the small attendance—sometimes there were no more than a dozen persons at a performance. Yeats, they said, produced only the plays of his friends, and since these plays usually were unpopular, they held that Yeats was killing the dramatic movement which they imagined they had founded.

Yeats repelled the accusation [wrote George Moore] by offering to submit those that he had rejected to the judgment of Professor Tyrell, a quite unnecessary concession on the part of Yeats, for Willie Fay is but an amusing Irish comedian and it was presumptuous for him and his brother to set themselves against a poet. They resigned, and one night Yeats came to me with the grave news that the Fays had seceded. . . . I told him, and without hesitation, that the secession of the Fays was a blessing in disguise, and that now he was master in his own house the Abbey Theatre would begin to flourish. . . .[7]

On January 13, 1908, the Fays left the theatre, and they did not return. They went to New York and produced a number of plays, claiming they were the Irish theatre. In the press, Yeats quickly contradicted this suggestion. He then called a meeting of The Irish National Theatre Society, at which were present himself, Synge, and Udolpho Wright. The following resolution was passed and transmitted to the Fays:

At a meeting of the Irish National Theatre Society held March 18, 1908, present Messrs. Yeats, U. Wright, J. M. Synge, you were suspended from membership of the society for breach of and under Rule V (R). Your breach of the rule might under different circumstances have been merely technical but recent misrepresentations have made this step necessary in the interest of the Society. Signed: J. M. Synge (Sec.).

Now Yeats was in absolute control, as Moore said, and the theatre prospered, although not exactly in the way Yeats had hoped.

Toward Freedom

Yeats never was in doubt on a question of policy. A poetic theatre which should be completely free of the stultifying influence of commerce was his obsession. He was guided always by intuition, rarely by reason or by expediency. His first, most urgent practical objective had been to demonstrate to the public that they must not presume to dictate to him. When the same challenge came from the actors, he answered it as he had answered the public: he drove the Fays from the theatre, even at the risk of killing the distinctive school of Irish acting which they had in part inaugurated. The artist must not compromise his freedom, and so the Fays had to go, leaving the theatre with only three or four actors, all inexperienced.

The belief was general that the Abbey Theatre would collapse after the Fays' secession. Yeats surprised everyone when he announced in February, 1908, that the season would open with two new plays, *The Man Who Missed the Tide* by W. F. Casey and *The Piper* by Norreys Connell (Conal O'Riordan). The Abbey was well filled—mostly by those curious to discover what attitude Yeats was taking. Many thought he would be in a defeatist mood, and they came to gloat over his misery. They were disappointed, for Yeats, with Lady Gregory, appeared in the foyer in full dress, beaming as if he had won a great victory.[1]

He had a new shock ready for the audience. *The Piper* would hurt patriotic sentiment as deeply as any of the earlier plays had done. It was based on an incident in the Insurrection of 1798, in which three Irish soldiers have captured an English soldier and are considering whether they should "bate" him. They quarrel among themselves as to whether they had won or lost, and as they are quarreling, a number of English soldiers return and shoot them all.

The audience did not know how to react; they had come to scoff at a contrite Yeats but discovered they were exposed to further insults instead. *The Irish Independent* reported:

Up jumped a man in the pit: "Is this what the National Theatre stands for?" he asked in loud tones. "Order," came the cry. "Sit down." "I won't sit down. I protest against this thing. It's rubbish. It's a damn shame to allow it to go on." [2]

The play was very short and consequently did not arouse the audience to riot. The press attacked the play. Yeats defended it in a letter to *The Freeman's Journal:*

The play, to my mind, meant a satire upon the nine years of the Parnellite split, years of endless talk, endless rhetoric, and futile drifting; years which were taken out of the history of the nation and made nothing. Further my imagination went back to the rebellion of Robert Emmet, the folly that surrounded him, the slackness as bad as treachery, which brought that heroic life to nothing. That also was satirised in the play. We are all agreed that it is worthy of satire, the most bitter satire; and that a national theatre is right in satirising upon the stage that endless, useless talk through which the lifeblood of the nation is wasting away.

Yeats must have realized that *The Piper* was a bad play, but it was important to convince the public they were incapable of forming judgment. Accordingly, it was essential that he defend it. In a leader, *The Irish Independent* of Saturday, February 15, appealed to Yeats to withdraw the play "now that it got a fair hearing." This, to Yeats, was a challenge to continue the play. He arranged that it be repeated the following week, with a matinee performance included. This was the final defeat for the Abbey Theatre audience and for the Dublin press. Obviously Yeats could not be intimidated. The audience, not Yeats, learned its lesson, and for the next seventeen years the public conducted itself in a humble manner. Whatever dissatisfaction it felt toward the theatre was expressed privately. The actors, too, took care not to protest to Yeats against his policy, even when many of them could see no sense in it. They preferred the broad comedies of Boyle to the lyrical plays of Synge, but Yeats had refused to produce Boyle's plays. In a letter to Boyle, Holloway wrote:

Every day I hear from the players their regret at missing seeing one or other of your plays. They are *the* plays of the movement up to the present no matter how they have been boycotted by the log-rollers of the exotic press that worship at the shrine of Yeats, Synge and the rest of the mystic or muck-producers of so-called Irish drama. All speak with pleasure of your plays, while they candidly confess that such works as *Deirdre* of Yeats make them quite ill, and as for Synge's late efforts, they shake their heads as if to say he is quite impossible as a dramatist of Irish character or thought.[3]

Yeats needed a producer to replace Willie Fay, and he gave the position to Sara Allgood, a brilliant young actress. A number of foreign masterpieces were performed: Sudermann's *Teja* (April 4, 1908), Molière's *The Rogueries of Scapin* (April 4), translated by Lady Gregory, and *The Scheming Lieutenant* by Sheridan (May 29). Earlier in the season Yeats had presented a new play of his own, *The Golden Helmet* (March 19); the characters all were taken from Irish legend, but the theme was mystical and obscure. Yeats was trying to give universal significance to a subject essentially Irish and even local. Lady Gregory's *The Workhouse Ward* appeared on April 20.

Lennox Robinson was the great discovery of that year. His first play, *The Clancy Name* (October 8), was far from being a notable one, but Yeats was able to see in it a spark of real talent. He encouraged Robinson to continue writing, and out of this encouragement emerged one of the most productive of the Abbey Theatre playwrights. Robinson also became a distinguished producer.

Robinson's second play, *The Cross Roads* (April 1, 1909), was praised even by the critics. Yeats wrote in his journal in 1909 that "Robinson should become a celebrated dramatist if this theatre lasts long enough. He does not argue like the imitators of Ibsen, though his expression of life is as logical, hence his grasp on active passion." [4] Robinson's plays were realistic, and Yeats, although he was aware that Robinson's success might eventually lead the theatre away from its path of poetic drama, would not hinder the development of a genuine artist.

Sara Allgood, recognizing her limitations, did not remain long as producer, and Norreys Connell was appointed in her place. In her short term as producer Sara Allgood had showed great promise and was responsible for discovering a fine actor, Fred O'Donovan. He might not have had the finesse of the Fays, but he was an invaluable acquisition to the company at this critical time.

In 1909 the Abbey Theatre suffered its greatest loss: J. M. Synge died on March 24, even before he had time to finish the writing of his play *Deirdre of the Sorrows*. He was never a happy man, and he spoke of *Deirdre of the Sorrows* as his last disappointment. He had not had time to marry Maire Quinn, the girl he loved, but she was the only one he would allow at his bedside in those last moments when cancer was eating his life away. He was in great pain, and when the nurse offered to give him injections to alleviate his suffering, he protested, "What's the use of giving me anything; all's up with me. It's better to let me die." [5]

Yeats was deeply moved by the death of Synge, and immediately he decreed a revival of *The Playboy*. Everyone associated with the theatre hoped it would be allowed to pass without protest. And so it did. The death of Synge in great agony seemed to soften the people's hearts, and newspapers which had previously attacked Synge's *Playboy* were now unstinting in its praise. Yet it was the same text that had been used in the first production. The only difference was in the casting; the part of Christie was now acted by Fred O'Donovan instead of by Willie Fay. This may have had some effect, for Fred O'Donovan was a tall, handsome fellow with whom any girl might fall in love; Willie Fay, on the other hand, for whom the part had been written, was about five feet, three inches tall, and it would be difficult to imagine any girl falling in love with him, particularly as he appeared in the play, dirty and disheveled, having slept in the ditches for a fortnight. Perhaps the real reason the play was well received was that Yeats had succeeded in educating the public. In any case, it was clear that Yeats had finally conquered the mob, who had hissed the play when first produced.

It was natural that Lady Gregory and Yeats should have been pleased. The reception of *The Playboy* gave them encouragement. Ireland was becoming educated. But Yeats feared it might be difficult to keep up the supply of vital Irish plays, and he decided that a taste might be created for translations of foreign masterpieces. In his diary for 1909 Yeats wrote:

If at all possible I will now keep at the Theatre till I have seen produced a mass of fine work. If we can create a taste for translated work—which we have not yet done—we can carry on the theatre without vulgarity. If not the mere growth of the audience will make all useless, for the Irish town mind will by many channels, public and private, press its vulgarity upon us. If we should feel this happening, if the theatre is not to continue as we have shaped it, it must for the sake of our future influence, for the sake of our example, be allowed to pass out of our hands, or cease. We must not be responsible for a compromise.[6]

Yeats was looking to the future; there was no immediate danger that the theatre would be swamped by vulgarity. Lady Gregory was still writing vital plays, and other new playwrights were arising. In 1909 Lord Dunsany wrote a play for the Abbey, *The Glittering Gate* (April 29); W. M. Letts, *The Challenge* (October 16), and R. J. Ray, *The White Feather* (September 16). In all, Ray turned out five plays for the Abbey Theatre, but none of them was published. This fact is significant, for it had been the policy of the theatre from its early years that only those plays which constituted literature and were worthy of publication would be accepted for production. In most instances Yeats's recommendation to a publisher was sufficient for a play's acceptance. That Ray's plays were never published indicates that Yeats did not think highly of them, although he did allow them to be played at the Abbey.

For some time Yeats had been worried because the theatre had been receiving the support of the Anglo-Irish, or more correctly, British element in Ireland. This group were delighted with Yeats's championing of *The Playboy* and with his attack on the sentimental sector of the nationalists. Such praise was distasteful to Yeats, and he had been considering how he might best reject it.

The opportunity came in the summer of 1909. The Abbey company had been in London, playing at the Court Theatre in June. Lady Gregory visited Shaw on this occasion, and he gave her a copy of his play *The Shewing-up of Blanco Posnet*, which had been banned by the English censor for alleged blasphemy. The chief character in it is a horse thief who shakes his fist at Heaven and afterward finds Heaven too strong for him. There was no censorship of plays in Ireland, and Yeats eagerly accepted the play for the Abbey, knowing that its production would shock the British element.

The Lord Lieutenant of Ireland, his attention drawn to it by the Protestant *Irish Times*, objected to its being performed at the Abbey and even threatened to withdraw the patent if Yeats persisted in his intention. The play, he contended, was not on an Irish subject. To this, Shaw replied that "the real protagonist in my play who does not appear in person upon the stage at all, is God. In my youth the Castle view was that God is essentially Protestant and English; and as the Castle never changes its views, it is bound to regard the divine protagonist as anti-Irish and consequently outside the terms of the Patent." [7]

Shaw was delighted with the publicity, and he kept Yeats and Lady Gregory well advised on what policy to adopt. "Do not threaten them with a contraband performance," he wrote Lady Gregory; "threaten that we shall be suppressed; that we shall be made martyrs of; that we shall suffer as much and as publicly as possible. Tell them that they can depend on me to burn with a brighter blaze and louder yells than all Foxe's martyrs." [8]

Yeats paid little attention to Shaw's advice; the play was produced against the wishes and orders of the Lord Lieutenant on August 25, 1909. The theatre was crowded with nationalists, who were pleased to see the Protestant Anglo-Irish chastised. When the curtain dropped, the audience rose to their feet and cheered. Many of the extreme Protestants were very angry at the performance, but they lacked the emotional temperament of the nationalists and allowed it to pass without any display of violence. "One old lady—a strict Protestant—thought that God would send down fire on the theatre at such rank blasphemy being indulged in." [9] Yeats was satisfied. He had shown his contempt for all sections of Irish public opinion.

The theatre needed a producer urgently. Miss Horniman, still exercising her authority as owner of the Abbey, had dismissed Norreys Connell, and Lady Gregory was obliged to produce *Blanco Posnet* herself. Yeats, in another display of unerring judgment, found the man for the job. He wrote Lennox Robinson, who by now had turned out three plays for the Abbey, and invited him to Dublin for an interview. After fifteen minutes' conversation Yeats said, "I am making you manager and producer of the Abbey Theatre. It will also assist you in learning your trade as a dramatist."

Robinson was astounded. It was an honor he had hardly hoped ever to attain. He was only twenty-one and had no experience whatever in production. He could not understand why he should be given so responsible a position. He was not even a poet, and the plays he had written were far from good. Yeats, however, was certain from the beginning of Robinson's ability, and when he saw Robinson's extraordinarily long legs he was further assured; it was a theory of his that all geniuses were built in a queer manner. Robinson hastened back to Cork, collected his baggage, and returned to Dublin to manage and produce.

Nineteen hundred and ten, Robinson's first year at the theatre, was the most successful in the Abbey's history. All its battles had been fought and won, and now it was settling down to produce solid work. The season opened with the première of Synge's *Deirdre of the Sorrows* (January 13, 1910). Then followed on February 10 *The Green Helmet* by Yeats; this was an heroic farce and was a revised version in ballad verse of *The Golden Helmet,* previously performed in 1908. Some of the other new plays produced in 1910 were Colum's *Thomas Muskerry* (May 12); *Harvest* (May 26), written and produced by Robinson; T. C. Murray's *Birthright* (October 27), and *The Suiler's Child* (November 24) by Seumas O'Kelly, who is better known as the author of the short story "The Weaver's Grave."

Murray's *Birthright* was the first important play to come directly out of the Irish peasantry. Murray, like Robinson, came from Cork. Robinson knew the Protestants in all their attitudes, while Murray was intimate with every phase of Catholic peasant life. He was a peasant himself and later became a schoolmaster. *Birthright,* written somewhat in the manner of Ibsen, told of a common problem in Irish family life—there are two sons, the elder loved by his mother, the younger loved by the father. Only one can remain on the small farm, and the other must go to America to find his fortune. The theme of the play is one of conflicting loves, and it ends tragically. Murray handles his story and his characters with delicate sympathy, and his dialogue has a poetic and authentic sound. Here for the first time, untampered with, the real language of the ordinary peasant was to be heard from the Abbey stage.

Much credit for the Abbey's success up to 1910 must go to Lady Gregory. After the Fays had departed, she had come to the rescue and performed every task associated with theatre work. Shaw spoke of her playfully as "the charwoman of the Abbey Theatre." Feeling great responsibility for keeping the Abbey open when it was in danger, she wrote play after play, sometimes three or four in one year. George Moore pointed out:[10]

Nobody could have done Lady Gregory's plays as well as she did them herself, and *The Workhouse Ward* must not be forgotten, a trifle somewhat sentimental, but just what was wanted to carry on the Abbey Theatre, which, for a moment, could do very well without the grim humours of Synge. We must get it into our heads that the Abbey Theatre would have come to naught but for Lady Gregory's talent for rolling up little anecdotes into one-act plays.

Miss Horniman, after her defeat by Lady Gregory in 1907, was maintaining with Ben Iden Payne her own Manchester Repertory Theatre. She continued to subsidize the Abbey as promised, but she did so grudgingly and was only awaiting an opportunity to withdraw. One can hardly blame her: it was hard for her to stand by urbanely and watch her rival, Lady Gregory, gain a reputation on her money. Yeats, she could forgive, but not Lady Gregory.

Miss Horniman's guarantee was scheduled to end in December, 1910. In the meantime Lady Gregory was trying to find someone among her English friends to endow the theatre. Lady Gregory herself was not rich, and despite all the publicity he was receiving, Yeats was making only thirty pounds a year from the sale of his poems.[11] Miss Horniman was becoming more bitter, and she was trying to damage Lady Gregory's prestige among the latter's English friends. She suggested that the Abbey Theatre was turning anti-British, and as evidence pointed to *The Shewing-up of Blanco Posnet*.

Miss Horniman's real opportunity came in May, 1910. King Edward VII died on May 7, and all the Dublin theatres closed on that day as a tribute to his memory; but not the Abbey Theatre. Yeats was away in France, visiting Maud Gonne, and Lady Gregory was at her residence at Coole, leaving Lennox Robinson in full control. Robinson would not admit any connection between the drama and the death of an English king, and consequently he kept the theatre open. He had some doubts, however, and he sent a telegram to Lady Gregory asking for definite instructions. Lady Gregory lived two miles from the nearest post office, and the telegraph messenger, being a nationalist and knowing the contents of the message, took three hours to travel the two miles. Lady Gregory's reply, "Should close through courtesy," was therefore delayed and the theatre remained open. Miss Horniman at once seized on this indiscretion and telegraphed on May 10:

Opening last Saturday was disgraceful. Performance on day of funeral would be political and would stop subsidy automatically.[12]

On the following day she further informed Lady Gregory by wire, and the public by letters to the press, that the subsidy would cease unless Robinson and the directors apologized publicly. Lady Gregory's apology was as contemptuous as possible and came as an aside to a program announcement:

Harvest, a play in three acts by S. L. Robinson, will be produced for the first time next week. . . . There will be no performance on Friday (the date of the King's funeral). The Directors and Manager regret that owing to accident the theatre remained open on Saturday last. Lady Gregory, who was in the country, had wired immediately on the receipt of the news of the King's death and a telegram asking instructions, desiring it to be closed, but this was too late in the day, the matinee had already been put on, and it was considered too late to stop the evening performance.

Miss Horniman was very angry with this slightly insulting apology. She read into the phrase "owing to accident" an implication that the directors were disappointed they had not kept open deliberately. She at once asked that Robinson be dismissed. Yeats arrived home from France at this point, and when he learned of the situation he rejected Miss Horniman's demands and refused to apologize further.

The nationalist press objected to any apology being made but was delighted with the stand taken by Yeats. The messenger boy was called a hero (but was dismissed by the post office). Miss Horniman could stand it no longer and she announced she was withdrawing the subsidy. Yeats persuaded her, however, to submit the question for arbitration to C. P. Scott, editor of *The Manchester Guardian*. Scott decided in favor of Yeats.

This was the final disillusionment for Miss Horniman. She had spent ten thousand pounds on the theatre, and now she felt that, instead of receiving thanks, she was being insulted. She refused to credit the integrity of the action taken by Lady Gregory and Yeats. However, at the end of the year she fulfilled her promise to hand over the theatre to the directors at the nominal sum of one thousand pounds. Then she broke completely her friendship with Yeats.

Certain legal formalities were necessary before Yeats and Lady Gregory could assume ownership. For this reason the National Theatre Society Limited was re-formed and registered under the Companies Consolidated Act of 1908. Records of the change were destroyed in the disastrous burning of the Four Courts during the Civil War, but the Articles of Association are still available.[13] The following are the most interesting articles:

4. The income and property of the Company, wheresoever derived, shall be applied solely toward the promotion of the objects of the Company as set forth in this Memorandum of Association, and no portion thereof shall be paid or transferred, directly or indirectly, by way of dividend, bonus or otherwise, by way of profits to the members of the Company.

   PROVIDED that nothing herein contained shall prevent the payment in good faith of remuneration to any officer or servant of the Company or to any member of the Company or other persons in return for any service rendered to the Company or the payment to any such person or persons of royalties or fees at current rates in respect of any play or plays written by any such person or persons and performed or made use of by the Company.

5. The number of directors shall be two, but the Directors may from time to time, increase such number by appointing an additional Director or Directors, but so that the total number shall never exceed three. Two Directors shall form a quorum. The first Directors shall be Dame Isabella Augusta Gregory and William Butler Yeats.

7. If upon the winding-up or dissolution of the Company there remains after satisfaction of all its debts and liabilities any property whatsoever the same shall not be paid or distributed among the members of the Company, but if and so far as effect can be given to the next provision, shall be employed in the furtherance in Ireland of Irish dramatic Art (whether the medium employed be the English or Irish language) or of some educational or artistic object to be determined by the members of the Company at or before its dissolution.

10. The qualifications of a Director shall be the holding in his own right, of 100 shares of the Company, and the office of a Director shall be vacated:—
   (a) If he becomes bankrupt
   (b) If he becomes lunatic or becomes of unsound mind
   (c) If he ceases to hold at least 100 shares in the Company
   (d) If he sends in his resignation in writing to the Board.

47. Every member shall have one vote for every share held by him.

60. Any notice required to be, or which may be, given by advertisement, shall be advertised in The Irish Times.

67. Any invitation to the public to subscribe for any shares or Debenture Stock in the Company is hereby prohibited.

[Signed] Isabella Augusta Gregory
William Butler Yeats

10th. March 1911.

The capital of the Company was fixed at one thousand pounds, consisting of one-pound shares, of which 390 were issued. Lady Gregory and Yeats held 376 between them. The original records were destroyed, but the shares probably were distributed in the same manner as on March 30, 1921:

Gregory, Lady	188
Yeats, W. B.	188
Wright, Udolpho	2
Allgood, Sara	4
Bourke, Edmund	2
Bailey, Rt. Hon. William F.	2
Hanson, Philip	2
Robinson, Lennox	2
Total	390

The directors planned to keep the theatre going by collecting money from friends and forming with it an endowment fund, which they hoped to fix at five thousand pounds. This was not an easy thing to accomplish, since those who might lend money for such an enterprise were either English or pro-English, and at that moment the Abbey was in disfavor with the British element in Ireland. For one thing, the British national anthem was never played at the Abbey, although it was heard in every other Dublin theatre. Miss Horniman's bitter criticism of Yeats and Lady Gregory had added fuel to the fire, prejudicing many English persons of wealth against them.

However, Lady Gregory wrote all her friends, and Yeats gave a series of lectures in London to raise money. George Bernard Shaw, though not a part of the Irish theatre, was very friendly toward it, and on this occasion he was chairman for one of Yeats's lectures. Edmund Gosse and Herbert Trench alternated as chairmen for the other meetings.

The campaign resulted in a sum of £2,169, and a financial committee was set up to administer the fund. The members were the Right Honourable William Frederick Bailey, Estates Commissioner; Philip Hanson, Commissioner of Public Works, and Edmund Bourke, Inspector of the Local Government Board for Ireland.

One important incident must not be forgotten: the old patent expired and a new one had to be applied for. All the commercial theatres in Dublin objected, as did the Theatre of Ireland. This was a rival nationalistic theatre started in 1909 by Edward Martyn, with the blessing of George Russell. They had no theatre building, and they acted their plays, which included James Stephens's *The Marriage of Julia Elizabeth,* in various halls about the city of Dublin. When the Abbey applied for a renewal of the patent, the Theatre of Ireland made the audacious proposal that they be granted the use of the Abbey Theatre for eighteen days in each year to produce their plays, and that they get forty per cent of the receipts therefrom. When Miss Horniman had been in control of the Abbey, she would not allow the Theatre of Ireland to rent the theatre on any condition. The proposal was thrown out and the patent granted the Abbey for twenty-one years.

Signed by Winston S. Churchill, then Principal Secretary of State in the Home Office, London, the patent differed in a number of details from the original one. Added to the kinds of plays the theatre might produce were "all acknowledged masterpieces of English dramatic literature of the eighteenth century and earlier." The clause governing the selection of plays, which previously had caused Yeats so much anger, was now altered to permit the Society to produce such plays "as shall be selected by the Board of Directors of the National Theatre Society." This further clause was also inserted:

And we further hereby strictly prohibit the holding or giving of representations or performances of any kind whatsoever on Sundays or on days proclaimed to be days of mourning.

The Abbey Theatre was at last securely in the hands of Yeats and Lady Gregory in September, 1911. Their endowment fund was not so great as they had hoped, but it was sufficient to allow the theatre to continue at least for a time. The Abbey was still dependent on British money; this was somewhat embarrassing, but at least Lady Gregory and Yeats had demonstrated that Miss Horniman was not indispensable.

A Poetic Theatre

During the early years of the twentieth century the minds of the Irish people were occupied with problems of business and politics. They were thinking only of how they might get on in the world. In the evenings, the peasants would gather round their fires—not to tell stories of romantic Ireland but to listen to someone read *The Freeman's Journal,* which told them of the struggle for home rule. They had become realists and were applying their newly discovered standard to everything: does it pay? Romance was departing from their lives, and Ireland, like England, was turning into a nation of businessmen.

Irish idealists perceived the danger in this heresy. The Gaelic League believed the best answer to it would be to make the country

81

completely Gaelic speaking. *Sinn Fein* maintained that an Irish republic would cure all her ills. Both groups were so concerned with discussing how Ireland could be saved that romance fled from them, and they consequently produced a negligible literature.

Yeats stood aloof from all their arguings. For him, a high art was the answer to everything; it was the only monument to a nation that no politician could stain nor any revolution destroy. Such a monument, he believed, was the Abbey Theatre, and he made every effort to see that it kept, at all times, its high dignity and purpose. He was constantly attacked for not encouraging playwrights to write about "realistic" subjects—politics and the problems of the Irish worker. But this was for Yeats a false realism; the true and highest realism was that of poetry. What Ireland needed was dreams, so that she might keep her eyes on the light that was ahead and not on the ditches along the way.

By 1911 it seemed as if Yeats's dreams of an Irish National Theatre had become reality—Irish plays played by Irish actors before an Irish audience in a theatre which he owned and dominated. Yet there was one disturbing feature: the Abbey Theatre movement was drifting away from his original conception of a poetic theatre. No dramatic poet of consequence had arisen, and the Abbey Theatre was dependent completely on Yeats for its poetic plays. The plays of Synge and of Lady Gregory were important, but they were strongly influenced by peasant drama and were directing the theatre away from poetry.

In 1909 Yeats had felt that if he were to avoid the degrading influence of politics and the market place, he would have to look for his inspiration outside Ireland—in some country, real or of the imagination, where the people were not snarled in the nightmare of self-consciousness, where life was not submerged under conventions and eternal debate. Obsessed always with the quest for truth, Yeats believed he could no longer penetrate it by continuing to write on Irish themes. He turned to the abstract and symbolist No plays of Japan. The plays he wrote under this influence were obscure from the first, and they became increasingly so until finally, in *Purgatory* (August 10, 1938), all was abstraction, and there was little that could be understood by an intelligent person.

Yeats believed that plays written under this new impulse were no less truly national than plays about Cuchulain and Kathleen Ni Houlihan. Truth, he believed, was a universal quality, essentially the same in every country. If a play was really good, it would automatically be nationalistic in the best sense if written by an Irishman, since enlightenment adds to a nation's prestige.

When Yeats became sole owner of the Abbey Theatre in 1911, he made one final effort to direct it back onto the road of poetic drama, to excite the imagination of the audience and bring the people into that most real of worlds, the make-believe world of the theatre. He, more than anyone else, knew it was as essential for a nation to feed its imagination as to fill its warehouses. Only through the imagination does a nation survive.

Had the Fays remained with the Abbey, Yeats's problem might have been easier, for they were excellent speakers of verse. At this time he might well have regretted their departure. Yet this minor obstacle was overcome by inviting Florence Farr, the English actress, to come over to the Abbey, if only for a short period, to chant the verse in his plays.

It was not only actors that Yeats needed; scenery and costumes would have to be in harmony with the spoken work, and no one at the Abbey had both the experience and the imagination to design suitable sets. Yeats was a friend of Gordon Craig, an experimenter in stagecraft, and was impressed with his work. He invited Craig to design costumes and scenery for a revival of his morality play *The Hour Glass*, with which he hoped to open the 1911 season. Craig believed in the beauty of extreme simplicity, and he designed a set of plain screens, following a mathematical pattern, which he forwarded to Yeats in Dublin. The screens were a success, but the dresses made from Craig's designs were very ugly, and Yeats came before the curtain after the play and apologized for them.[1] Craig's screens were used for many years at the Abbey, but his help was not again asked. Yeats was well satisfied, however, with the production of *The Hour Glass*, and he delighted to tell his friends how the earlier version so influenced a music-hall singer that he attended Mass every day for six weeks.

The Abbey Theatre was now dependent for its financial support on people of fashion. Yeats's slightly obscure verse plays were exactly what was needed to attract middle-aged, aristocratic ladies. Once again, in this small matter, Yeats showed his genius as a diplomat. When the 1911 season opened on January 12, Yeats was to be seen in the vestibule of the theatre in full dress, receiving his upper-class guests.[2] He needed their money, though he would make no fundamental concession to obtain it. If they contributed to the endowment fund, he would be pleased; if they enjoyed his plays he would also be pleased; but whatever they might do, Yeats was insistent that they keep quiet during the performances and avoid shuffling their feet or talking while the actors were onstage.

Yeats now undertook to rewrite his earlier poetic plays. Many of them had been written when he was young and inexperienced in the art of the theatre. Before he would allow them to be staged again, he would have to alter them to correspond with his more developed principles. *The Land of Heart's Desire*, his first play to be staged, had not been shown at the Abbey, despite the need for poetic plays. Yeats now reworded it, and the revised version was performed at the Abbey Theatre on January 26, 1911. It was very successful, and it found a permanent place in the Abbey repertory.

On the same program was performed a new play, *King Argimenes and the Unknown Warrior* by Lord Dunsany. Dunsany, as much as Yeats, believed in the significance of romance in contrast with the realistic plays of Ibsen and his imitators. There was this difference, however, between the ideas of Yeats and those of Dunsany: while Yeats informed his romantic plays with a high purpose, Dunsany believed in employing fantasy for its own sake. *King Argimenes and the Unknown Warrior* was a play of this kind. It was a pure fantasy, with an Eastern setting, and took for its theme the belief that there is something in the blood of a king which makes him royal and distinguishes him, however low he may fall, from the ordinary man. It had some appeal for the audience, but it lacked those essential qualities of sincerity and truth which must appear even in fantasy if it is to be successful on the stage. Dunsany was not the answer to Yeats's demand for a poetic dramatist.

Yeats also rewrote *The Countess Cathleen* and began a translation of *Oedipus Rex*. Although he had the assistance of a good Greek scholar, the translation was not to his liking and it was not played or printed. Sir Gilbert Murray had advised against translating this play by Sophocles and had himself refused to translate it for production in Ireland. "I will not translate Oedipus Rex," wrote Sir Gilbert, "for an Irish theatre. It has nothing Irish about it; no religion, not one beautiful action, hardly a stroke of poetry. . . . It has splendid qualities as an acting play, but all of the most English–French–German sort . . . it is all construction and no spirit. . . . It ought to be played . . . at the Lyceum with a lecture before and after. And a public dinner. With speeches. By Cabinet Ministers. . . ." [3] Yeats later returned to the task and in 1926 produced a translation under the title *Oedipus the King* at the Abbey Theatre.

Another new playwright, St. John Ervine, came to the Abbey in 1911. He belonged to the school of peasant playwrights, but Yeats welcomed him. Yeats's theories of a national theatre did not extend so far as to demand poetic plays to the exclusion of all other types; he wanted only to make them the dominant influence. Ervine was a North of Ireland Protestant, and his *Mixed Marriage* (March 30, 1911) was the first play produced at the Abbey Theatre dealing with the peasant of that region. Yeats hoped Ervine might be able to do for the North of Ireland what Synge and Lady Gregory had done for the west. His hope was not realized; Ervine wrote competent plays on Irish subjects but had not enough sympathy with Ireland or with her people to write well about them. He possessed the qualities of the critic rather than of the creator.

Mixed Marriage, aptly enough, dealt with an extremely vital problem—the consequences of a marriage between a Catholic and a Protestant in Ireland. It is not easy for a person outside Ireland to understand the violence such a union can create among the relatives of married persons. In some of its aspects it is comparable to the furore caused by the marriage of a white girl to a colored man in Georgia. Ireland is all tensions, political, religious, social. An incident which to an American writer might be of passing interest only, to an Irishman writing for an Irish public might have in it the seeds of revolution. George Russell's alleged description of an Irish literary movement as consisting of a number of writers living in an Irish city, fighting continuously with one another, was more than a quip on the part of George Moore, who recorded it.

It was the policy of the Abbey Theatre at this time to re-create interest in poetic plays, yet the business aspects were not neglected. On the contrary: few businessmen could have handled its affairs with the expert skill which Yeats demonstrated. He was always on the alert, and it has been said of him that he could judge the important features of a balance sheet as soundly as he could judge a play or a poem.

Up to 1911, Abbey playwrights had not been paid royalties. They were happy to give their work free, and they felt that having their plays produced in a theatre of such artistic integrity as the Abbey's was more than adequate compensation. This attitude may surprise people abroad who have dealt with Irish poets and playwrights; it is not unusual for the latter, in their relations with the non-Irish, to display extraordinary interest in money. In Ireland their attitude is quite different: they would rather have their work printed in impecunious magazines of high standards than in popular magazines which pay well. Even Yeats adopted this attitude in relation to his own work, although he was often badly in need of money. But he felt he was being somewhat compromised as a consequence of not paying royalties to other Abbey playwrights: they might consider Yeats and the other directors under obligation to them, and the suggestion was implicit in the situation that the playwrights had the right, even if extremely tenuous, to a voice in the theatre's direction. The implications were intolerable to Yeats, and one of his first moves at this time was to pay royalties, however small, to every playwright. The effect upon the directors, exercising their authority, would be significant.

Still more essential to Yeats's absolute control of the Abbey

86 *A Poetic Theatre*

was his control of the actors, stage designers, and all other persons connected with the theatre. He would pay the actors and all the others. He would compel them to work under contract, and thus develop in them a sense of responsibility to the directors—and, perhaps more important, a sense of their subservience. This arrangement would make the organization so efficient that it could carry on during Yeats's extended absences in England and Lady Gregory's in her west Ireland mansion.

In July, 1911, Yeats with Lady Gregory took the company on tour in England. Dublin was Yeats's emotional home, but London was where he found intellectual excitement. Most of his friends were there and he kept in close contact with them. He had reason to be friendly with them, for in April of 1911 they arranged with the British government that Yeats should receive a Civil List pension of £150 per year. Although he needed the money badly, he was in some doubt as to whether he should take money from a British king. When he decided to accept it, the nationalist press in Dublin jeered. *The Leader* always referred to Yeats thenceforth as "Pensioner Yeats" and the same paper published a parody on his play *The King's Threshold,* in which it portrayed Yeats lying on the doorstep of the king's treasury demanding a pension. Part of it ran:

BARD:

> Here will I lie
> Before the golden palace of my dreams
> And take no food until I get a pension.
> How long, I wonder, will their flinty breasts
> Hold out against my fasting at their door?
> If they do think my proud heroic soul
> Will from its Pagan purpose budge an inch
> Until its wistful longings are appeased
> With fat donations from the public purse
> They make a vast mistake. If so they think
> They little know the economic sense
> That rules the raptures of a Celtic Bard.
> Upon these rocks in hunger I will stretch
> Until the State becomes the goose to me
> That lays the golden egg.

(Enter TWO LORDS)

1ST LORD:

    I bring thee, Bard, a fairy wand of old
    To conjure visions out of Tir-na-nOg
    I prithee take it and depart at once.

BARD:

    I tell thee, man, I'm here for minted dross.
    A golden lever, not a magic wand,
    Will lift me from these stones. . . .
    Here will I remain
    Until I get a pension.

The Abbey company's English tour was a success in many ways. Not only did they make five hundred pounds profit,[4] but they received an offer to tour America with *The Playboy*. All expenses were guaranteed, and the company was to receive thirty-five per cent of all profits. Though this offer came at an awkward time—Yeats was experimenting with the poetic play—yet it was too generous to turn down. It had always been the ambition of Yeats and Lady Gregory to take the company to America, for they were justly proud of their achievements and were anxious to display them to the world. At one time it had even been agreed upon by Yeats and Lady Gregory that if ever it seemed the Abbey Theatre was in danger of dying, they would collect all possible funds and take the company to America. If the Abbey Theatre were to die, then it would die dramatically.

Yeats started planning how he could best continue his propaganda for a poetic theatre while the company was in America. He decided to organize a second Abbey company and brought over to Dublin, Nugent Monck, organizer of the Norwich Players, to become director of a school of acting. Monck, an Irishman residing in England, had learned his art under Poel of the Elizabethan Stage Society. He favored simplicity of staging and insisted on clarity of diction from his actors.

Yeats left Monck at the Abbey and went off with the players to America. He had received a promise from Lady Gregory that she would follow in a week and relieve him in the tedious tour of that country. Yeats returned to Dublin as soon as possible after Lady Gregory arrived in America. He then set about helping Monck produce a series of mystery and morality plays, while he supervised the revival of his own *The Countess Cathleen*.

The Abbey second company opened its 1911 season with two mediaeval plays: *The Interlude of Youth* (November 23) and *The Second Shepherd's Play* (November 23). For these two plays Monck built a triple stage: back of the regular stage was a small platform raised a few feet above the normal level; beyond the footlights was another platform on a lower level, extending out into the auditorium. The stage was beautifully and simply hung. Backstage, a choir sang "Sumer is y-cumen in," illustrating secular delights, in contrast with a very devotional "Ave Maria" of 1545, which was also sung. *The Interlude of Youth*, a short morality play, depicts Youth alternately swayed by the seductions of Riot, Pride, and Lady Luxury, on the one hand, and by the injunctions of Charity and Humility, until finally he surrenders himself to the Virtues.

The Second Shepherd's Play, from the Wakefield Cycle, included a traditional "Gloria in Excelsis." Between the two plays, Monck gave a lecture on mediaeval drama. An imprudent remark almost caused a disturbance in the Abbey. In speaking of *The Second Shepherd's Play*, he mentioned that the author drew the shepherds on the model of Yorkshire shepherds, and he had no doubt that many people then protested it was an insult to draw Yorkshiremen like that. This was a pointed reference to Synge's portrayal of Irish characters. A member of the audience called out, "Better not introduce that!" Other members of the audience joined in: "You must not make a disturbance," "Shut up," "I'll not shut up. I'll do as I please," "Throw him out." The incident developed into a minor scuffle and then died down.[5]

On November 30 a one-act play by Douglas Hyde entitled *The Marriage* was performed, and the following week *Red Turf* (December 8) by Rutherford Mayne. *Red Turf* was disliked by everyone. The scene was placed in the west of Ireland, and according to the critic of *The Irish Independent* (December 8), "It relies on curses and swear words to give distinction to a dreary dialogue. . . . It is a wretched attempt at drama—the only dramatic incident was the explosion of a cartridge and that happened off the stage. . . . *Red Turf* is redolent rubbish."

Monck's production of the revised version of *The Countess*

Cathleen (December 14) enjoyed a good reception. This time there was no need to have police in the house. Yeats did not alter the play in any of its essential parts, and we find the Protestant *Irish Times*, a Dublin sheet, protesting against the heresy contained in it.

Monck put on a play in Gaelic, *The Tinker and the Fairy*, by Douglas Hyde on January 15, 1912. Immediately after Christmas, *The Annunciation* had come, and *The Flight into Egypt* (January 4). Monck staged another morality play, then a short sketch by Lady Gregory, *MacDonagh's Wife* (January 11), the title of which was later changed to *MacDarragh's Wife;* Lady Gregory had written this on the boat that took her to America. With this, Monck brought to an end his season with the Abbey.

Yeats had a motive in offering these religious plays. He had come to the conclusion it would not be possible to make the poetic drama a dominant feature of the Abbey Theatre unless he received help, and the help he now was willing to solicit was that of the Catholic Church. His first move being to stage some religious plays, he then approached Edward Martyn and asked him for his opinion. Would the Church help if he were to continue having the second company perform religious plays?

Martyn replied that the Church still was suspicious of the Abbey Theatre and of Yeats, and he might expect no help from that quarter. Yeats was disconsolate. When Lady Gregory returned from America, he let her assume complete control of the Abbey and he went off to England. His attempt at bringing back poetry to the stage had failed, and he would waste no more time on the experiment. From now on, the Abbey was to become a "people's theatre."

Yeats had wearied of the effort to make the Abbey exclusively, or at least primarily, a poetic theatre. His hopes of an Irish dramatic poet arising were not realized. Reluctantly he became reconciled to the idea of producing prose plays of a high standard. If this much could be achieved, then he could periodically restate the original purpose of the theatre by offering a poetic play written by himself.

Touring America

When it was announced that the Abbey Theatre Company was to tour America with *The Playboy*, protests came once more from the noisy nationalist press in Ireland. This, they said, was an act of treachery. The production of *The Playboy* in England was bad enough, but it did no essential damage to Irish prestige there; it only confirmed the English in their belief that the Irish native was a half savage who would be expected to kill his father and be praised for his heroism. Performing *The Playboy* in America was a much more serious matter. National Ireland was looking to the Irish in America for help in the struggle for independence. The Irish-American was trying hard to become "respectable," to live down the idea that he was an uneducated, drunken, irresponsible person, fit only to be a servant. If a company of players claiming to represent national Ireland came to America and represented the Irishman as the kind of person drawn by Synge, it would damage the Irish-American's prestige, they thought, and might prejudice others against the Irish cause. The nationalists in Ireland determined that this must not be allowed to happen, and they alerted their friends in America so that they might be ready to drive the Abbey company out of that country at once, or at least discredit it as a national theatre company.

Irish-American papers attacked the Irish players long before they arrived, and J. B. Yeats, then living in New York, wrote home to his son in August, 1911:

I send you a paper in which some priest makes an attack on the theatre, evidently a priest—when you come here I hope they *do attack you.* It would make your fortune—all your poets and writers and actors and actresses would become famous. People would rally to you. People that never heard of you before would gather round you. It would be a fine fight for a fine principle.

At this time Yeats was not greatly interested in a fight; already he had proved to himself that he was able to handle a violent mob, and the prospect of teaching a lesson to the Irish-Americans did not appeal to him; it was such an easy and insignificant problem that it was unworthy of his energy and talent. It would, however, be something novel for Lady Gregory, and he was pleased when circumstances demanded that she go to America with the company.

Maire O'Neill, Synge's fiancée and the original Pegeen Mike of *The Playboy* had married shortly before the company set sail and decided not to go on the tour. There was no actress with sufficient experience to take her place, and it was decided to take along a young girl, Miss Magee, and train her for the part in America. The Abbey company then found itself in a situation which was both comic and embarrassing; they were going to America as the Irish National Theatre Society, yet there was no one in the company capable of teaching Miss Magee how to speak the Anglo-Irish dialect used in Synge's play. Yeats spoke with a Bloomsbury accent, and although he was constantly writing of the beauties of the Irish dialect, he was unable to speak a word of it. Lennox

Robinson had even less knowledge of the dialect, for he belonged to an educated family and was brought up to speak Trinity College English.

In a desperate effort to save the situation, Yeats wired Lady Gregory, who had made a study of how the peasants spoke, to follow him by the next boat to America and take on the task of teaching Miss Magee. This suited Lady Gregory well; she packed her bag, put on her best Paris gown, and set off for Boston.

She arrived on September 29, 1911, and was met at the dock by Yeats. He told her the latest news: how *Birthright* by T. C. Murray and her own *Hyacinth Halvey* had been produced successfully but had been attacked by a writer in *The Boston Post* as "Vulgar, vile, beastly and unnatural, calculated to degrade and defame a people and all they held sacred and dear." This came as a surprise to Lady Gregory, for neither play had been attacked in Ireland: *Birthright* was a sensitive play about a common problem in an Irish peasant household, and *Hyacinth Halvey* was merely an amusing comedy. It was clear that the attack by the Irish-Americans was going to be indiscriminate, so Lady Gregory surveyed the scene like a general and prepared herself for battle.

Americans were now to witness a phenomenon unique in their country but common in Ireland—a fight over a work of art. From the time St. Columchille fought a bloody battle over the copyright of a book in the sixth century and went into voluntary exile on account of it, down to our own day many of the greatest battles waged in Ireland have been over some artistic ideal. Even as late as 1940, when the existence of London as a city was being threatened by the continuous bombings of the Germans, Dublin writers were cracking each other's skulls over the worth of Louis Mac-Neice's new book of poems.

Non-Irish Americans were somewhat mystified by the attack on the Abbey players; they could understand a fight over a woman or over a million-dollar estate, but that anyone should bother to fight over a play was then something entirely novel to them. Many of them explained it away by reverting to the popular misconception that the Irish love to fight irrespective of the cause.

The production of *The Playboy* in Boston was announced for October 16, and Lady Gregory threw all her energies into preparing to meet the certain assault which would be made on it. The players were instructed to save their voices if there was an attempt to shout them down, and be prepared to repeat the scene. A claque in support of the play was organized among the students of Harvard University, and when *The Playboy* came on, the boohs of the Irish-Americans were drowned by the cheers and hand-clapping of the Harvard students.

The Playboy was therefore a success in Boston. Yeats, satisfied that Lady Gregory would be able to deal with all situations that might arise on tour, returned to Ireland to continue his work on the poetic play.

Before proceeding to New York, the Abbey company paid visits to neighboring towns where they gave *The Playboy* despite local protests. Even when they played at Yale University there was opposition, and the police chief, after attending a matinee performance, demanded certain cuts in the play. He thought it was *The Playboy* he had seen, but only when he had announced his decision did he learn that the play he had censored was not *The Playboy* but Shaw's *Blanco Posnet*.

From Yale the company went to Washington, D.C. The priests there, mostly of Irish descent, condemned the plays from the altar, and the Aloysius Truth Society distributed a pamphlet at the church doors, part of which read:

Nothing but hell-inspired ingenuity and a satanic hatred of the Irish people and their religion could suggest, construct, and influence the production of such plays. On God's earth the beastly creatures of the plays never existed.

Such are the productions which, hissed from Dublin, hawked around England by the "Irish Players" for the delectation of those who wished to see Irishmen shown unfit for self-government, are now offered to the people of Washington. Will Washington tolerate the lie?

Lady Gregory and her troupe of players arrived in New York on November 18. Trouble was expected at once, for the United Irish Societies had already pledged themselves to "drive the vile thing from the stage." *The Gaelic American* announced that "The Playboy must be squelched" and a lesson taught to Mr. Yeats and his fellow agents of England.

The Playboy went on the boards in New York on November 28. The editor of *The Gaelic American* was there with about forty of his friends as a bodyguard. They boohed and hissed and threw potatoes at the players. When they ran short of potatoes, a number of them threw their rosaries onto the stage as their ultimate dramatic gesture, and one man hurled his watch. Concluding that his watch was too expensive a weapon of protest, he called to the stage door after the performance to claim it. The police had been called in but, being Irish, they were not anxious to arrest anyone. Protests continued through the week but the play was continued. A stranger, seeing the crowd of police outside the theatre, inquired what was wrong. He was informed that "There's a Jew-man inside has a French play and he's letting on it's Irish, and some of the lads are inside talking to them."

From New York the company went to Philadelphia. There an Irish saloonkeeper and his brother, who was a priest, had them charged before the court with producing "immoral and indecent plays." The charges were easily disproved, and the plays were continued. Opposition in Chicago was better organized, but once more it failed to have any serious effect. The city council demanded that *The Playboy* be prohibited. During the debate at the council meeting, one Alderman McInerney, on being asked if Lady Gregory was not Irish, replied, "There's a difference in being from Ireland and being Irish. . . . If you're born in a stable that doesn't make you a horse." The mayor of Chicago did not ban *The Playboy*, despite the entreaties of his friends, and Lady Gregory won the battle.

Many threatening letters had been received; in New York a big Kerryman invited Robinson to Robinson's own wake, and in Chicago, Lady Gregory received an anonymous letter, adorned with a picture of a gun and a coffin, which stated that her "doom was sealed."

George Bernard Shaw did not let the opportunity pass without making a statement. In an interview with a correspondent of the *New York Sun* he stated:

SHAW: In the plays of Mr. Yeats you will find many Irish heroes, but nothing like "the broth of a boy." Now you can imagine the effect of all this on the American pseudo-Irish, who are still exploiting the old stage Ireland for all it is worth, and defiantly singing: "Who fears to speak of '98?" under the very nose of the police—that is the New York police, who are mostly Fenians. Their notion of patriotism is to listen jealously for the slightest hint that Ireland is not the home of every virtue and the martyr of every oppression, and thereupon to brawl and bully or to whine and protest, according to their popularity with the bystanders. When these people hear a little real Irish sentiment from the Irish Players they will not know where they are; they will think that the tour of the Irish company is an Orange conspiracy financed by Mr. Balfour.

INTERVIEWER: Have you seen what the Central Council of the Irish County Association of Greater Boston says about the Irish Players?

SHAW: Yes; but please do not say I said so; it would make them insufferably conceited to know that their little literary effort had been read right through by me. You will observe that they begin by saying that they know their Ireland as children know their mother. Not a very happy bit of rhetoric that, because children never do know their mothers; they may idolize them or fear them, as the case may be, but they don't know them.

Lady Gregory and the Abbey company arrived back in Dublin in March, 1912, like heroes returning from a great victory. A gala public reception was held at the Royal Hibernian Academy. Speeches were made and everyone praised one another.

The American tour taught Lady Gregory many things. It taught her she was capable of handling opposition almost as well as could Yeats, it taught her confidence, and above all it taught her that money could be made by taking the company on tour. No longer would it be necessary to beg money from her friends to keep the theatre going.

After staging three new plays, *Family Failing* by William Boyle (March 28) ; *Patriots* by Lennox Robinson (April 11), and *Judgment* by Joseph Campbell (April 15), the Abbey company set out once more for England. They played for five weeks at London's Court Theatre, producing for the first time *Maurice Harte,* a new play by T. C. Murray (June 20), and *The Bogie Man,* also a new play, by Lady Gregory (July 4).

Supporters of the Abbey Theatre in Dublin felt hurt that London should be given the honor of an Abbey Theatre première. But, unwittingly, the Abbey company was accepting the ideal of the businessman, "does it pay?" Lady Gregory was now practically in full control. In future, the Abbey would pay its way, and it could accomplish that end only by touring. Dublin, in future, would be a place to which they would return as to a base. Had Yeats and Lady Gregory depended on Dublin for financial support, the Abbey Theatre would not have survived. In the early years, English friends had supplied the money; now America was to act as sponsor of the company. Dublin would have to be satisfied with the second company and feel honored when the first company paid them a visit.

The Abbey company returned to Ireland for the autumn of 1912 and played at the Abbey Theatre up to Christmas. Two new plays were performed: *The Magnanimous Lover* by St. John Ervine (October 17), and *Damer's Gold* by Lady Gregory (November 21). Lady Gregory was now the centre of attraction rather than Yeats. Everyone wanted to speak to her, but with the Abbey Theatre's money box full she could afford to be disdainful even of people of fashion. Holloway's description of the scene at the revival of Lady Gregory's *The White Cockade* on October 24, 1912, exemplifies the new attitude:

As Lady Gregory came into the stalls she was button-holed by two old women. She spoke courteously to them for a moment but as the curtain went up she moved back towards the Pit. A woman came in during the first act with a regular cart-wheel of a hat and sat directly in front of Lady Gregory. When the act was over Lady Gregory went out and soon after an attendant came in and asked those ladies who had not already removed their hats to do so. Yeats came in by the side-staircase—pausing for a while to gaze at the stalls before descending—he looked very dreamy. He sat in a seat and scanned the audience.[1]

At Christmas, Lady Gregory and the company set sail once again for America. They took Nugent Monck with them and left Lennox Robinson at the Abbey to entertain the Dublin audiences. Robinson was interested in continental drama, and he experimented with plays by Strindberg, Paternoster, Hauptmann, and Tagore. Yeats liked Tagore, and the production of the latter's play was obviously at his suggestion.

Lady Gregory took the Abbey company direct to Chicago, as if to say to the Irish-Americans in that city, "Here I am again, and you better like me for I will keep visiting you until you do." Chicago received the players with enthusiasm, and when they revisited New York *The Playboy* was greeted by a cheering audience. The critics gave great praise to everyone associated with the company; Nugent Monck, they singled out as the greatest actor of the group. This was absurd, for Monck had a hard English accent, but American people, particularly the critics, find the English accent irresistible.

It was late in the spring of 1913 when the Abbey company returned to Ireland, but they proceeded almost at once to England, where they played for several weeks. They were back in Dublin that autumn, but in accordance with their new custom they set sail once again for the United States to make some more money. Monck stayed in Ireland with the second company this time, and Lennox Robinson accompanied Lady Gregory as business manager.

They played in many small towns and in Chicago, Toronto, Boston, and New York. The plays were applauded in New York, but with some dissent. During the performance of Murray's *Birthright,* when one of the brothers chokes the other, John Devoy, leader of the Irish-American patriotic organization *Clann na nGael,* jumped up in the stalls and shouted out, "Son of a bitch, that's not Irish."

Despite all this publicity, the tour was not a financial success, and Lady Gregory returned home disgruntled. She blamed Robinson for the failure. Actually, she had never liked Robinson's sombre personality, and she had now a legitimate opportunity to persuade Yeats to agree to dismissing him as manager. Robinson was glad to leave, for, as he stated in his autobiography, *Curtain Up,* "After four and a half years of ceaseless work there I felt I had become stale as a producer; production and management left me little time for writing."

It really was Lady Gregory who had failed as an Abbey director, and not Robinson as manager. From the time she assumed virtual dictatorial power over the Abbey Theatre's destiny in 1912, up to the summer of 1914, she had succeeded in twisting the theatre from its true path. Instead of keeping it close to the ideal of a poetic theatre, she allowed it to become a peasant theatre.

The new policy of the Abbey came in for angry criticism from the Dublin intellectuals, who at last realized the directors had become contemptuous of the opinion of even the best minds in Dublin. Some hoped Edward Martyn would apply for a patent for a new theatre. "It would be a well-spent £50," wrote Holloway,[2] "and would frighten the life out of these other potentates, Lady Gregory and Yeats neither of whom has even a sense of humor."

An article by Ernest Boyd in *The Irish Review*[3] was representative of the general line of criticism. He pointed out that in the early days of the Abbey Theatre few concessions were made to public prejudice, and a firm stand had been made against those who wished to make of the theatre a vehicle for the propagation of their political and religious ideas:

It would be impossible to over-estimate the importance of this victory in a country where religion and politics have too long been the sole manifestations of intellectual activity. It has at least been demonstrated that there is in Ireland a literary conscience which must not be violated with impunity. But if the Irish dramatic movement has resisted the onslaught of the artistically illiterate it seems in danger of succumbing to a more insidious enemy—popularity. Dublin will soon cease to be anything more than the nominal headquarters of the Abbey Players. Most of their time is spent abroad, where some of them even compete with Russian dancers or Japanese jugglers for the applause of music-hall audiences. . . . It seems, however, incredible that the financial position of the Abbey Theatre should be so unsound that it must remain vacant for the greater part of the year, while the company travels round in search of cash. Touring, which used to be purely incidental, has now become the mainstay of the theatre. In the intervals between one tour and another Ireland has to be content with such crumbs as fall from the dramatic feast prepared for foreigners.

The new "peasant" play also was attacked by the intellectuals, and it is significant that the attack came from the Abbey Theatre supporters and not from its enemies. Heroic tragedies and symbolistic fantasies, it was pointed out, were no more. Synge had introduced the "peasant" play and had revealed the potentialities of this *genre,* but those who imitated Synge unfortunately lacked his genius; their plays, which aimed at realism, succeeded only in being melodramatic. George Russell was outspoken on this subject:

We have developed a new and clever school of Irish dramatists who say they are holding up the mirror to Irish peasant nature, but they reflect nothing but decadence. They delight in the broken lights of insanity, the ruffian who beats his wife, the weakling who is unfortunate in love and who goes and drinks himself to death.[4]

The playwrights whose work came in mostly for attack were Robinson, Murray, and Ervine. Had the attack been directed toward the plays of R. J. Ray, it would have been more justifiable. Writing of the later Abbey dramatists in *The Irish Review* of February, 1912, G. Hamilton Gunning declared:

They have just gorgeously vulgarised the sources of inspiration of the first dramatists, for they have made such a cheap and ugly traffic of peasant Ireland that no serious writer can venture to present a peasant in literature for the next ten years.

The later Abbey dramatists have steeped the peasant play in all the horrors and paraphernalia of ancient melodrama. At present a loud and stirring gun-shot rocking the house with horror is so much the recognised ending of a play among these writers and their imitators that their work may be suitably classified in the history of the Abbey Theatre as "the gun-shot school of drama."

Most of this criticism was well founded. It was particularly annoying because it came from sources friendly to the Abbey Theatre. But Lady Gregory and Yeats, acting as if they were unconscious of it, continued with their plans. Dublin intellectuals had been disappointed, for Yeats had so often led them to believe he would be satisfied with nothing less than an intimate poetic theatre. Now it seemed Yeats had given up the struggle and was allowing Lady Gregory to make the folk comedy the dominant influence. This was exactly what was happening, but the critics failed to discern that Yeats countenanced it only because Ireland was not producing dramatic poets. Colum and Dunsany were not the answer to this difficult problem.

Despite criticisms, it was only Yeats and Lady Gregory who had achieved anything permanent; the critics themselves were barren. Even Edward Martyn recognized the accomplishments of Yeats and Lady Gregory. His appreciation which follows, though touched with a gentle sarcasm, sums up the situation very well:

The qualities by which Mr. Yeats has made the theatre are Napoleonic and consummate. A fine poet and subtle literary critic, he has, above all, a weird appearance which is triumphant with middle-aged masculine women, and a dictatorial manner which is irresistible with the considerable bevy of female and male mediocrities interested in intellectual things. In this way he practically dictates to the critics who reproduce his opinions. Lady Gregory, although not intellectually profound, is intellectually acute in the most extreme degree. She has a knowledge of mankind and a social mastery and tact that can only be described as genius. Thus equipped she sympathetically leads the leaders and parasites of society who may affect letters, to make the theatre fashionable. A combination of two such unique and efficient personalities for the special work they had to do, I suppose, the world has never seen before. The result is that Mr. Yeats and Lady Gregory have defied opposition, and have built up from nothing at all a remarkable and lasting structure.[5]

The outbreak of the World War in 1914 put an end to the American tours. Another reason, of course, was that Lady Gregory was advancing in age, being in her sixty-third year. She needed a rest. Yeats had already disconnected himself in part from the Abbey, so that he might give more attention to writing poetry. He still was vitally interested in the theatre, but he felt his energies should not be expended on the mechanics of theatre management. He depended on Lady Gregory's judgment to see that the Abbey was kept alive, and when she had suggested dropping Robinson as manager he did not object, although he recognized it as a serious mistake. Lady Gregory's choice of a manager to replace Robinson, A. Patrick Wilson, an actor of no distinction, was a poor tribute to her judgment. The Abbey seemed on the way down.

The only notable feature of Wilson's term was the production of a new play by Lennox Robinson, *The Dreamers* (February 2, 1915). He attracted no new dramatist to the theatre worth mentioning—certainly no one who was ever heard from again. He staged *The Critic* by Sheridan (December 26, 1915) and a new play by Lady Gregory, *Shanwalla* (April 8, 1915). For the latter, he deserves no credit.

Wilson's most important achievement was to run the Abbey into debt. During his first term the theatre suffered a loss of £500. For the first time, the Abbey was mortgaged. The amount was £600. Yeats had to forego his verse writing and return the theatre to a sound financial status. He gave lectures and approached his friends for help. This necessity was most distasteful to him at this time. England was fighting a war with Germany, and Ireland was not greatly sympathetic toward her. *Sinn Fein* was opposing Irish conscription, and others were openly on the side of Germany. It was not easy to collect money from wealthy English people without making some compromise.

Now, the British government would gladly support the theatre if Yeats would allow it to be used as a medium for British propaganda. This, he refused. From the early years, even before the Abbey Theatre was built, the British foreign office had made attempts through George Wyndham, Chief Secretary for Ireland, and through others to buy Yeats over to the English side, but Yeats would not compromise with any side. His only concession in 1915 was to postpone production of Shaw's antirecruiting play, *O'Leary, V. C.*, in deference to the wishes of the English government. He and Lady Gregory had considered inviting the viceroy to the Abbey in his official capacity, but they finally thought better of it and rejected the idea. Yeats was afraid of what the Pit might think of it; in fact, he knew the theatre might be burned down if the viceroy were allowed in. The Irish people would not condone such a sacrilege. The viceroy was so anxious to come, thinking it would help his recruiting campaign, that Yeats had to force him to keep away unless invited. Then Yeats was asked to support the recruiting of Irishmen for the English army, but once more he refused, although it was hinted he might be given a knighthood for doing so. Yeats wrote home to his sister on this matter:

I have just refused a Knighthood. Lady Cunard has already sounded the authorities and asked me about it. Please keep it to yourself and it would be very ungracious of me to let it get talked about in Dublin. It was very kindly meant. I said: "As I grow older I become more conservative and I do not know whether that is because my thoughts are deeper or my blood more chill but I do not wish anyone to say of me, 'Only for a ribbon he left us.' "

Yeats collected some money for the theatre, and his only compromise was to dismiss A. P. Wilson and bring in St. John Ervine, a rabid pro-Englishman, as manager of the Abbey Theatre.

Ervine had no sympathy at all with Ireland or her ideals. He was English in every way except by birth. Holloway said of him, "When a northerner has talent combined with cheek there is no standing him." He was already well known to Dublin audiences and critics from his plays, and he was universally disliked. One newspaper had dismissed his play *The Magnanimous Lover* (October 17, 1912) in a few sentences, the critic stating he was not "a sanitary inspector." Ervine tried to reply to his critics in his short skit *The Critics* (November 20, 1913), but this had no merit, being too vulgarly abusive, and was partly ignored.

When Ervine came to the Abbey as manager in the autumn of 1915, he announced his intentions of teaching the dramatists how plays should be written. His method was to produce world masterpieces as examples to be followed. He was not to remain long enough to carry out this policy. His object seems to have been to insult the National Theatre. The Abbey Theatre, he said, must not stand alone; it must have no individuality, certainly no national ideal. It was his hope to Anglicize it by making it merely one link in a chain of repertory theatres throughout Great Britain and Ireland. The Abbey must, if possible, be submerged in the British theatre movement, or in whatever corresponded to a movement in England.

It was evident from the start that Ervine would not get very far with a Dublin audience, and Yeats must have gently cawed to himself in expectation of the public's reaction. Yeats had not sold out to England; he was allowing the theatre to drift with the tide for a time. He could always save it when he wished.

The one notable production during Ervine's term as manager was his own play *John Ferguson* (November 30, 1915). This was Ervine's best play. It attempts to demonstrate the innate religious quality of the North of Ireland Protestant, as exemplified in the character of John Ferguson. Unfortunately, Ervine strains its verisimilitude by having John Ferguson overcome and treat with equanimity trials more severe than those which tested Job.

Ervine had only contempt for Irish dramatists, and possibly for this reason he discovered no new playwrights; contempt, like hatred, is barren. The best he could find was two dull farces by Bernard Duffy, which were more suited to the Queen's than to the Abbey Theatre. Early in 1916, he took the company to Liverpool for a two-week engagement, returning in Easter week with the intention of continuing at the Abbey till summer. However, the Insurrection broke in on his plans.

A large part of central Dublin was burned down, but fortunately the Abbey Theatre escaped; this was partly because the theatre stood on the corner farthest from the centre of the city, and on two sides was divided from all other buildings by unusually wide streets.

Most of the actors and staff of the Abbey Theatre supported the Rising. Nellie Bushell, chief usherette, took a prominent part in the fight. She carried dispatches from Padraic Pearse, commanding officer of the Insurgents, and even used a rifle at Jacobs factory and Marrybone Lane. Only Ervine was pro-British. He was intelligent enough to realize that, despite its literary nature, the Abbey Theatre was essentially a rallying point for extreme nationalists. Augustine Birrell was not quite accurate when he stated to the Royal Commission on the Rebellion of 1916 that the Abbey Theatre did not contribute in any way to the Insurrection:

The Abbey Theatre made merciless fun of mad political enterprises and lashed with savage satire some historical aspects of the Irish Revolutionary. I was often amazed at the literary detachment and courage of the playwright, the relentless audacity of the actors and actresses and the patience and comprehension of the audience. A little more time and but for the outbreak of this war new critical temper would, in my belief, have finally prevailed, not indeed to destroy national sentiment (for that is immortal) but to kill by ridicule insensate revolt.

It is true the Abbey Theatre was independent of all political parties, but revolutions are born in the mind and the Abbey Theatre helped to develop the thought of the nation. Padraic Pearse and Thomas MacDonagh, the two most influential leaders of the

Rising, were strong supporters of the Abbey. It must not be forgotten that Pearse praised *The Playboy* when the sentimental nationalists were trying to drive it from the stage. MacDonagh considered it the greatest play of the century.

Ervine advised Yeats and Lady Gregory that because of the Insurrection the theatre should be shut down. They succumbed to the hysteria of the time and surprisingly agreed. People were shocked when they read the following advertisement in *The Irish Times* of May 16, 1916:

THE DIRECTORS OF THE
ABBEY THEATRE
Are Prepared
TO LET THEATRE AND MECHANICS' INSTITUTE
Together or Separately
for business premises
Apply to Abbey Theatre, or Fred J. Harris, 39 Lower Ormond Quay, Dublin.

No one at first could understand why the Abbey Theatre should close down at the height of its popularity. They suspected that Ervine was responsible, though it was not easy to imagine, from his sleepy, half-awake, almost bohemian appearance, that he could be guilty of such intrigue. They were quickly to be assured. Ervine audaciously invited to the theatre General Maxwell, the man who had ruthlessly shot Pearse and all his comrades. The truth was now out; Ervine was the real evil influence. Protests were so violent over his invitation to the British general that even he decided it would be too much of a risk. Had he persisted in his intention, there is no doubt that the Abbey Theatre would have been burned down.

The same day that the advertisement appeared in *The Irish Times* the Abbey opened for a matinee performance with *The Mineral Workers* and *The Coiner,* but there were only thirty people present. Ervine next announced they would go for a week to Limerick, in the hope that Dublin would be more settled when they returned. While in Limerick, the players, indignant with Ervine's hostile attitude, picked a quarrel with him and decided to rebel. He at once informed them their contracts were terminated.

The company returned to Dublin, where *The Playboy* was billed for May 29, 1916. Ervine was so little in touch with Irish emotion that he imagined that the players would continue with their work. He was shocked when he arrived that evening at the Abbey and, like the regular patrons, was handed a pink slip of paper as he was entering. It read:

TO THE PATRONS OF THE ABBEY THEATRE

The Players regret to disappoint their public this week as they cannot appear under the present manager, Mr. St. John Ervine; full particulars will appear in the Press.

The players had wired Lady Gregory informing her of what they intended to do and asking her to reply before the evening performance. She did not reply until the following day, and the players refused to perform in *The Playboy*. In her letter to the rebellious players Lady Gregory explained she had ceased to take any active part in the management and could not see how she could go against the manager's decision.

It had always been the policy of the directors to support the manager against the complaints of the actors. Perhaps it might not be altogether unreasonable to suspect there was something more in this action than the respecting of a convention. The war had the effect of emphasizing Lady Gregory's sympathy with England— her son Robert was killed in the fight—and she must have felt, at least subconsciously, that an Irish National Theatre was in some subtle way an anti-British theatre. Hence the advertisement in the paper and hence her support of Ervine.

The players stood firm against Ervine. They asked Lady Gregory for permission to take over the theatre for a repertory season but of course were refused. Then, under the leadership of Arthur Sinclair, the Abbey Players left the theatre and did not return. They held together as a company and toured England as the Irish Players. They were very successful, and in the autumn they returned to Dublin and played at the Gaiety and Empire Palace Theatres. The Abbey directors sought an injunction to restrain Sinclair and his company from playing *Duty* by Seumas O'Brien, the rights of which were held by the Abbey. The case was not pushed and Sinclair was allowed to play it for a week.

Later the Irish Players toured America and Australia. They were always a financial success, but their failure was that no one of importance wrote plays for them. They remained mere players to the end.

The departure of all the actors left Ervine with nobody to manage. Lady Gregory and Yeats could do nothing except ask him to resign, which he did some months later. Everyone was happy to see Ervine leave the Abbey. He was a dictator but was a dictator without genius. He had done his best to destroy the personality of the Abbey but he did not succeed. Driving out the actors wrought no essential damage, for the genius of the theatre was not in the players, as they themselves learned when they broke away as a separate company. Yeats was the centre, and all depended on him. In fairness to Ervine it must be stated he was sincere in everything he did. He loved England, not Ireland, and when he left the theatre he pushed his pro-British sentiments to their logical conclusion—he went out to the battlefront, where he lost a leg.

Lady Gregory and Yeats were in a difficult position regarding the Abbey Theatre. Many replies had been received to the advertisement offering the theatre for a business premises, but they were all turned down. After 1916 it became clear that a new Ireland was being made, and Yeats wished to keep the theatre open for the coming of the dramatist who would give it expression. He did not know who that dramatist might be, but he was confident he would come. In the meantime the theatre would struggle along. J. Augustus Keogh was asked to be manager and to organize a new company of actors. He took control in September, 1916, and the Abbey was to return gradually to its normal function of being the National Theatre of Ireland.

Intermission

The European war was only half over and the Irish wars just beginning as J. Augustus Keogh moved in to manage the Abbey Theatre. He was completely without talent for production, being more fitted, as Holloway remarked, to run a tea shop than a theatre. Appointing this kind of person to take charge of the Abbey was so unlike Yeats that one must attribute the appointment to Lady Gregory. A safe man was needed, she must have thought, and a man without talent is easier to direct than a man of genius.

Yeats had almost cut himself adrift from the affairs of the theatre. He was living most of the time in London, experimenting with the Nō drama of Japan. He had been introduced to this by Ezra Pound. Kathleen Ni Houlihan was almost completely forgotten, and his philosophy had been reduced to its essentials, the circle and the straight line. The mysterious religion of pre-Christian Ireland he had shoved aside for something deeper still, something which was beyond the power of words to express. He would try to communicate in future by means of the dance. He made the acquaintance of a Mr. Ito, a Japanese dancer, and enlisted his help in a new play for dancers, to be called *At the Hawk's Well.*

For months Yeats and Mr. Ito were to be seen regularly outside a hawk's cage at the London zoo, imitating the movements of the bird. Their antics were a greater source of amusement to the visitors than many of the exhibits within the cages.

Yeats's new play was not written for the Abbey but rather for a few of his select friends in London. It was performed in the drawing room of Lady Cunard's London mansion in March, 1916, before a very fashionable audience. It was badly received—even though the proceeds were in aid of a war charity.

Yeats loved this kind of society, though he despised their intellectual attitude. His associating with upper-class British society had one good result: he was able to collect funds in aid of the Abbey Theatre whenever there was danger of its collapse.

The Rising of 1916 almost altered the whole course of his life. Maud Gonne's husband, Major Sean MacBride, had taken part in the Insurrection and had been executed by the British. Maud Gonne was a widow now and Yeats was interested, as always, in marrying her. Before acting in a matter of this personal nature he consulted Lady Gregory. She surprised him by reacting violently against the idea. It was unthinkable, she said, that he should marry Maud Gonne, a rebel against English rule in Ireland. What would happen to the Abbey Theatre? Would their British friends continue to support it? Yeats could see the truth of the arguments, but he was too deeply in love with Maud Gonne to be moved by logic. Seeing he was not to be deterred in his purpose, Lady Gregory made him promise he would marry Maud Gonne only on condition she renounce all politics and cease demanding amnesty for political prisoners in English jails. Yeats reluctantly agreed and set sail at once for France to invite Maud Gonne to marry him. He expected to find her in a mournful mood, disconsolate over the loss of her husband. He was to be surprised, for he discovered she was in fighting form, and her only anxiety was to find not a husband but a passport, so that she might return to Ireland and continue the struggle against England. She told Yeats she would not marry him and that even if she did, she would make the conditions. Yeats then asked her daughter, Iseult Gonne, to marry him. She also refused.

Yeats was defeated and he returned to London sad. Lady Gregory's aristocratic mind was shocked that a commoner such as Maud Gonne should refuse to marry the greatest poet of the century. It was an insult to Lady Gregory's pride even more than to Yeats's that Maud Gonne should act as she did. Lady Gregory would find Yeats a wife.

In the meantime she was thankful the Abbey Theatre was saved; it would still receive the support of the British. J. Augustus Keogh was therefore the ideal person to have charge of the Abbey Theatre at this time; he would do nothing wrong and would not, like Robinson, keep the theatre open when others, out of respect to an English king, might be shut.

Keogh had been fairly well known as an actor in the plays of Shaw, and it was to be expected he now would favor producing them. Yeats had never favored Shaw and had refused his *John Bull's Other Island,* on the excuse that an actor to play the part of Broadbent could not be found. For Yeats, there was too much propaganda and not enough poetry in Shaw.

Keogh, having organized a troupe of actors, decided to open his season on September 25, 1916, with *John Bull's Other Island.* In an interview with the press in September, Keogh announced a new policy: "In future there is no phase of Irish life which will not be faithfully portrayed on the boards of the Abbey Theatre. In addition to peasant life, which has already received a good deal of attention, plays dealing with the middle and upper classes of the country will be presented."

Keogh's intentions could not be carried into effect except in the particular instance of Shaw, since there were no plays of upper-class Irish life in existence, and Keogh was not the person to inspire anyone to write such plays. When Shaw learned that his plays were to receive preferential treatment at the Abbey he wrote to Keogh advising him that he considered it best not to have his plays produced at the Abbey until such time as the native dramatic works had emptied the theatre. Then, he said, his plays might appropriately be produced to bring back the audience. But Keogh went ahead and staged six plays by Shaw: *John Bull's Other Island* (September 25, 1916), *Widowers' Houses* (October 9), *Arms and the Man* (October 16), *Man and Superman* (February 26, 1917), *The Inca of Perusalem* (March 12), and *The Doctor's Dilemma* (May 26).

The season's most notable production was Robinson's *The Whiteheaded Boy,* a pleasant comedy. It was badly produced, for Keogh had no knowledge nor sympathy with Irish plays: his enthusiasm began and ended with Shaw. However, Robinson's comedy was a success and in later years was one of the most popular plays at the Abbey Theatre.

Shaw's plays did not fill the theatre as their author had prophesied; they did not even half fill it. Those associated with the Abbey grumbled at the small audiences and blamed Keogh. Holloway, who had always the popular ear, wrote in his *Diary*:

Larchet [director of the orchestra] longed for the return of the days when Irish plays would be staged with loving care. People were tired of Shaw. (There was a very small house tonight for The Doctor's Dilemma). Arthur Sinclair said that's a lot of money to be spending on Shaw without an adequate return. It was a mistake wasting such a lot on them and starving out Irish plays and neglecting Irish dramatists to cater for the manager J. A. Keogh's liking for Shaw productions.

Keogh was intelligent enough to perceive he was not a success and should leave. Accordingly he departed in the summer of 1917, and Lady Gregory appointed Fred O'Donovan, one of the actors, in his place. O'Donovan showed intelligence, and during his tenure as manager (ending in March, 1919) the public showed more active interest than ever before in the Abbey Theatre. There was even a profit to show, although a small one.

O'Donovan introduced the policy of changing productions twice weekly. He staged two plays of real importance, *Spring* by T. C. Murray (January 8, 1918), a delightful lyrical piece, and *The Lost Leader* by Lennox Robinson (February 9), about Parnell and modern Ireland. The Abbey seemed to be progressing toward financial success. But once more it was decreed otherwise.

Meanwhile, Lady Gregory persisted in her efforts to find a suitable wife for Yeats. She believed he would write better plays if he were relieved of the constant search for a mate. Some time earlier, Lady Gregory had introduced him to a well-to-do young English woman, Miss Hyde-Lees, and now Yeats decided to marry her. They were wedded in October, 1917. Miss Hyde-Lees was fairly rich, and it was well she was; Yeats had only eight pounds in his pocket when they married, although he was one of the best-known writers of his time.

Yeats settled down at Oxford to cultivate his Nō plays, and for the moment the Abbey was forgotten. When it became apparent his wife was going to have a child, he took her to Ireland so that the child would be born in that country. They stayed for the greater part of the summer of 1918 in an old tower near Lady Gregory's mansion, and in the winter they moved to Dublin.

Yeats now was less interested in the theatre than in his new "philosophy" of the antithetical self and its expression. The same could not be said for his wife. Being the wife of Yeats, she assumed the right to dictate to O'Donovan, manager of the Abbey. She would come in during rehearsals and give directions. Interference such as this was not allowed to pass. Neither O'Donovan nor the actors were pleased to be criticized by an Englishwoman and, worse still, by an Englishwoman who knew little about the stage. They protested, and for a while George (as Yeats called his wife) was more careful in what she said at the Abbey. O'Donovan felt there was never a time when there should be less criticism, now that the theatre was prospering.

O'Donovan discovered no new dramatists of note and was inclined to favor foreign plays. Yeats objected. He had changed his mind on this subject. Though he believed in giving the Dublin public a knowledge of foreign masterpieces he felt it was not the business of the Abbey to undertake this task. He had founded the Abbey as an Irish National Theatre and as such it must remain. He recognized that the standard of the new plays had dropped, but he was content to wait until a good dramatist came along.

To satisfy the demand for foreign plays, Yeats organized the Drama League. Yeats became president and Lennox Robinson secretary. Its first production took place at the Abbey Theatre on

February 17, 1919, with *The Liberators* by Srgjan Tucic. The policy of the Drama League was to have four or five productions during the season. Each play would run for only two nights at the Abbey Theatre—on Sunday and Monday. The Drama League ran for ten years—up to the time of the Gate Theatre Company's formation by Hilton Edwards and Micheál MacLiammhóir, when it became superfluous. During its existence the Drama League produced plays by Strindberg, D'Annunzio, Sierra, the Quintero brothers, Eugene O'Neill, L'Normand, Andreyev, Benevente, Euripides, Dunsany, Shaw, Cocteau, Bjornson, Schnitzler, Chekhov, Jules Romains, Evreinov, Pirandello, Philip Barry, Stark Young, Toller, Gribble, Cannan, Verhaeren, Flecker, Chesterton, Glaspel, and Hughes.

Mrs. Yeats had stopped interfering directly in the affairs of the theatre, but she gave advice to Yeats on what should be done. Yeats carried out her instructions. This was even more annoying to the company than direct interference, and O'Donovan was planning to resign. Finally, when Lady Gregory reappointed Miss Magee at a salary of five pounds a week "because we want some beauty on our stage," O'Donovan marched out of the theatre, taking most of the good actors with him. He formed a company and went on tour.

The Abbey was once again left without a company. Yeats had become tired of reorganizing the theatre and wanted to close it; he had lost his vigor for a fight. Not so, Lady Gregory. Although she was sixty-seven she refused to allow the theatre to close even if she was compelled to manage it herself. One of the factors that urged Lady Gregory to continue the fight was that she realized her forcing the appointment of Miss Magee contributed to O'Donovan's resignation.

As luck would have it, Lennox Robinson was anxious to return to the Abbey as manager. Yeats agreed, because he felt that youth must be allowed to have its turn in running the theatre. Both he and Lady Gregory had lost the violence of youth, and there was no better plan than to hand over the management to Robinson, who was by now a distinguished playwright. Yeats wrote Lady Gregory, then in London, informing her of his idea. Lady Gregory agreed— but only with reluctance, for she still cultivated the self-deception that Robinson, not herself, was responsible for the losses on the last American tour. So great was this obsession that it blinded her to Robinson's capacity, and she could see little in his delightful comedies except morbidity. Robinson was at the time secretary of the Carnegie Trust, and he hoped he would be allowed to work part time as secretary and full time as manager and producer at the Abbey. This was arranged, and Lady Gregory struck a hard bargain with him. He was to receive five pounds a week as salary, but Lady Gregory made him agree to accept half pay during the off season. Robinson wanted a two- or three-year contract to safeguard himself against capricious eviction, but Lady Gregory refused, saying that even in marriage settlements each side had for practical purposes to consider the other a possible rogue. "So had we in case he should take to drink or use the theatre for the purposes Lord French is said to use the mansions he hires in London." Robinson agreed to a one-year contract.

Although he had had to force his way back into the managership of the Abbey, Robinson's return gave great hope. No man of thorough competence had occupied the position since he left in 1914, and the theatre had been drifting downward. Robinson took up where he had left off and attempted to bring the Abbey back to the high position it had held. He had a difficult task ahead of him. For one thing, Lady Gregory was domineering and unfriendly. Again, not being a poet, he could not hope to inspire a great poetic drama; but he was a sincere writer, and he made no pretense at emphasizing this aspect. Under Robinson, the Abbey consolidated its position as a folk theatre. Yeats saw the inevitable but did not seek to turn the tide. He was confident Robinson would lead the theatre, though on a different road, with a dignity in keeping with the ideals of its founders. In an open letter to Lady Gregory in *The Irish Statesman*[1] Yeats wrote what seemed his farewell to the Abbey:

My dear Lady Gregory:
 Of recent years you have done all that is anxious and laborious in the supervision of the Abbey Theatre and left me free to follow my own thoughts. . . . We have been the first to create a true people's theatre and we have succeeded because it is not an exploitation of local color or of a limited form of drama possessing a temporary novelty, but the first

doing of something for which the world is ripe . . . the making articulate of all the dumb classes each with its own knowledge of the world, its own dignity, but all objective with the objectivity of the office and the workshop, of the newspaper and the street. . . . Yet we did not set out to create this sort of a theatre and its success has been to me a discouragement and a defeat. . . . You and I and Synge, not understanding the clock, set out to bring again the theatre of Shakespeare or rather, perhaps, of Sophocles. . . . I want to create for myself an unpopular theatre and an audience like a secret society where admission is by favor and never too many. Perhaps I shall never create it, for you and I and Synge had to dig the stone for our statue and I am aghast at the sight of a new quarry, and besides I want so much—an audience of fifty, a room worthy of it (some great diningroom or sittingroom), half a dozen young men and women who can dance and speak verse or play drum and flute and zither. . . . I desire a mysterious art always reminding and half-reminding those who understand it of dearly loved things, doing its work by suggestion, not by direct statement, a complexity of rhythm, colour, gesture, not space pervading like the intellect but a memory and a prophecy; a mode of drama Shelley and Keats could have used without ceasing to be themselves and for which even Blake in the mood of "The Book of Thell" might not have been too obscure.

This letter might more properly be taken as a statement of Yeats's position at this time rather than as a farewell to the Abbey Theatre. He loved the Abbey too much ever to desert it completely, and he lived to fight more than one battle for its continued existence.

Cuchulain and His Hound: the Abbey Emblem

Ghostly Musicians in Yeats's "The Dreaming of the Bones"

William Butler Yeats

In 1890

ts, Mr. Ito, and the Hawk

Lady Gregory, *by Mancini*

Alice Boughton

At Her Desk

In 1893

John Millington Synge

Sean O'Casey, *by Augustus John*

Off Guard

A Study

George Moore, *by Mark Fisher*

George Russell

Annie Elizabeth Horniman, *by J. B. Yeats*

Frank Fay

Lennox Robinson

Paul Vincent Carroll

Edward Martyn, *by Sara Purser*

The Abbey

The Stage

The Green Room

Rehearsal Time

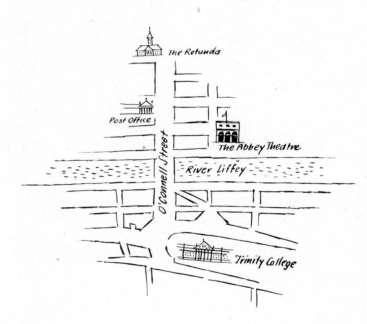

The Rotunda

Post Office

The Abbey Theatre

O'Connell Street

River Liffey

Trinity College

Taking "The Playboy" to England

Frank O'Connor

Padraic Colum

Sara Allgood

Barry Fitzgerald

Dudley
Digges

Arthur Shields

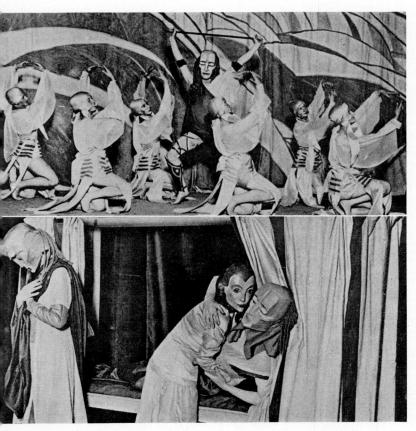

Yeats's Ballet "Fighting the Waves"

Joseph Holloway

A Page from His Diary

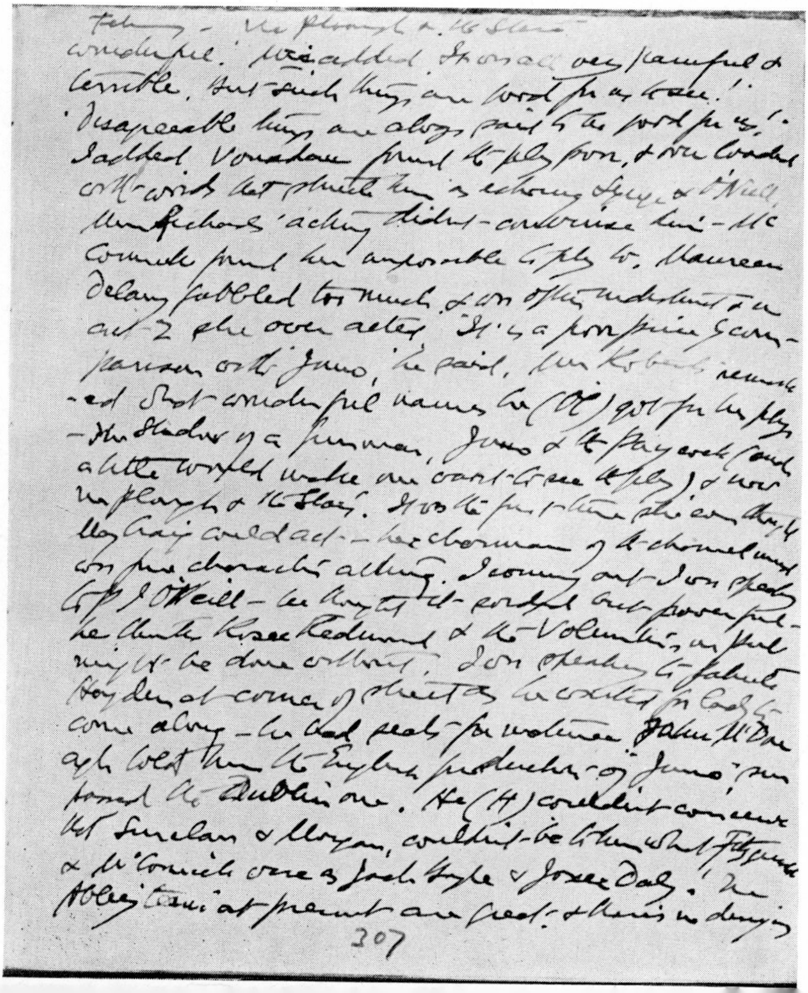

Talking — the Plough & the Stars
wonderful.' He added, 'It was all very painful &
terrible, but such things are good for us to see.'
'Disagreeable things are always [illegible] for us.'
I added. Vaughan found the play poor, & we wonder
with wide [illegible] that struck him as echoing Synge & O'Neill.
Miss Richards' acting didn't convince him — Mc
Cormick found him impossible to play to. Maureen
Delany gabbled too much, & was often indistinct in
act 2 she over acted. 'It's a poor piece of com-
parison with Juno,' he said. Mrs Roberts remark-
-ed what wonderful names he (O'C) got for his plays
— The Shadow of a Gunman, Juno & the Paycock (and
a little word would make one want to see the play) & now
The Plough & the Stars. It was the first time she saw that
May Craig could act — her charwoman of the [illegible]
was fine character acting. I coming out I was speaking
to J. J. O'Neill — he thought it sordid but powerful —
he thinks Rosie Redmond & the Volunteers in pub
might be done without. I was speaking to [illegible]
Hayden at corner of street as he waited for Lady G to
come along — he had seats for volunteer. Father McDon-
agh told him the English production of 'Juno' sur-
passed the Dublin one. He (H) couldn't conceive
that Sinclair & Morgan couldn't be better than what Fitzgerald
& McCormick were as Jack Boyle & Joxer Daly. 'The
Abbey team at present are great & there is no denying
307

Maude Gonne

The Abbey During the Civil War

The period from 1919 to 1925 was one of the most crucial for the Abbey Theatre and for the Irish nation. The national spirit, awakened by the 1916 Rising, had spread to all Ireland. All were united in a desperate and final attempt to achieve political freedom for the country. It was a period of war, of passive resistance, of hunger strikes, and of pestilence. That the Abbey Theatre survived was possibly the greatest achievement of all, and a tribute to its directors. The Abbey, though not directly concerned in the fight, suffered seriously because of it and received a blow which at the time seemed superficial but later turned out to be mortal.

The Abbey was a national theatre and it could not, even if it so wished, dissociate itself from the political struggle for a free Ireland. It had contributed much to the change in national sentiment, but in so subtle and fundamental a way that its influence was not clearly apparent. For twenty years it had been molding the intellect of Ireland to accept an attitude of independence.

Pearse and MacDonagh, leaders of the 1916 Rising, had recognized the importance of the Abbey and were among its most enthusiastic supporters. Later, Michael Collins, the man who led Ireland to eventual freedom, considered it almost a patriotic duty to patronize the Abbey, and he took time off from shooting English spies to attend the plays. It was no secret that he went there, and on more than one occasion he had to be smuggled out of the building when it was surrounded by Black and Tans who had come to arrest him.

Michael Collins was an exceptionally intelligent patriot. Many of his colleagues, because they had awakened too suddenly to a consciousness of national Ireland, looked with less sympathy on the Abbey and could not see that it was in any way a national theatre. Thus, we find General Mulcahy, chief of staff of the Irish Republican Army, stating in an Abbey Theatre speech in October, 1921, that "we have been deserted, at the present time, and all through the fight put up in the country, by our literary people." This attitude toward the work of the Abbey Theatre, on the part of a section of the nationalists, created the greatest problem for the Abbey leaders during this period. Irish writers were expected to be "of use"; they were to forget all their ideas of art and turn the theatre into a weapon of direct and obvious propaganda. The Abbey had never condescended to propaganda, and even in this moment of crisis Yeats would rather have closed its doors than desert his ideals. He knew, and so did Robinson and Lady Gregory, that if they deserted their ideals they would have only a hollow shell when the fighting was over and the shouting had died down. The attitude of the soldiers was understandable—for them, the real drama was being enacted on the streets of Dublin—but it might have been disastrous for literature and consequently for Ireland if Yeats and his friends had accepted this essentially shortsighted view. Sean O'Casey might never have arisen, and Ireland would have been the poorer.

The battle for national independence begun in Easter week,

1916, reached its greatest intensity from 1919 to 1921. Even the extreme Anglo-Irish were disturbed by the savage methods employed by the British government. Lady Gregory, whose son died for England, supported *Sinn Fein,* and so did AE, Yeats, Robinson, and all the leading writers. The prolonged hunger strike of Terence MacSwiney, lord mayor of Cork, ending in his death, drew world attention to the Irish struggle.

The military battle was at its height when Robinson rejoined the Abbey, and prospects for guiding the theatre safely were not encouraging. To make matters even worse, a virulent 'flu epidemic was raging, and only the bravest would come to a theatre when they were subject to contracting the 'flu or to being shot by the Black and Tans. Abbey audiences, already very small, were bound to become smaller. In his autobiography *Curtain Up,* Robinson described the condition in which he found the theatre:

When I returned to the Abbey Theatre as manager I came back to a theatre very different from the one I had left. I had left it prosperous, with a fine company, lacking exciting plays perhaps, but, given time, such plays would be sure to come. Instead came the War, that war which killed every Repertory theatre in England and almost killed the Abbey. The audience dropped . . . dropped. The players' salaries had to be reduced and further reduced; the starriest of the players sought their living elsewhere. Sara Allgood went, Arthur Sinclair went, and J. M. Kerrigan and Sydney Morgan. Finally Fred O'Donovan left, taking with him the best of the players who were still at the theatre and when I was asked to come back, just after the Armistice, there was but a handful of young players and a balance in the bank of one hundred pounds.

Yeats had gone off to live in England, offering the excuse that he wanted to give Robinson a free hand at the Abbey. This was a sensible view; all Ireland was being directed by youth, and the Abbey Theatre might be revitalized by a young man. Lady Gregory took a different attitude: as long as she lived she would not relinquish any of her control. So she came to Dublin to order Robinson around.

Robinson quickly collected a company of actors and continued the work of the theatre as if no break had occurred. He would begin by reviving Yeats's *Kathleen Ni Houlihan.* An actress to take the part of Kathleen could not be found, and Lady Gregory, in a fighting mood, decided to play it herself, which she did with some success. Next was *John Bull's Other Island,* and there was again difficulty in finding capable actors—particularly for the part of Broadbent. Only her sex prevented Lady Gregory from pitching in once more. However, a young man was coached in the part, and everything went well.

Lady Gregory wrote a new play, *The Dragon,* produced April 21, 1919. This play, like her next two, *The Golden Apple* (January 6, 1920) and *Aristotle's Bellows* (March 17, 1921), was a fantasy and thus an entirely new departure for Lady Gregory. The three plays were well received by the audience, but many thought them childish. Larchet, the musical director, told Holloway these plays were an indication that "the old lady has reached her dotage." Yet, whatever their merit as drama, they added to the repertory and brought people to the theatre to see them, if only out of curiosity.

Robinson opened the autumn season of 1919 with a series of new plays, some good and some not good; at least they were a relief from the tedium of popular revivals. *A Night at an Inn* by Dunsany (September 2) was staged, and *The Labour Leader* by Daniel Corkery (September 30). Corkery was far from being a considerable dramatist, but his play about the problems of labor touched on a vital subject.

The most notable offering of the season was *The Player Queen* by Yeats (December 9). This play, Yeats explained in a note to the printed version, was begun as a tragedy "where every character became an example of the finding or not finding of . . . the Antithetical Self." It mystified the audience, and after the performance everyone was asking one another in the foyer what it was all about. No one knew, and everyone assumed it to be high art.

Mystery always draws a crowd, and *The Player Queen* attracted a large audience. Robinson was encouraged, and he believed the discovery of a good playwright would save the theatre. Not having Yeats's genius for discovering a poet even before the poet arrived, Robinson thought he would discover a dramatist by producing all the new plays he could put his hands on. Accordingly, in

1920 he produced six plays by authors mostly unknown in the theatre. *The Land for the People* (November 30) by Brinsley Macnamara, a novelist, was the best play in this group. Macnamara was a minor discovery, and he was to write many plays for the Abbey.

The theatre was making progress now and was avoiding serious debt. Yeats was on a lecture tour in America in early 1920 and was publicizing the Abbey everywhere he went. In a lecture at Hart House, Toronto, he made the amusing statement that *Twenty Five* by Lady Gregory could not be performed for two years; in it a man returned from America with £100, and this was objected to because it might encourage emigration. He also said *The Rising of the Moon* could not be performed either, because a policeman was portrayed as holding patriotic sentiments.

Yeats made sure never to lose touch with Ireland, and we find him at an Abbey revival of *Kathleen Ni Houlihan* (August 2, 1920). Holloway writes:

W. B. Yeats came in spectre-like during Kathleen Ni Houlihan and stood inside the door leaning against the pillar for a time. After the little play he moved across to the other side meeting Larchet on the stairs coming down to conduct the orchestra and Robinson came in and followed him into the scene door having first exchanged a few words with Larchet as he stood by pious. They returned for the third act of *Mixed Marriage* which Yeats heartily applauded. After this act they returned again.

Lest it might ever be said the Abbey did not do its bit for national Ireland in the hour of its trial, *The Revolutionist* by Terence MacSwiney, the man who had died on hunger strike, was performed (February 24, 1921). It was an extremely bad play, but it packed the theatre for two weeks because of the author's popularity.

The theatre was surviving, but the coming of the Black and Tans and the consequent imposition of an eight-o'clock curfew meant the Abbey would be compelled to close. In this state of affairs, English friends once more came to the rescue. A series of lectures in aid of the theatre was arranged by J. B. Fagan in the large drawing room of his London mansion. The lecturers were Yeats, Lady Gregory, Shaw, and St. John Ervine. The chairmen were

John Galsworthy, John Drinkwater, Fagan, and Lennox Robinson. The proceeds of the lectures (including donations) were almost enough to pay off the £500 debt which the Abbey had incurred in consequence of the troubled times. Then Lady Ardilaun, hearing of the Abbey's plight, sent a check to Lady Gregory clearing the theatre completely of debt. The Abbey was now able to continue for a time, irrespective of the war.

The war for independence was drawing to a close. England had asked for a truce, and after negotiations Home Rule was granted to twenty-six of the thirty-two Irish counties. Most Irishmen were delighted, especially those associated with the Abbey, for it meant the theatre could open again. Now they would have a free theatre in a free Ireland. Arthur Griffith was elected president of the new Irish government, with Collins, Cosgrave, and others as his ministers. Griffith, though for years at enmity with Yeats, recognized the importance of his contribution to the freedom of Ireland and at once offered him a nomination to the new senate. Yeats readily accepted.

Later, AE also was offered a seat in the senate, but he reacted somewhat differently. The story is told[1] that the evening before the Official Gazette was to go to press, the secretary to the president and another civil servant were dispatched to AE's house in Rathgar to ask if he would accept a seat in the Senate. Apparently AE was holding a séance when they arrived, and instead of coming to the door he put his head out the window and inquired sharply, "What do you want?" The president's secretary answered, "We want to know will you accept a nomination for the senate?" AE considered for a while and said, "Before making any decisions I always consult my deities." The civil servant, who was responsible for getting out the Gazette, was irritated by what he considered AE's facetiousness, and he burst out, "Coddin' apart, will you take it or leave it?" AE did not reply; wrapping himself up in his spiritual toga, he shut the window and returned to his meditations. Not till the next day did he give his decision: he would not accept the honor.

Suddenly, when all Ireland seemed happy and content with her newly won freedom, De Valera, who had fought in 1916, decided he would not accept the Treaty and initiated a civil war. Irishmen were struck with consternation at the folly, almost criminality, of his action. AE was particularly shocked; he wanted someone to write a play about how the generations for seven hundred years fought for the liberation of the beautiful Kathleen Ni Houlihan, and how, when they set her free, she walked out a vituperative old hag. Robinson was deeply moved; he felt like writing the play and leaving Ireland forever the day before its production.

Yeats, no less than AE, was shocked by the civil war. He wanted to close the Abbey, go live in Cork, and start all over again. He was completely disillusioned and depressed. Lady Gregory dissuaded him from the idea, but he suggested as an alternative that the Abbey be handed over to the new government. Ireland, he felt, was not worthy of his theatre. Desperation brought on by the civil war had caused Yeats to lose his judgment. And Lady Gregory agreed to this proposal, thus failing to give him sound advice in the hour of his need.

To their surprise, Eoin MacNeil, minister of education, refused the theatre, saying he had troubles enough to contend with. Yeats would then have closed the theatre, but Lady Gregory would not hear of it, and it was decided to carry on. Only in this extreme emergency did Lady Gregory concur in making Lennox Robinson a director, thus filling the vacancy caused by the death of Synge in 1909.

The honor of being made a director encouraged Robinson to greater efforts. Unlike Yeats, his measure of success was more or less that of popularity. To him, a large audience was no indication of a drop in taste, and he made every effort to attract the public. He opened the season of 1922 with a new play by T. C. Murray, *Aftermath* (January 12). It dealt in an Ibsenish manner with Murray's favorite theme of parental love. It was not very successful. Robinson followed with a play of his own, *The Round Table* (January 31). It was an interesting experimental play of personality, but it also failed to please.

Robinson tried to determine whether a Shaw play would lure the public to the theatre, and he staged *Man of Destiny* (March 6), but to little avail. Meanwhile he was writing a new comedy, believing he had to come to his own rescue. It was *Crabbed Youth and Age* (November 14), and it did extremely well.

On October 3 another peasant play had been performed. It was *Paul Twyning* by George Shiels. Shiels was a promising playwright from the North of Ireland who gave hopes of becoming a major dramatist if he could be directed away from dramatic journalism. *The Grasshopper,* an adaptation by Padraic Colum (October 24), particularly pleased Robinson, because it brought in a large and distinguished audience. The crowd brought back memories of the old days at the Abbey Theatre as they stood in the foyer discussing the play. Holloway records that all literary Dublin was present, and his list is interesting, even if time has not honored all the names with immortality:

Present in the foyer were W. A. Henderson, T. C. Murray, John Burke and his niece Miss Burke, Brinsley Macnamara, Frank Hugh O'Donnell, Mr. and Mrs. Paul Henry, Mr. Maguire, Mr. and Mrs. Caufield, W. B. Yeats, Captain Bryan Cooper, Lennox Robinson, Dermot O'Brien, the Misses Young, Dorothy Macardle, P. Kirwan, Mr. Corrigan, Mrs. Colum (Padraic was in London), and F. R. Higgins.

Robinson's heroic efforts seemed of little avail. The civil war was having disastrous effects on the theatre's finances. Now that Yeats was a senator in the new government, De Valera's irregulars were threatening his theatre. Occasionally a command would be issued by the irregulars to close the theatre on a certain night, only to be countermanded by the government. Soldiers would be sent to enforce the order, and in the circumstances the public thought it safer to stay away. The situation had deteriorated so far that Lady Gregory thought the most discreet and practical move would be to close down the theatre and rent it for a few years to a film company. The money accruing from the rental might, she thought, be saved up so they could later open unencumbered by debt.

It is instructive to note that the civil war had affected people so perversely that many were delighted to learn the Abbey was about to pass away. Val Vousden, a music-hall entertainer, was particularly pleased. He told Holloway it was the greatest blessing that ever occurred for the theatre in Ireland. Now, he said, there will be great hope for the little theatre in the future.

Supporters of the Abbey were disconsolate. There was an overdraft on the bank of 1,153 pounds, 16 shillings, 10 pence on June

17, 1924. Checks drawn on the Abbey's account were being dishonored. In a last desperate effort the Abbey building was mortgaged; this cleared the overdraft and lodged £500 in the bank to the Abbey's credit.

Lady Gregory continued to press the government to take over the theatre, and finally Ernest Blythe, minister of finance, agreed to consider giving the Abbey an annual subsidy. Blythe was a strong supporter of the Gaelic League and he had to consider whether the money might not be better spent in promoting the aims of that society.

The accounts of the Abbey were examined, and it was discovered that between the years 1912 and 1924 the Abbey had lost £4,000. Blythe consulted with his government colleagues, and it was agreed to make an annual grant of £850 to the Abbey. At the same time an annual grant of £600 was made to An Comhar Dramíochta, an organization which promised to found a Gaelic drama. One condition of the Abbey subsidy was that the government be allowed to appoint a special director to look after its interests. This was readily agreed to, and George O'Brien, a very brilliant young professor of economics, was appointed as the government's nominee on the Abbey Theatre board of directors.

Lady Gregory was very proud of her success in getting the government subsidy. It was entirely her own idea, but the acceptance of the conditions were also her responsibility. Yeats was touring in Italy for the sake of his health and was giving the theatre little attention. He would have been happier, perhaps, if the Abbey had closed down entirely, for he was astute enough to see that a government subsidy meant some interference with policy, and this he would never tolerate. He wanted the Abbey to remain an intellectually independent theatre or stop completely.

Lady Gregory, on the other hand, knew the subsidy would relieve her of the onerous duties of begging money from her friends; with her advancing age this process was increasingly arduous. It was her belief that she and Yeats could prevent the theatre from being swamped by any government influence.

Blythe, the minister of finance, seemed a friendly and reasonable person, without much education, perhaps, but simple and without guile; or so it appeared at the time. George O'Brien, the new director, was a bit too intelligent to be safe, but since his field was economics, it would be easy to override any objection he might make. The only feature of the new arrangement pleasing to Yeats was that the Abbey Theatre, after twenty-one years of struggle, was finally recognized officially as the National Theatre of Ireland. His dreams as a youth were completely fulfilled; he had done what seemed almost impossible—the creation of a distinctive national theatre and the education of an audience, however few in numbers, to appreciate good drama.

The twenty-first anniversary of the Abbey's founding was celebrated with great rejoicing on December 27, 1925. Three plays were revived: *The Hour Glass* by Yeats, *In the Shadow of the Glen* by Synge, and *Hyacinth Halvey* by Lady Gregory. All past bitterness was forgotten, and Frank Fay was brought back to play his old part as the Wise Man in *The Hour Glass*. An elaborate program was printed and speeches were made from the stage. Ernest Blythe proposed a vote of thanks to the players, past and present, and promised to increase the subsidy the following year. The chairman, Thomas Johnson, a labor leader and a member of the new Irish government, added a few words of praise, then Geróid Ó Lochlain, leader of the Gaelic Drama League, supported Blythe's motion; he spoke in Gaelic.

Lady Gregory, replying on behalf of the players, ended her speech with a quotation from Yeats, hoping "that the long-remembering harpers have matter for their song." Yeats was there with his tall hat and dress suit, but he did not make a speech. Perhaps he feared that the unpopularity he had brought on himself by supporting the Divorce Bill in the senate some months before might encourage some member of the audience to heckle him and thus spoil what should be an occasion for general rejoicing. Maybe the real reason for his silence was that he sensed that the presence of Blythe on the stage was a bad omen for the future of his theatre. He was sixty years old and his fighting days were over. In future it would be Robinson's duty to fight, but Yeats did not wish it should ever be said he sold an ideal for money.

Yet the truth is, that is what actually happened to the Abbey Theatre. The enemy had sneaked in unnoticed in the cloak of a friend, and only too late was he recognized. Yeats would be dead before the enemy revealed himself. The acceptance of the subsidy was the beginning of the end of the Abbey as a theatre of the imagination. The tragic irony of it was that the subsidy came just when it was not really needed, for the Abbey had already come to its own aid unknowingly, by discovering Sean O'Casey.

Sean O'Casey

Sean O'Casey was the first and only great playwright who wrote
for the Abbey Theatre about the real Ireland. Yeats wrote about
the Ireland of his imagination, and Synge imposed his genius on
the peasants. But O'Casey was of the people and sang of their
sorrows and joys—less to entertain an audience than for his own
inner satisfaction. He had not read of Ireland's history and legend,
as Yeats had done, before he wrote, nor had he gone to the west of
Ireland as Synge had gone. He was Ireland himself. When he
wrote sincerely out of his own life and its emotions, he was expressing the inner spirit of Ireland.

All Ireland, including the cities, is dominated by the land. Because of this, every truly Irish writer, whether he be city dweller

or countryman, is in the larger sense a peasant. O'Casey, born in the Dublin slums, was therefore a peasant.

The Dublin tenement dwellers are the most essentially Irish group in the nation. The peasants who live on the land are so dominated by the land that many of their native qualities are submerged, and they have little left but dreams. Dreams, it is true, are the final reality and the essence of every work of genius, but they must be free and detached from every sordid influence which would enclose them. Sometimes it is the intellect which is the sterilizing influence; at other times it is lust for material things; in the case of the Irish countryman it is the unholy love of the land. The Irish peasant loves the soil so much that he is usually undistinguishable from it. His spirit leaves him and he becomes a part of the clay.

Every Irish peasant writer of genius has had to flee to the city from the tyranny of the farm before he could give his dreams expression. A writer born in the Dublin slums has no such problem. He has not to fight off that savage love for the soil which would engulf his spirit. His only problem is one of poverty, and poverty in moderation is good for the soul. In the Dublin slums is therefore to be found what might be called the disembodied spirit of Ireland. James Joyce recognized this and attempted to give it expression. Joyce failed where O'Casey succeeded, because Joyce was not of the slums; at best he was a sympathetic observer. His mind was dominated by the intellect, by the knowledge one finds in books, and his writings of Dublin life, despite their brilliance, never catch fire from the emotion of the people. Joyce gives the impression that he is writing to be heard; O'Casey in his early plays is writing for himself.

O'Casey was a typical Dublin slum dweller. He lived with his mother in a shabby tenement in the back streets of the city. He had no formal schooling and, like his neighbors, he made a living as well as he could by working at any casual job he could find. Sometimes he would be idle for long periods, unable to find a job. Unemployment did not bother him greatly for poverty was the normal state in that society. There was no such thing as frustration, and the people accepted their struggle as a commonplace of living. It was obvious to them that by no effort of their own could they ever become rich, and this diverted their minds from making money to discussing ideals. All were intensely aware of the struggle for a new Ireland and could appreciate why someone like Pearse or Connolly was willing to sacrifice everything for an ideal.

O'Casey was one of the organizers of the citizen army and an active member of the labor movement. He seldom had enough money to buy himself a shirt, yet like many others he spent much of his time and energy learning the Gaelic language—an occupation which offered no material advantage at that time. He was interested in what Yeats and his associates were trying to do and for many years attended the Abbey regularly. The plays excited him and finally he experimented with writing one himself.

After many attempts he finished a play, *The Crimson in the Tricolour,* dealing with the labor movement, and submitted it to the Abbey directors. That it was badly handwritten on dirty paper was the kind of thing to interest Yeats; it was a theory of his that only from the unlettered was there hope of getting fresh dialogue. O'Casey's play was read carefully but rejected with the notation "not far from being a good play." Lady Gregory further advised him that he should concentrate on characterization, which she discerned to be his strong point. O'Casey was disappointed with the rejection of his play but was not discouraged. He began another, a play about the civil war, which he entitled *The Shadow of a Gunman.* He submitted it to the Abbey, and this time the play was accepted. This was in 1923, when the Abbey was considering closing down completely.

Yeats did not need to consult the stars to discover troublesome signs on the advent of this new dramatist. While *The Shadow of a Gunman* was in rehearsal Robinson received a typed order from the "Government of the Republic of Ireland" signed by Padraig Ó Ruitléis, "Minister for Home Affairs," stating that because of the acceptance of the Free State and the executions and imprisonments, "it is hereby decreed that the present be observed as a time of national mourning, that all sports and amusements be suspended and that all theatres be closed."

All theatres closed except the Abbey; the government of the Free State gave the Abbey military protection, and when Lady

Gregory arrived for the opening night of O'Casey's play, she found soldiers inside and out. One soldier was behind the scenes showing an actor the correct way to hold a revolver he was using in the play.

Lady Gregory escorted O'Casey to a seat in the stalls. They sat together for a time, and O'Casey, being a typical peasant, kept his cap on. No Irish countryman would ever consider taking off his cap in a house. After a while Yeats arrived, as usual in full evening dress. Lady Gregory gave him her seat and he sat beside O'Casey throughout the first act without making himself known to him. Yeats spoke to O'Casey later but he maintained his aristocratic role. O'Casey was not a poet, and Yeats greeted him with bored enthusiasm.

After the play Yeats dismissed O'Casey, and he and Lady Gregory sat on the oak bench in the vestibule, discussing what they might do with the theatre. Should they close down? It did not seem to have occurred to them that the savior of the theatre had arrived. On the following nights the Abbey was so filled that many could not find seats and had to stand at the back of the Pit.

The scene of the play was laid in a one-room tenement in Dublin. The central character, Seumas Shields, a peddler in spoons, braces, and other small goods, caused the most entertainment. He had taken in as a lodger a poet who everyone thought was a gunman "on the run" but in the end turned out to be only the shadow of a gunman. For the first time the Abbey audience recognized on the stage an Irish dialect which was not only authentic, but artistic. The Abbey Theatre was at last reaching all the people.

O'Casey was encouraged by his success and he started work on a new full-length play which he was to name *Juno and the Paycock*. In the intervals, when not working on this play, he completed a sketch of little account, *Cathleen Listens-in,* which the Abbey produced in October, 1923. It was so slight that it was given little attention even by the author; what really mattered was his new play, *Juno.* When it was finished it was submitted to the directors of the Abbey and accepted with enthusiasm. Yeats said it reminded him of Tolstoy. It was put into rehearsal and everyone looked forward to its production.

132   *Sean O'Casey*

When the night came for its première on March 30, 1924, the theatre was crowded. O'Casey was to be seen sitting with one of his working companions in the stalls, both wearing their caps. *Juno and the Paycock* stirred the audience and it was clear to them that a genius had arrived who could penetrate to the heart of the Irish people. Lady Gregory remarked after the final curtain, "This is one of the evenings at the Abbey that makes me glad to have been born."

Once more it is a play of character; the story, which is tragic, matters little. One is so busy laughing at the characters that one forgets to be shocked by the tragedy. There is the Captain, the lazy good-for-nothing who is looking for a job and praying to God he will not get it. There is his friend "Joxer Daly," of much the same type, and of course Juno, the brave, struggling woman who works to keep an invalid son and a drunken husband from starvation. Here at last was a play the ordinary man could understand and enjoy—a play which satisfied the high standards of Yeats and at the same time amused the audience.

Hundreds had to be turned away because there was no place for them in the theatre. The play was run a second week—an unusual procedure then, unless it happened that a play was particularly displeasing to the audience. The Abbey was becoming a truly national theatre, or so it seemed to the public. Even the most extreme nationalists began to patronize the plays. Country folk who once attended the melodramas at the Queens when they came to the city went now to the Abbey. The result was that a play such as *The Would-be Gentleman,* Lady Gregory's translation from Molière (January 4, 1926), drew even a larger audience than did *Juno and the Paycock.*

Large audiences still did not please Yeats—even though the play which drew them in was a good one. The poetic play had almost completely disappeared from the Abbey, and it was for the production of such plays that the theatre had been founded. An audience, like a woman, is most attractive when it is beaten into humility, and Yeats was considering afresh how the new large audiences could be chastized and humbled. Plays which would do this come only from the pen of a poet, and it seemed the responsibility for writing one would have to be his own.

Sean O'Casey   133

To his amazement and delight O'Casey supplied the weapon. He had submitted to the Abbey a play, *The Plough and the Stars,* treating of the Insurrection of 1916. From the moment the play reached the directors it caused trouble. Even Dolan, the producer who succeeded Robinson in the position when the latter became a director, wrote to Lady Gregory, "At any time I would think twice of having anything to do with it. The language is—to use an Abbey phrase—'beyond the beyonds.' The song at the end of the second act, sung by the 'girl of the streets' is impossible." Dolan, in keeping with the theatre's policy, was dismissed for his insolence. The job was given back to Robinson, who needed extra money since he had been expelled from the secretaryship of the Carnegie Trust for writing what was considered an obscene story.

The serious danger of interference consequent upon accepting the government subsidy became quickly apparent. George O'Brien, the government nominee on the board of directors, objected to certain portions of the play, especially to the character of Rosie Redmond, a prostitute. O'Brien protested that a prostitute must not be introduced on the Dublin stage, that the song she is made to sing is totally impossible in holy Ireland. Lady Gregory took a strong stand:

Our position is clear. If we have to choose between the subsidy and our freedom, it is our freedom we choose. And we must tell him [O'Brien] there was no condition attached to the subsidy, and though in connection with it another Director was suggested, I cannot be sure whether by me or by Blythe, there was no word at all of his being a censor, but only to strengthen us on the financial side, none of us being good at money matters or accounts.

A directors' meeting was called to settle the dispute, and O'Brien was put in the awkward position of having to defend his point of view against the combined opposition of Yeats, Lady Gregory, and Robinson. O'Brien's argument was quite logical: the play would cause annoyance to a Dublin audience and, apart from that, the introduction of a prostitute seemed to his mind indecent. What he failed to realize was that Yeats was uninterested in what the Dublin audience might think and was eager to teach them a lesson once again.

O'Brien sat straight up in his chair, his weak eyes focusing on any object other than on his co-directors. He listened to the skillful arguments of Yeats but contented himself with repeating at intervals, "That song is objectionable," "And that word 'bitch—' " Yeats tried to persuade him of the artistic propriety of the prostitute, but O'Brien was obstinate. Finally, Robinson, who had been sitting back in his languid way enjoying the embarrassment of O'Brien, suggested that the matter be submitted to a majority vote. O'Brien's objections were voted down and he graciously admitted that he had mistaken his position as being that of a censor.

The situation was reminiscent of Edward Martyn's objection to *The Countess Cathleen,* for it was said O'Brien had also submitted *The Plough and the Stars* to a theologian. The public in this instance, however, were unaware in advance that there was anything objectionable in the play, and when the night of its first performance arrived on Monday, February 8, 1926, there was a queue a quarter of a mile long outside the theatre hoping to see the new play by the author of *Juno and the Paycock.* The Abbey was thronged, and O'Casey had to content himself with standing room in the gallery. The audience included the lord chief justice and his wife; Kevin O'Higgins, and of course members of the literary world: Liam O'Flaherty, F. R. Higgins, and others.

The song to be sung by the prostitute had been omitted, mainly because Yeats realized there was sufficient in the play which would cause offense. The performance was a great success, and the players were called and recalled several times; but it was clear that when the public recovered from the shock administered them by their popular dramatist, they would protest loudly. Joseph Holloway, as always representative of the Dublin audience, was disgusted and was not afraid to say so. Going out the door when the play was over, he said to a Mr. Donaghy:

"It is an abominable play."

"I see nothing abominable in it," replied Mr. Donaghy.

"Then you have a dirty mind."

"No, I haven't."

"Well you have a filthy mind. There are no streetwalkers in Dublin."

"I was accosted by one only last night."

"There were none in Dublin till the Tommies brought them over." [1]

The following night, four or five people in the Pit, more brazen than the others, protested, while the play was in progress, when the Volunteers brought the flag of the Citizen Army into a pub. It was only a minor protest, but it was an indication of more to come on subsequent nights. Holloway, who suspected trouble, was present at this performance also. He commented in his *Diary*, "It will be alright if Yeats in his desire to uphold the freedom of the stage doesn't get the players to dance on the flag in future." Encouraged by the protests on Tuesday night, a group of extreme nationalists, mostly women, arranged to make a major protest on Wednesday. Holloway gives the following account of what happened:

The protest on Tuesday having no effect on the management a great protest was made tonight and ended in almost all the second act being played in dumb show and pandemonium afterwards. People spoke from all parts of the house and W. B. Yeats moved out from the stalls during the noise; Kathleen O'Brennan who came in afterwards told me Yeats went round to the Irish Times Office to try to have the report of the row doctored. On his return to the theatre he tried to get a hearing on the stage but not one word he spoke could be heard. I am sorry to say I was incorrect in my judgment as to what the Abbey audience would stand when I told George O'Brien on Monday before act 2 that they would stand even the devils in Hell exhibiting their worst pranks in silence sooner than make another objectionable play like the Playboy burst into notoriety by their disapproval. But alas! tonight's protest has made a second Playboy of The Plough and the Stars, and Yeats is in his element at last. It is really dirt for dirt's sake. After act one the first I heard that a row was brewing was from Dan Breen who was speaking to Kavanagh and said: Mrs. Pearse, Mrs. Tom Clark, Mrs. Sheehy-Skeffington and others were in the theatre to vindicate the manhood of 1916. . . . O'Casey sneaked out during the row. Some of the players behaved with uncommon roughness to some ladies who got on the stage and threw two of them into the stalls. One young man thrown from the stage got his side hurt by the piano. The chairs of the orchestra were thrown on the stage and the music on the piano flittered, and some four or five tried to pull down half of the drop curtain. The players headed by McCormick as spokesman lined up on the stage and McCormick asked that the actors be treated as distinct from the play. . . . Only for the fact that arrangements had already been made to produce certain plays next week there is no doubt that Yeats would have run The Plough and the Stars a second week as he did The Piper.[2]

Wrath was directed not so much at Rosie Redmond (though shocking epithets were hurled at her) as against the political significance of the play, its brutal description of what took place in the homes of Citizen Army members while the leaders were out making speeches. Holloway's account of what happened, though adequate, is not subtle. When Yeats left the theatre during the disturbance to visit the newspaper office, his business hardly was to have the report of the incident suitably edited but, what is more probable, to hand in a copy of the speech he had prepared for delivery, which he realized would not be heard above the protestations of the people. Yeats must have been prepared for the emergency, and here is what he said (according to the newspaper accounts) as he waved his hands dramatically before the screaming audience:

I thought you had got tired of all this which commenced about fifteen years ago. But you have disgraced yourselves again. Is this to be an ever-recurring celebration of the arrival of Irish genius? Synge first and then O'Casey. The news of the happenings of the last few minutes will go from country to country. Dublin has once more rocked the cradle of a reputation. From such a scene in this theatre went forth the fame of Synge. Equally the fame of O'Casey is born here tonight. This is his apotheosis.

The Abbey was protected by police for the remainder of the week, and protests in the theatre were not allowed. However, an attempt was made to kidnap Barry Fitzgerald, one of the principal actors, because he was the person who had knocked a protester right into the stalls with a punch to the chin. Mrs. Sheehy-Skeffington, who led the protesters, explained her position in a letter to The Irish Independent:[3]

I am one of those who have gone for over twenty years to performances at the Abbey, and I admire the earlier ideals of the place that produced "Kathleen Ni Houlihan," that sent Sean Connolly out in Easter Week; that was later the subject of a British "Royal" Commission; the Abbey, in short, that helped to make Easter Week, and that now in its subsidised, sleek old age jeers at its former enthusiasms.

Yeats's defense of O'Casey was different in many ways from his defense of Synge. Synge was one of Yeats's intimate friends, born into the same society as himself, and when Yeats defended *The Playboy,* he was defending a friend as well as an artistic principle. Yeats was young then, trying to build up a theatre, and he realized he had to fight desperately for certain principles of freedom or accept defeat. When he defended O'Casey, he did so as a matter of routine—it was the thing to do. An artist must continually assert his independence and his contempt for the crowd or lose his soul. By the time of O'Casey, Yeats had fulfilled his ambition to found a theatre, and with the government subsidy it was assured survival. His championing of *The Plough and the Stars* was as much a warning to the government that it must not presume to interfere with his theatre as it was a gesture of contempt for the crowd.

O'Casey as a person never was considered by Yeats. He was a slum dweller, not a garreteer, and Yeats, who had become growingly aristocratic in behavior, could not consider becoming a close friend of O'Casey, who was not even a poet. O'Casey, for his part, considered Yeats a poseur, though he recognized his ability as a poet. O'Casey could not respect a man who came to the theatre in full evening dress and patronized only the company of titled people. Genius recognizes no rank other than itself, and O'Casey continued to protest Yeats's attitude by refusing to dress otherwise than in his cap and sweater.

There was no sense of camaraderie between O'Casey and Yeats —no human relationship—and since O'Casey had proved himself a playwright of the first order, his future obviously attached permanently to the Abbey, he felt he could only retain his sympathy for it by living well away from it. Accordingly, he went to live in London. Dublin, while it produces writers, has no sympathy for them, and it is difficult to survive there and produce good work. Even among the writers there are too many factions to allow for pleasant living. Because of its size, London has fewer tensions than Dublin, and O'Casey was happy there. He married and settled down to write a new play. This was to be on the subject of World War I, and the setting was to be away from the Dublin tenements he knew so well. It was an experiment in a new mold for him. O'Casey wished to prove himself a dramatist to whom no part of life was alien. Any subject, in any setting, could be made to serve his genius.

He called the play *The Silver Tassie,* and in a letter to Lady Gregory of February 28, 1928, he told her of his new play and advised her that he was sending a copy of it. "Personally I think it is the best work I have yet done," he said. "I have certainly put my best into it, and have written the work solely because of love and deep feeling that what I have written should have been written."

Everyone thought O'Casey would never write another play after he left Ireland, and it was with some distrust that the directors read his new play when it appeared. Robinson disliked it and wrote in his report, "I'm glad that he is groping towards a new manner—he couldn't go on writing slum plays forever and ever, but I wish the second half of his play was better." Lady Gregory agreed, and this pleased Robinson, for he told her, "If you had disagreed with me I should have suspected myself of all sorts of horrid subconscious feelings." The play was then sent on to Yeats, who was resting in Italy. Yeats also disliked the play, and in his report he said:

My dear O'Casey,—Your play was sent to me at Rapallo by some mistake of the Theatre's. It arrived just after I had left and was returned from there to Dublin. . . . The mere greatness of the world war has thwarted you; it has refused to become mere background, and obtrudes itself upon the stage as so much dead wood that will not burn with the dramatic fire. . . . You were intensely interested in the Irish civil war, and at every moment of those plays wrote out of your own amusement with life or your sense of its tragedy; you were excited and we all caught your excitement. . . . But you are not interested in the Great War; you never stood on its battlefields, or walked its hospitals, and write out of your opinions.

While his play was going the rounds of the directors for their comments, O'Casey was in London busily correcting proofs. He was anxious that the Abbey produce it, but he was having it published in advance. He was now a literary figure, recognized by everyone as a first-rank dramatist. The Abbey, he wrote Lady Gregory, was going to get the first choice of producing his play.

After a long delay Lady Gregory, acting as secretary, had received the reports of Yeats and Robinson, and with some sympathetic remarks of her own sent the lot to O'Casey. The decision of the directors was that the play be rejected. As if to make matters worse, Yeats wrote a second letter to O'Casey, advising him in a very patronizing way what excuse he might make to the public for the Abbey's rejection of the play. Yeats and his fellow directors, if they had not misjudged the play, at least misjudged O'Casey. O'Casey was expected to be disconsolate but resigned to the decision and advice of his betters.

O'Casey had more spirit in him than was thought. He turned the tables on the Abbey directors by reporting on them, and it was Yeats's turn to be disconsolate. O'Casey unashamedly informed the press of what had happened and sent the complete correspondence to *The Irish Statesman* for publication in its June 9 issue. Yeats was so worried over this that he threatened to sue both AE and O'Casey under the Copyright Act if the letters were published, but to no avail. AE published them. Part of O'Casey's letter to Yeats in reply to his report on *The Silver Tassie* ran as follows:

Dear Mr. Yeats,—There seems to me to be no reason to comment upon whether you read my play in Rapallo or in Dublin, or whether you read my play before or after reading your fellow-directors' opinions, or whether the Abbey owed or did not owe its prosperity to me—these things do not matter, and so we'll hang them up on the stars. . . . You say—and this is the motif throughout the intonation of your whole song—that I am not interested in the Great War. Now, how do you know that I am not interested in the Great War? Perhaps because I never mentioned it to you. Your statement is to me an impudently arrogant one to make, for it happens that I was and am passionately and intensely interested in the Great War.

To complicate the affair still more, Walter Starkie, a Trinity College professor who lived in Spain and who had replaced George O'Brien as government representative on the Board of directors, in a belated report advised that the play be produced. Starkie was annoyed that his opinion had not been sought before the reports were sent to O'Casey, and that he was thus debarred from the publicity consequent upon O'Casey's information to the press.

Starkie was not to be by-passed in this manner, and the report which he submitted later read as follows:

In *The Silver Tassie* the characters seem to come from a shadow world; they are not beings of flesh and blood. . . . I feel that the author had a great idea at the back of his mind and fugitive symbols presented themselves to him but he was not able to create, as he did before, living men and women. The play seems to me to decline act by act from the beginning. . . . In spite of all this I feel that the author is experimenting in a new world of drama; for this reason I feel strongly that the Abbey Theatre should produce the play. Sean O'Casey has given us so many fine works that we ought to leave the final decision with the audience that has laughed and wept with him. He is groping after a new drama outside the conventional stage; at any moment he may make a new discovery.

The rejection of *The Silver Tassie* was of sufficient importance to draw a statement from Shaw. Writing to Lady Gregory in June, 1928, he said:

Why do you and W. B. Y. treat O'Casey as a baby? Starkie was right, you should have done the play anyhow. Sean is now hors concours. It is literally a hell of a play; but it will clearly force its way on to the stage and Yeats should have submitted to it as a calamity imposed on him by the Act of God, if he could not welcome it as another *Juno*. Besides, he was most extraordinarily wrong about it on the facts. The first act is not a bit realistic; it is deliberately fantastic chanted poetry. This is intensified to a climax into the second act. Then comes a ruthless return for the last two acts to the fiercest ironic realism. But that is so like Yeats. Give him a job with which you feel sure he will play Bunthorne and he will astonish you with his unique cleverness and subtlety. Give him one that any second-rater could manage with credit and as likely as not he will make an appalling mess of it. He has certainly fallen in up to the neck over O'C.

When the play was published, AE (under the pseudonym Y. O.) reviewed it in *The Irish Statesman*. "I think I have been as deeply moved," he wrote, "by *The Silver Tassie* as by any of Sean O'Casey's plays, both by its intensity and its incapacity. I think that the dramatist has brought into the writing of this play a greater intensity of feeling than he brought even to *Juno and the Paycock* or *The Plough and the Stars*. But that very intensity of feeling has carried him into regions of the soul to which his art is unable to give adequate expression." Once again O'Casey answered his critic. He replied:

"What is wrong with Y. O. is that he wants the old and much caressed familiarities. He wants *The Silver Tassie* to be a copy of *Juno* because it was a copy (it wasn't) of actual life. . . . He believes that the play was rejected through a desire that O'Casey's reputation should not suffer. That is a cold and wretched statement to make. It was rejected because W. B. Yeats and Lennox Robinson couldn't see or wouldn't see, that the play was worthy of production by the Abbey Theatre; that was the ethical reason for the rejection. The concern for O'Casey's reputation vanishes with its tail down when we remember that the replies to the Abbey's criticisms showed that O'Casey was prepared to risk his reputation, which was all his own business and none of theirs, to which they refused to respond by producing the play to show whether their opinions were right or wrong. . . .

Sean O'Casey wrote no more plays for the Abbey Theatre. Yeats's decision was possibly his greatest mistake in tactics. Granted that *The Silver Tassie* was a bad play, this was no excuse for its rejection. O'Casey had earned the right to have a bad play produced. Yeats adopted the presumptuous attitude of acting as guardian of O'Casey's reputation. There might have been greater justification for this if the theatre at the time was swamped with fine poetic plays demanding production. Actually, there was a severe shortage of good plays. Yeats had temporarily adopted the attitude that only himself and Lady Gregory had the right to use the Abbey Theatre for experimental purposes.

But one must not blame Yeats too much, even though his mistake had disastrous consequences for the Abbey and serious ones for O'Casey. Yeats had been right so often that when he made an error, people cried out more in surprise than in anger. Yeats had been right in defending *The Plough and the Stars*, even though most of the literary critics had condemned it. Liam O'Flaherty had stated in a letter to the press that it was a bad play; F. R. Higgins, the poet, that it was "an all-Abbey burlesque, intensified by 'diversions' and Handy Andy incidents . . . a laborious bowing on a one-string fiddle"; and Austin Clarke, speaking on behalf of "several writers of the new Irish school," believed that "O'Casey's plays are a crude exploitation of our poorer people in the Anglo-Irish tradition that is now moribund."

Yeats had a clearer vision than any of his contemporaries. His blunder with respect to *The Silver Tassie* was one of tactics, not of judgment. It is useless to speculate what might have happened had *The Silver Tassie* been accepted and O'Casey continued to write solely for the Abbey Theatre. This much, however, can be said as one views it from a distance of twenty years, that the rejection of *The Silver Tassie* marked a weakening in the organizing faculty of Yeats's mind and a turning point in the Abbey Theatre's career as it moved down the hill to its ultimate collapse with the death of Yeats in 1939.

The Subsidized Theatre

When the Abbey Theatre received the government subsidy, Lady Gregory was an old woman—well advanced in her seventies. The subsidy relieved her mind of worry as to how the theatre was to be supported and gave her the pleasing assurance that the Abbey, for which she had worked so hard, would continue after her death. She could settle down now at Coole, attending her garden with the gratifying knowledge that she had led a full life.

She was unable to travel with comfort to Dublin, and she did somewhat resent having to relax her control on the theatre. However, she would never consider delegating her authority, and she still read all the plays submitted to the directors. She would retain a vital interest in the Abbey to the very end; it was her theatre as

145

much as it was Yeats's, and she would guide its destiny as long as she was alive. The loss of Sean O'Casey to the Abbey worried her most of all, and she regretted often that she did not insist on production of *The Silver Tassie*.

Yeats was paying small attention to the theatre. This was partly because he was in poor health and partly because the Abbey had not fulfilled his ideal of a poetic theatre. He lived mostly abroad, in Italy or in England, and his chief interest was in experimenting with verse forms. Like every great artist he was never satisfied that he had reached perfection, and he continued to correct and rewrite much of his earlier work. He was still working on a translation of Sophocles' play *Oedipus*, which he had begun more than ten years before. He was in his sixties now, and there was much to do before he died. The theatre was going along successfully; not as he might wish it, perhaps, but it was in a state from which it might be possible to lift it whenever he felt so inclined. He had fought enough battles for it, had spent much of his time and energy creating it and keeping it alive, and he too, like Lady Gregory, wanted to relieve himself of the continued strain of managing it. Lennox Robinson was a young man of exceptional capabilities, and Yeats would give him a free hand.

Robinson was a brilliant producer and a writer of fine comedy, but he did not possess the quality of leadership. Accordingly, he was not a completely successful manager of the theatre. He had no enthusiasm except for his own work. This is true of most writers. It was true also of Yeats, but he made the discovering of writers his work and exulted over every discovery. Robinson did not seem to care whether new dramatists came along or not. His attitude was that the Abbey was an established theatre and there was no need to look for talent. When it came along he would recognize it and give it an outlet. With Yeats, it was otherwise; he sought out the writer with talent, and he inspired and encouraged him to write well.

Robinson lacked the passion necessary in a leader. Perhaps this was because he was a writer of comedy and as such was an observer of life rather than a part of it. He could not stir up an emotion for a movement and sweep young writers along with him as Yeats and Lady Gregory had done. He was too inclined to smile, at a moment when a great leader would be infuriated by passion.

Robinson was only at the beginning as a writer of comedy, and he was looking forward to his own career rather than to the future of the theatre. But a theatre will die if fed too much comedy; only passion keeps it alive, and the lack of serious drama and the concentration on the comic element was one of the causes which eventually drove the Abbey Theatre bankrupt artistically.

Robinson's comedies were an important contribution to the repertory of the theatre. They were written sincerely and out of a deep feeling for human life and an awareness of certain incongruous elements in it. There is never an attempt to be loud or broad, and the appeal is always an emotional one which approaches pity. It might be said they are lyrical comedies select in their appeal. Robinson succeeded as a writer of comedy while many of his contemporaries failed, because he seems to be writing out of an inner demand and satisfying a personal integrity.

The same cannot be said of George Shiels, whose plays were the great vulgarizing influence on the Abbey Theatre during the late 1920s and all through the 1930s. In his early years as a dramatist his plays were seldom revived at the Abbey Theatre and were never allowed to dominate the repertoire. Unfortunately, later on the directors relaxed their vigilance, and the public demand for Shiels's plays was satisfied. Shiels had acquired suddenly the knack of amusing a crowd without any apparent effort. Confined to his home in the north of Ireland as a cripple, he had begun to write plays to relieve boredom. His first play to be produced was *Bedmates* (January 6, 1921). Almost every year thereafter he gave the Abbey a new play.

Shiels was a dramatic journalist rather than a playwright. His work proved vastly amusing to audiences interested only in the superficialities of life. Any subject was good enough; many of his plays had really no subject at all. There was never any danger of his offending the crowd, and everyone was satisfied except those interested in genuine comedy. Thousands flocked to the Abbey to be amused by Shiels's *Professor Tim* (September 14, 1925). The Abbey was making money.

Robinson was not foolish enough to imagine that Shiels was the answer to the theatre's demand for good drama. He always had wanted to stage translations of famous continental plays and ancient classics, and now Yeats did not bother to object as he had done some years earlier, when Robinson suggested these plays as the only means of maintaining a high standard. The Dublin public now had the opportunity of seeing Ibsen's *A Doll House* and Goldsmith's *She Stoops to Conquer* (April 22, 1923); Sierra's *The Two Shepherds* (February 12, 1924) and *The Kingdom of God* (November 3, 1924); Shaw's *Fanny's First Play* (April 21, 1925); Chekhov's *The Proposal* (April 28, 1925); Molière's *The Would-be Gentleman*, translated by Lady Gregory (January 4, 1926); Jules Romains's *Doctor Knock* (February 16, 1926); Wilde's *The Importance of Being Ernest* (November 6, 1926); Sophocles' *Oepidus the King* translated by Yeats (December 16, 1926); Eugene O'Neill's *The Emperor Jones* (January 24, 1927), and various other famous plays. Dublin intellectuals were interested in seeing the plays of other countries, and Robinson satisfied that demand. It was at least better than reviving the plays of Shiels, but it was not for this that the Abbey Theatre had been established.

The climax to this policy of staging non-Irish masterpieces came with the performance of Shakespeare's *King Lear* (November 26, 1928). It failed completely. Yeats had agreed to its production, and for once Lady Gregory had not been consulted, to her great annoyance when she heard of it. The producing of *King Lear* had been given to Denis Johnson, a young Irishman and a product of the English public-school system, as a recompense for the rejection of his impressionistic play on Robert Emmet. Lady Gregory had been responsible for turning this down, and Johnson retitled the play *The Old Lady Says No* and had it produced at another Dublin theatre. It was indicative of the careless attitude of Yeats toward the theatre that he was prepared to make sacrifices to avoid hurting the feelings of Denis Johnson, who was never more than a man of talent, while in the same year he ruthlessly rejected O'Casey's *The Silver Tassie.*

Foreign classics were abandoned in 1928, when the Gate Theatre Company was founded in Dublin with the specific object of producing them.

The government subsidy was having a subtle effect on Abbey Theatre policy. It was turning it into an institution as conservative as the National Gallery or the National Museum. The Abbey was now secure against failure and was gradually becoming conscious of its national importance in a bourgeois sense. It was tending to interest itself in how it looked to the world. The seeds of decline were already sown, and Yeats was too interested in other things to have the energy to uproot those seeds.

Typical of the new attitude was Robinson's opening in 1928 of a small experimental playhouse, The Peacock Theatre, in a building adjacent to the Abbey, at a cost of £4,094. "It is not the intention of the Abbey Company to produce plays in this theatre," Robinson announced. "The new theatre is intended for the convenience of the general public interested in the writing or production of plays." The intention was to enable anyone interested in writing a play to rent this small building at comparatively little cost and with the help of friends have the pleasure of seeing his play on the stage. It was objected that the money spent on the Peacock Theatre was wasted, that there was no need for it, since the Abbey Theatre had been founded expressly as a theatre where the young dramatist could have an opportunity of learning his trade. The Abbey, it was repeatedly argued, was an experimental theatre in the best sense and should remain so, while the Peacock was an insult to Dublin writers.

Yeats supported the Peacock as a training school for young actors. He had always wished to have a second Abbey company, so that if ever it became necessary to dismiss the first company for insolence (as often happened), he would have a group of actors who could take its place immediately. The Peacock Theatre was even more acceptable to Yeats for the production of his own plays than the Abbey was. It was more intimate and had seating accommodation for one hundred persons—the maximum size he wished his audience to be. A still more important reason why Yeats gave his consent was that he hoped to have trained there a group of Irish men and girls in ballet, who could perform in his plays for dancers. The Abbey Theatre, to his great disappointment, had become a folk rather than a poetic theatre, but Yeats would reassert his ideas to the end, and he never gave up hope even in his old age that he would be able to direct it back to its original path. Yeats had been aware of this trend for a long time, and as early as 1916 he had asserted in a note to the first performance of *At the Hawk's Well*:

. . . I have begun to shrink from sending my muses where they are but half-welcomed; and even in Dublin where the pit has an ear for verse, I have no longer the appetite to carry through the daily rehearsals. Yet I need a theatre; I believe myself to be a dramatist; I desire to show events and not merely to tell of them; and two of my best friends were won for me by my plays, and I seem to myself most alive at the moment when a room full of people share the one lofty emotion. My blunder has been that I did not discover in my youth that my theatre must be an ancient theatre that can be made by unrolling a carpet or marking out a place with a stick, or setting a screen against the wall. Certainly those who care for my kind of poetry must be numerous enough, if I can bring them together to pay half-a-dozen players who can bring all their properties in a cab and perform in their leisure moments. . . . Whatever we may lose in mass and in power we should recover in elegance and in subtlety. Our lyrical and narrative poetry have approached nearer, as Pater said all the arts would if they were able, to "the condition of music"; and if our modern poetic drama has failed it is mainly because, always dominated by the example of Shakespeare, it would restore an irrevocable past.

Yeats had realized too late even his *Kathleen Ni Houlihan* had made too many concessions to the public and so could never win over the theatre for poetic drama. The public liked most of his early plays, and that in itself was a condemnation. That Shakespeare's audience liked his plays did not affect the present problem, for the Elizabethan audience had still their intellectual innocence, and their imagination had not been dulled by book knowledge. The true art of the theatre, Yeats continued to assert, began in ritual and must remain so to the end. The theatre must be continually resanctified to poetry of the intensest kind if it is to remain pure. If the Abbey Theatre was to be saved it would have to produce plays exaggerating the poetic and ritualistic elements. Poetry allied to music and the dance would be the answer to the problem. The dancers would wear masks, so that their human faces would not distract the audience from the poetic emotion. In 1921 he had published four plays for dancers and in the preface had stated:

Should I make a serious attempt, which I may not, being rather tired of the theatre, to arrange and supervise performances, the dancing will give me most trouble, for I know but vaguely what I want. I do not want any existing form of stage dancing, but something with a smaller gamut of expression, something more reserved, more self-controlled as befits performers within arm's reach of the audience.

Forming a school of ballet at the Peacock Theatre, where the students would be trained with a consciousness of Irish tradition, was therefore of utmost interest to Yeats. His plays for dancers, and other plays which he would write on the same pattern, now could be performed in a mode more in keeping with his ideals. In September, 1928, the School of Ballet produced Yeats's *The Player Queen.* He did not expect perfection with the first attempt, nor did he get it; accordingly, he rewrote in prose his *The Only Jealousy of Emer.* Rearranged so as to admit many dancers, it was planned to be immediately intelligible to the average audience.

It was performed on August 13, 1929, under the new title *Fighting the Waves,* and it puzzled the people who came to see it. The play was not intended to be a conventional one: Yeats had stated in a preface to it that it was "a mere occasion for sculptor and dancer, for the exciting dramatic music of George Antheil." It was the beginning of what he hoped might be a new influence in the theatre.

The following year, Yeats returned to a slightly more conventional form with his play *The Words Upon the Window Pane* (November 17, 1930), based on the life of Dean Swift. The scene of this one-act play is laid in the rooms of the Dublin Spiritualists' Association. Actually it is less an attempt to justify spiritualism than it is an effort by Yeats to associate himself with the Anglo-Irish writers of the eighteenth century, whom he had long ignored. The romantic Ireland visualized by himself and by John O'Leary in the late nineteenth century was degenerating into a smug democracy, now that it had found its independence. Yeats could never accept government by anyone except of the highest intelligence, and he was coming to believe that the ideals of Swift, Goldsmith, Burke, and Berkeley were perhaps nearer his own. In an introduction to the printed text of his play he wrote:

I turned from Goldsmith and from Burke because they had come to seem a part of the English system; from Swift because, being a romantic, I acknowledged no verse between Cowley and Smart's *Song of David*, no prose between Sir Thomas Browne and the dialogues of Landor. But now I read Swift for months together, Burke and Berkeley less often but always with excitement, and Goldsmith lures and waits. I collect material for my thoughts and work, for some identification of my beliefs with the nation itself, I seek an image of the modern mind's discovery of itself, of its own permanent form, in that one Irish century that escaped from darkness and confusion. I would that our fifteenth, sixteenth, or even our seventeenth century had been the clear mirror, but fate decided against us.

Yeats had become disillusioned. The Abbey Theatre no less than politics had contributed to that disillusionment. It seemed to him that he had been hewing the wrong kind of stone for his statue and now was aghast at the prospect of a new quarry. But Yeats was too good a poet to acknowledge defeat by laying down his hammer and chisel; he would write to the end, out of his newly found convictions, and would put on record in the dramatic form his more mature ideas.

In 1931 Yeats completed *The Resurrection* (July 30, 1934), dealing with the Resurrection of Christ. In September, 1931, his play for dancers, *The Cat and the Moon*, was performed—a play so obscure, as he admitted in a preface, that "no audience could discover its dark, mythical secrets." Two months later another play for dancers, *The Dreaming of the Bones*, was also put on by the School of Ballet. The conception of this play, Yeats explained, was derived from the worldwide belief that the dead dream back, for a certain time, through the more personal thoughts and deeds of life. "All solar natures, to use the Arabian terms, during the life move towards a more objective form of experience, the lunar towards a more subjective."

These plays were exactly the kind of strong purgative needed for an audience which was coming to believe that the plays of Shiels were the highest kind of drama. They were produced at the Abbey rather than at the Peacock. Many were so sickened by the first dose that they made certain not to get another, and they carefully avoided in future all plays by Yeats. Up to the time of his death, Yeats continued to bring periodically before the Abbey audience these new, obscure plays, half dance and half music. They at least had the effect of reminding the public that the Abbey was a poet's theatre, even though it might have fallen on lean years.

It is somewhat surprising that Yeats never liked the sensitive plays of T. C. Murray. Perhaps the reason was that Murray modeled his plays on Ibsen, and Yeats disliked Ibsen. Murray's *Autumn Fire* (September 8, 1924) has for its theme the tragic consequences of an old widower's marriage to a young woman—who is loved by her husband's son. Unlike Ibsen, Murray merely creates the situation and makes no attempt to resolve it.

The chief merit of Murray's plays is the beautiful dialogue. It is realistic yet has a faery quality; it is as poetic as Yeats's but more Celtic in tone. It is indicative of the Abbey Theatre's attitude toward Murray that they allowed their production rights to *Autumn Fire* to lapse. In October, 1927, another Murray play, *The Pipe in the Fields*, appeared at the Abbey. This was a one-act fantasy describing how the artistic perception in a boy's soul has been awakened by listening to faery music. Once more the dialogue is distinctive and much higher in quality than that of most Abbey plays.

In 1931 Robinson decided it was time the company displayed its talents once more in America, and he made arrangements for a winter tour. It was now almost twenty years since they had last been to the United States, and it was hoped all antagonism had died down. However, it was known that the Irish people, more particularly the Irish-Americans, had very long memories. Robinson considered it best to approach them obliquely, by visiting only the smaller towns and avoiding the big cities. He hoped that in this manner the players would ingratiate themselves gradually into the confidence of the Irish immigrants. Jack Quigley, an enthusiastic young supporter of the theatre, was sent ahead of the company to organize support in the small towns where they hoped to play. Robinson and the Abbey company set out for America in October, 1931, leaving the Abbey Theatre to the School of Ballet and to any other organization that might care to rent it.

Thanks to Quigley's fine organizing abilities, they had large audiences wherever they went. They intended to visit the West

Coast, but arrangements for a tour in that part of the country broke down, and they returned by way of Ottawa and Montreal.

While Robinson and the company were away in America, the solicitors for the theatre applied for a renewal of the patent, which had now expired. The application (which was granted) was signed not by the King of England but by James MacNeill, governor general of the new Irish Free State. The conditions of the patent differed slightly on this occasion from those of the previous one. Thus, the bombastic opening of the 1904 document—"Right Trusty and Right well-beloved Cousin and Councillor We greet you well"—was omitted. So were the stipulations about fire hatchets, fire curtains, water buckets being kept in the theatre, and the ban on Sunday performances. Amusingly enough, the admonition not to bring wild beasts on the stage nor hang women from the wings was retained. (See page 227.)

The conditions relating to the kinds of plays the Abbey was entitled to perform were also slightly altered. The significant part of this clause now read that Lady Gregory and Yeats, the patentees, might perform plays by Irish authors "and works by authors of any nationality on Irish subjects and works by foreign (not including English) authors and English dramatic works of a period prior to the year 1830 "PROVIDED HOWEVER that performers other than those engaged by the National Theatre Society Limited performing in the Abbey Theatre shall in addition be entitled in any one year to give up to a maximum of one hundred performances of other dramatic works not coming within the limitations aforesaid. . . ." The patent was granted for the customary twenty-one years.

Lady Gregory died on May 22, 1932. Her obituary appeared extensively in the press, and the Abbey Theatre paid appropriate respect on the occasion. But apart from Yeats, Robinson, and her other friends, no one seemed to care. To the Abbey audiences she had become in her latter years a mere name, a someone who had helped to organize the theatre and who had written many plays for it. The public read of her death with a slightly bored expression, and literary folk casually discussed her over a pint of porter. It seemed as if she were no more than another of those wealthy women who amuse themselves by associating with theatrical celebrities. Her pleasant little comedies were at best only an echo of Yeats's genius. She was just another female writer with no excitement and no message. Actors and their associates remembered her only as a domineering, self-centred, snobbish person who sometimes treated them to excellent currant cake in the Green Room. Sentimental nationalists said no prayers for her. She was an impostor, an English titled lady who used Gaelic Ireland for her own vain ends. The peasants around Coole thought only of how they might grab her estate and steal her trees. Other peasants, when they read of her death in the paper, merely inquired, "Who could that lady be who just died? She must be someone great to get her name in the paper. She be to be a Protestant landlord."

In England, Miss Horniman celebrated Lady Gregory's death by publishing in *John O'London's Weekly* a letter full of venom and disparaging allusions to her. Her hatred had not mellowed with the years; the wound apparently had been too deep.

Lady Gregory needed no defense against this thoughtless and unkind gossip. She had written her name into history, and time would take care of all criticism of her. It is unfair to judge her only as a playwright: pleasant as many of her comedies may be, they are not great drama. Lady Gregory contributed, though indirectly, to literature—first, as a patron of Yeats, the greatest poet of his time; secondly, as the most energetic organizer of the Abbey Theatre. While many were sneering at Yeats, she had the insight to recognize in him a major poet, and though she had not a great amount of money she gladly shared with Yeats what she had, so that he might continue to write poetry. She modestly stated in her diaries that, even though all else she did be forgotten, perhaps she might be remembered as the person who persuaded Yeats to finish his *The Wind Among the Reeds*.

Lady Gregory defended Synge at home and fought for the right to produce *The Playboy* in America. She fought Dublin Castle when they attempted to prohibit the production of Shaw's *Blanco Posnet*, and she earned a tribute from him on that occasion: "I am a conciliatory person and was willing, as I always am, to make every concession in return for having my own way. But Lady Gregory and Mr. Yeats not only would not yield an inch, but insisted within the due limits of gallant warfare, on taking the field with every circumstance of defiance, and winning the battle with every trophy of victory."

When the theatre was in need of money, she begged from her wealthy friends and always succeeded in getting enough to carry on. When Yeats dismissed the whole company for insolence, she did not object but proceeded to build a new company better than the previous one. When in 1923 Yeats wanted to give up the struggle to maintain the Abbey, Lady Gregory refused to acknowledge defeat and persuaded the government to grant an annual subsidy to the theatre. She encouraged Sean O'Casey to write his best plays and was present in the theatre to cheer them to victory on their first performance. In addition to all these things, and many more, she wrote twenty-nine original plays for the theatre and translated nearly a dozen from foreign languages. Her contribution was great and her death a severe loss.

American Sojourn

The death of Lady Gregory must have reminded Yeats sharply of his own advancing years. He had accomplished a great deal with her help, and there was so much still to be done, and he would have to do it unaided. His deepest conviction was that he was a natural dramatist; the Abbey Theatre, he regarded as his most important creation. It had developed differently from what he had hoped, but it was his child and he would never allow it to be degraded. The lack of interest in the work of Lady Gregory, as shown by the casual attitude of the public at her death, infuriated him. Attendance at the theatre had even fallen off; on the night of a first performance there would be a fairly large audience, consisting mostly of loud-voiced women who fluttered around the edges of literary society, but on other nights the attendance seldom averaged more than fifty or sixty.

All would have been well if this poor attendance had been the result of violent dislike on the part of the public toward the plays. Yeats had gloried in the smallness of the audience when he was defending Synge's plays. A small audience then was the sign of distinction. Now the situation was different; the public stayed away through apathy, and this Yeats would never allow. Dublin was not worthy of the Abbey Theatre. He would cast his pearls elsewhere. The Abbey Theatre company would go to America and stay there until the Dublin public was humbled sufficiently to beg them to return. The tour of the small towns of America in the winter of 1931-1932 had shown there was much interest there. Accordingly, it was arranged that the centre of activity be moved from Dublin to New York.

From October, 1931, to June, 1935, the company spent most of its time in America. The Abbey Theatre building in Dublin remained closed for part of that period, and when occasionally it did open, it was occupied by a much inferior Abbey second company or by the School of Ballet. The Dublin public was being taught a lesson.

Renewed Irish-American opposition to the Abbey Theatre plays added further interest to the tour. Mr. de Valera and his Fianna Fail party had recently carried the elections in Ireland, and this success was partly due to the Irish-Americans who had financed his campaign. When the Abbey company came to America in the autumn of 1932, the Irish-Americans demanded of De Valera, as payment for their support, that he control the activities of Yeats and his group of "anti-Irish propagandists." This time they did not throw potatoes at the players but adopted the conservative attitude of protesting officially through the Irish consul in New York. According to the *New York Times*,[1] the United Irish-American Societies and Fianna Fail, Inc., New York, protested that *The Playboy of the Western World, Juno and the Paycock, In The Shadow of the Glen,* and other plays presented orgies of "filthy language, drunkenness and prostitution" and thereby maligned the Irish people. They requested that the Irish government withdraw the subsidy to the Abbey Theatre.

Not all the Irish-Americans were so inclined, and many were angry with those who objected to the Irish plays. Consequently we find a counterprotest being made to the Irish government by Patrick Farrell, director of the Irish Theatre and of the Museum of Irish Art in the Barbizon Hotel, New York. "I myself and those I represent here in America," he said, "feel that it is not a matter of what types of life or outlook the plays present. We do not recognize that the plays presented by the Abbey Theatre malign Ireland or its people. But even if they did, there is no reason why they should be barred so long as they represent worthwhile Irish art." Farrell's protest could have no more than academic importance, for he was at best only a bohemian who had certainly not contributed to Mr. de Valera's election funds, and his counterprotest could carry no weight with the Irish government.

Before De Valera could reply to the protests, Yeats, who had just returned from America, made a very astute statement designed to appeal to the Irish government and to direct them in the attitude they might adopt. In an interview with *The Irish Press*,[2] Yeats said:

Irish political organizations in the United States are breaking up and are being replaced by societies interested in Irish culture—poetry, drama, literature and the Irish language. . . . The Abbey Players went to America as Ambassadors of Irish taste. I went on the lecture tours with the same object. We have got to keep the Irish in America linked up with our nation, we must not lose them. We cannot have them linked up to us by political parties any longer; Ireland must decide her political destinies for herself in future. But they can be linked to us culturally: that is what we have been working for, and we have been successful.

The influence of the Irish-Americans was too strong for Yeats, and De Valera reacted by reducing in April, 1933, the annual government subsidy to the theatre from £1,000 to £750. This did not satisfy the philistines. They would not be content unless the government assumed complete control of the Abbey. Replying to a question asked by a Gaelic-speaking deputy in the Dail on April 26, 1933, De Valera admitted that certain Irish societies in America had protested against the kind of plays produced by the Abbey company. However, he said, "the government has no power

American Sojourn   159

to influence directly the selection of plays intended for the American tour but the government has made certain representations to the Abbey Company indirectly and it is hoped that if the Abbey Company goes to America again plays of the kind objected to by the American Irish will not be produced." This reply caused great excitement in Dublin literary circles, and Lennox Robinson, who had not gone on tour with the company, issued the following statement to the press:

You can completely deny the story of government interference with the Abbey. President de Valera who was guarded in his reply in the Dail, is friendly to the Abbey. The Company at present in America will return in May after a highly successful season. They went to Chicago for two weeks and were obliged to remain for seven. I do not know what plays are being produced in America which are objected to there. All the plays in the repertoire already are very successful here. What is good enough for Dublin ought to be good enough for New York. The agitation of certain people against some of the Abbey plays has been going on for the past twenty-five years. These people want beautiful romantic drama, showing Ireland as an idyllic place, against the truer idealism of Synge and O'Casey who bring the greater glory of the country to their art. Synge and O'Casey plays are preferable to third-rate romantic plays written by third-rate people.

It was clear to the public that Yeats and Robinson were getting the better part of the argument with the government. Suddenly the government thought of something new. It had come to their attention that Starkie, the previous government's representative on the Abbey Theatre's board of directors, was being made full director to fill the vacancy left by the death of Lady Gregory. De Valera then tried to appoint one of his own political friends as the new government representative on the board, but both Yeats and Robinson took a firm stand and refused to appoint him even at the risk of losing the subsidy. De Valera had not expected to be repulsed, but he realized he had overestimated his authority, and in a statement to the Dáil in June he was extremely cautious. "No government representative," he said, "has yet been chosen to the Abbey directorate. It is the Abbey Theatre board, with the approval of the Minister of Finance, who chooses the representative. However, when the election is being held the Minister of Finance will see to it that the person chosen will be suitable in every way."

De Valera made good his promise when in February, 1934, he persuaded the Abbey's directors to appoint Dr. Richard Hayes as the government representative. This was an extremely astute move by De Valera. Richard Hayes seemed at the time no more than an innocuous medical practitioner who was interested in books, and Yeats and Robinson readily agreed to his appointment. Only too late was it discovered that Hayes was in the opposite camp and was a brilliant intriguer. De Valera had won the argument and no one realized it. At the same time he continued his public objections to the plays which were being produced abroad by the Abbey.

Early in April, 1934, plans were made for another tour in America, and De Valera on this occasion made personal representations to the Abbey Theatre directorate as to the kind of plays they should produce there. Replying to a question in the Dail on April 18, he stated:

I am aware that the Abbey Theatre Company intends to travel to America this year and I have informed the directors of the theatre that it is my opinion if they produce certain plays that are on the list for production in America, if they produce these plays then it is clear that they will damage the good name of Ireland and they will cause shame and resentment to the Irish exiles.

The Abbey directors then made a public statement: the matter had been "amicably settled" on condition the directors make it clear to American audiences that the Irish government was not responsible for the plays selected by the Abbey Theatre. This statement so infuriated the government paper, *The Irish Press*, that it wrote editorially:[3]

The directors of the theatre are evidently determined to produce any plays they consider fit without regard to the fact that some of these plays, as President de Valera said in the Dail, arouse shame and resentment among Irish exiles. If in spite of that feeling on the part of the elected leader of the people, the Abbey directors are still going to cause shame and resentment among millions of Irish exiles in the United States, their responsibility is very grave and will not be easily evaded.

All this controversy was good publicity for the Abbey, and the violence of the opposition pleased Yeats, for it was a sign that the Abbey was still a vital institution. Lest there might be any thought in the minds of Americans that the Irish government had censored the Abbey program for the American tour, he announced shortly before the company sailed:

Dr. W. B. Yeats to-night declared that the directors emerged from the controversy with their freedom of action unimpaired. "Our original program has not been altered in the slightest," he said. "Synge's *Well of the Saints* and O'Casey's *Juno and the Paycock* are also included. The Government, however, pointed out that in our previous tour we gave the impression that our plays were being produced under its authority and we agreed to make it clear on the following tour that the government is in no way responsible for the plays." [4]

The Abbey company's tour, lasting from October, 1934, to June, 1935, was extremely successful. No opposition was offered by the Irish-Americans, and on December 16, 1934, Barry Fitzgerald, one of the leading actors, was presented with a scroll by Mayor La Guardia, Padraic Colum, Walter Winchell, and Lowell Thomas, in which he was described as "the most versatile character actor in the world."

While the first company was in America, several interesting plays were produced for the first time at the Abbey by the second company. The most important were *Men Crowd Me Round* by Francis Stuart, a writer of promise and sensitivity (March 13, 1933); *Drama at Innis*, an amusing comedy by Lennox Robinson (February 16, 1933). In May of the following year Robinson had his finest play, *Church Street*, performed (May 21, 1934). The scene was laid in the small town so favored by Robinson, and his evocation of its atmosphere was so successful that *Church Street* was regarded as the best Abbey play of its kind.

While the first company was away in America that winter, an Englishman, Brandon Peake, was brought to the Abbey to stage foreign and classical plays. He put on Shakespeare's *Macbeth* (October 25, 1934); Schnitzler's *The Gallant Cassian* (November 12); Molière's *The School for Wives* (November 12); Pirandello's *Six Characters in Search of an Author* (December

3), and C. K. Munroe's *At Mrs. Beam's* (December 26). He also produced on interesting play on Parnell, entitled *Parnell of Avondale*, by W. R. Fearon, a Trinity College professor (October 1).

Brandon Peake, at best, was a competent producer without inspiration, and the standard of acting, on the part of the second company, was very low. It was gradually dawning on the Dublin public that they deserved much better. As Yeats had expected, the people were learning their lesson and were coming to an appreciation of what the Abbey Theatre had really accomplished. By 1935 public apathy had fled. Letters were appearing in the press protesting the Abbey policy of absenting itself from Dublin for such long periods.

Yeats was satisfied. The public seemed ready for a second coming of the Abbey. The exile would be brought to an end and the Abbey directorate reorganized for the reawakening. To many, though not to Yeats, it seemed as if a new dramatist was about to arise.

Because of the shortage of good plays by new writers, the Abbey Theatre in 1931 set up a prize competition. There were a great many entries, even though the Abbey was almost universally disliked in Dublin. About one tenth of the population had written at some time in their lives a play intended for production there.

All entries were eliminated but two: *The Bed of Procrustes*, later changed to *Things That Are Caesar's*, by Paul Vincent Carroll, and *Temporal Powers* by Teresa Deevy. The prize was divided between these two, though there was a slight leaning toward Carroll's play, which was the first of the two to be performed. Carroll was not altogether unknown. The Peacock Theatre on November 17, 1930, had staged a short play of his, *The Watched Pot*. But Peacock Theatre plays awakened little public interest, and if Carroll's name was known at all, it was probably because he was able to win the poetry contest in *The Weekly Independent's* "Poets' Corner."

Carroll was born in the most historic part of Ireland, close to Dundalk on the edge of Baile's Strand, famous in all the great Irish sagas. Yeats had placed one of his plays in this setting, and it might be supposed that Carroll's play would be strongly influenced by the romantic background of his birthplace. It was far otherwise, for Carroll was not a romantic. He was concerned with social problems, particularly with the relationship between the clergy and the ordinary people. One reason for his real obsession with this problem was that, although he was highly qualified as a teacher, he had been compelled to seek employment in Scotland: his integrity would not allow him to adopt the conventional procedure of going cap in hand to the local priest or Christian Brother in quest of a job.

Because of his attitude, Carroll was attracted to the plays of Ibsen, and he made an exact study of their philosophy and technique. He returned every summer vacation to his native Dundalk, and as he walked along the strand reading a book, strangers might be forgiven if they smiled—not at his small stature and bald head but at the incongruity of the man in his setting.

Long before he had even written a play, Carroll was convinced he was a major artist and never hesitated to say so. The announcement that he had won the competition, together with Teresa Deevy, was no surprise to him.

The Abbey was crowded for the opening night of *Things That Are Caesar's* (August 15, 1932), and before the final curtain came down most of the audience recognized that the play was a new and distinctive kind of contribution. Carroll was the first writer to give the Abbey a play on an anticlerical theme which was handled with such skill that it could give no offense. It was far from being a truly good play, but it was a bold beginning, and rarely in the history of the Abbey had any play received such enthusiastic applause. For almost twenty minutes the audience clapped, cheered, and stamped.

As if to herald a new era at the Abbey, after the play was over Carroll and his friends adjourned to a neighboring pub to celebrate the success of the play. In earlier years, Yeats, Lady Gregory, and Robinson would have taken the new author to the Imperial Hotel after the première. They would have occupied a table in the centre of the lounge, deposited their hats, cloaks, and staves beside them on the floor, and ordered coffee. The conversation would revolve around intricacies of style, the poetic play, and perhaps the legends of Ireland.

The conversation at Carroll's party was far otherwise. But this break with tradition was of little account. What really mattered was that Carroll had arrived as a dramatist, and the Abbey was hopeful.

Carroll went back to his school in Scotland determined to write a play superior to *Things That Are Caesar's*. It would be so successful it would enable him to retire from teaching and devote all his energies to literature and the drama. He tried various subjects. He began by writing a play on Robert Emmet, but the characters would not come to life. He then took up Dean Swift as a subject. Certain incidents in this play were amusing, as when Swift drinks a toast to Ireland from a chamber pot, but the final result was disappointing. Eventually he returned to the subject he knew best—the priests and their relations with their parishioners. The scene of his next play on this topic would be the district around Dundalk, and its conflict would be one between the romantic ideals of a church canon and the somewhat practical ideals of a radical schoolmaster. The interests of both centered on a young girl who saw visions of Saint Brigid.

He called his play *Shadow and Substance* and submitted it to the Abbey Theatre. It was accepted at once and was staged January 25, 1937. As before, Carroll drew a full house, and all literary Dublin was present. *Shadow and Substance* was beautifully produced and the central character of Brigid was so sensitively played that the audience were convinced they saw a masterpiece unfolding before them. They were sure this was one of the greatest plays ever to have appeared at the Abbey. Not so, Yeats. When he was asked for his opinion of the play, he ignored the question. To everyone else, however, Carroll seemed the savior of the Abbey Theatre. He possessed more strength than Murray and more lyricism than O'Casey, it was said, and it seemed a great tragic dramatist was beginning his career.

Carroll delighted the audience when he announced from the stage that he would submit all his first productions to the Abbey. No amount of money, he declared, could persuade him to give a first production to any other theatre.

The Abbey directors were less enthusiastic. The following year they turned down Carroll's next play, *The White Steed*. Carroll was astounded by this apparent lack of sound judgment, and he announced he would offer no more plays to the Abbey. He had *The White Steed* produced at the Cort Theatre in New York on January 10, 1939. It failed, and this might have been the factor that motivated Carroll to try the Abbey once more. His next play, *Kindred*, was accepted by the Abbey and performed for the first time on September 25, 1939. To his consternation this play also failed. He deleted certain ghostly characters for the second and subsequent performances, and it still failed.

Carroll's failure lessened the life expectancy of the Abbey Theatre. A major dramatist was needed at just that time, and had Carroll developed in that direction the Abbey might have been saved for another generation. Carroll had learned studiously from Ibsen how to construct a play, but unfortunately he had very little to say. He had said everything in *Things That Are Caesar's*, and each subsequent play was but a repetition. The brilliance of his technique was not enough to disguise the superficiality of his thinking. He relied too heavily on his ability as a technician, as the ending of *Shadow and Substance* demonstrates. There, he allowed truth to be sacrificed for the sake of a dramatic situation. He allows the girl to die in the presence of a priest without any thought of having the priest administer the last rites of the Church. How gloriously and with what pomp would Shakespeare have handled such a situation.

Even Carroll's characters never varied from play to play, and those who were unable to recognize the sterility of thought did at least tire of looking at his Canon. Carroll might desert the Abbey, but he would never desert the Canon. It was his misfortune and his limitation.

The Abbey's hopes did not rest solely on Carroll. The younger writers were finding places on the board of directors, and there was the possibility they would continue the tradition.

New Directors

When Yeats celebrated his seventieth birthday in 1935, he knew he had very few years more to live. He was in poor health, and he could prolong his life only by spending winters in the South of France. This meant he would not be able to give the Abbey Theatre much personal attention. It still remained the centre of his life's interest, and as he looked around he felt a little sad that there was no one of sufficient stature to take his place in guiding its policy. Robinson was an artist but had not the dominating qualities of a great leader. He could build, but he lacked the energy to defend. There was no one with the astuteness of Yeats himself who would know when to make a stand against degrading influences. Yeats, when he had had the energy of youth, could often see such influences before they arrived and would be prepared for the assault.

167

He decided to resolve the problem by doubling the number of directors, hoping the combined intelligence of many lesser men might equal in some way the genius of a real leader. It was not that he had become converted to democracy: he still disliked it intensely. As long as he remained alive he would be the supreme authority, and at any moment he could step in and dismiss all the directors if necessary. He could, of course, have allowed things to remain as before, with Robinson, Starkie, and Hayes in control, but he had an intuitive feeling that Hayes was a philistine and Starkie unsound, and that in a very short time they would dominate Robinson and the Abbey Theatre. The wisest thing seemed to be to appoint two or three others who would act as checks on Hayes and Starkie. Accordingly, the Articles of Association were altered to provide for a maximum of four additional directors.

Yeats was somewhat careless in his selection of new directors, but in the circumstances he was not worried; it was only to be an experiment, and he could end it at will. His young friend F. R. Higgins had written some delicately derivative lyrics and was a Protestant with an Anglo-Irish outlook, which pleased Yeats, so he appointed him a director. The second man he selected was Brinsley Macnamara (whose real name was John Weldon); he appealed to Yeats because he had written a novel which infuriated many people.

Ernest Blythe, the minister of finance who had been responsible for the Abbey's annual subsidy, had been out of a job since the general election in 1932, and it seemed the charitable thing to appoint him also to the board of directors. He knew absolutely nothing about drama, but in the present circumstances it did not really matter. It was of little account who was at the helm so long as the captain was aboard. As a final move, Yeats, on the suggestion of John Masefield, the poet laureate, brought over Hugh Hunt, an energetic Englishman, to act as producer. Then Yeats left the directors free to follow their own ideas and departed for the South of France.

One of the first decisions of the reorganized board of directors was to produce Sean O'Casey's controversial play *The Silver Tassie*. The decision caused much comment in the press, and the public anxiously awaited the opportunity of seeing the play and of judging for itself if Yeats and his fellow directors had been right in rejecting this play in 1928. On opening night, August 12, 1935, the Abbey was crowded with distinguished people from the literary, political, and religious worlds.

The opinion of most people was that *The Silver Tassie* was merely a badly written play. Pious Catholics, however, were deeply shocked with what they considered its blasphemy, and Catholic organizations all over the country passed resolutions condemning O'Casey and the Abbey Theatre. In Galway, for instance, the Catholic Young Men's Society by resolution denounced the Abbey "in so far as it infringes the canons of Christian reverence or human decency, and in so far as it injures the nation's prestige at home and abroad." [1]

A Dominican priest, Father Gaffney, declared before the same meeting that by producing *The Silver Tassie* "Dublin has once more to bear the ignomy of its condonation of disreputable drama." The Abbey Theatre, he said, "has been playing fast and loose with our most sacred loyalties."

The sentimental nationalists joined in the cries of "horror," and the president of the Gaelic League, taking his cue from Father Gaffney, wrote a letter to the Press, stating: "The Abbey Theatre . . . is intolerable and must be swept aside. . . . I have never seen its latest horror, but I remember some years ago going to see *The Plough and the Stars* and having to leave before the second act from a fit of nausea. As to the Abbey itself, I am inclined to echo the prayer that I once heard an embittered old farmer utter on hearing of the death of his landlord: 'A speedy race down with him.' "

Here was a situation which would have delighted Yeats in his early years. He would have baited the public until they collapsed from exhaustion. It was easy to estimate what Yeats would do in the circumstances, and the public was curious to see what attitude the newly formed board of directors would take. Would they adopt a fighting attitude and continue the play for three or four weeks, or would they merely ignore the criticism?

The suspense was broken on the morning of August 29 when Brinsley Macnamara published a two-column announcement in *The Irish Independent* in which he denounced not only the play but also his fellow directors. People were astounded when they read: "I did not see the play until the second night of its production and my immediate feelings were that an outrage had been committed." As they read down the column they were further surprised to find Macnamara stating that as a Catholic he took exception to certain portions of the play, including "the travesty of the Sacred Office in the second act." It was well known that Macnamara was a Catholic, but no one suspected he was so undiscerning a Catholic. Macnamara went on to explain that he was so shocked he called a special meeting of the directors the following day and "it was agreed that the objectionable portions already indicated by me should be amended."

Macnamara did not confine his tirade to the play but attacked his fellow directors and even denounced the Abbey audiences because, he said, for more than ten years they had shown "a wholly uncritical, and I might say, almost insane admiration for the vulgar and worthless plays of Mr. O'Casey."

Most people imagined at first that the announcement was not authentic, and many of Macnamara's friends dashed down to Fanning's Pub to meet him and see if he were of sound mind. They found Macnamara there, his obese body sitting on the customary stool, sipping a glass of porter and discussing in his nasal voice with David Charles, the literary attorney, the worthlessness of O'Casey. He seemed sober and otherwise normal and apparently believed that his statement was of the first importance.

Yeats compelled Macnamara to resign immediately from the Board.

Macnamara's outburst had embarrassed the other directors, particularly Walter Starkie, who was a Catholic and had been chiefly responsible for having *The Silver Tassie* produced. "I think the whole purpose of the play has been misunderstood," Starkie wrote. "It shows that the common soldier has a feeling of religion and is not blasphemous." Intelligent Catholics came to the defense of O'Casey and his play. For instance, Robert Speaight, dramatic critic for *The Catholic Herald,* summed up the campaign against the play in this way:

The soul of the bourgeoisie has betrayed itself. And this surely is the essence of the bourgeois mind—that it cannot look tragedy in the face;

for O'Casey has seen into the heart of the horror of war and wrenched out its dreadful secret: that the co-heirs with Christ destroy one another in the sight of the Son of Man.

Macnamara's resignation became of great importance to the Abbey: it left a vacancy, and the vacancy was filled by Frank O'Connor,[2] a brilliant writer of short stories. Yeats would probably have appointed O'Connor in the first instance, but O'Connor was a "discovery" of AE, and Yeats always had had a prejudice against the AE school. But Yeats was too big to allow such a prejudice to influence him permanently to his own detriment, and soon O'Connor was one of his most trusted friends.

O'Connor quickly became the vital force in the Abbey; he was the only director who had both genius and the intuitive ability to do the right thing. Higgins had talent, but he could never apply it to the stage. He wrote a play and had it produced at the Abbey under the title *A Deuce of Jacks* (September 16, 1935), but it was a complete failure. It was the only play ever performed at the Abbey which the audience forgot to applaud. *A Deuce of Jacks* lacked every quality essential to a play. It had not form nor plot nor poetry.

O'Connor rightly believed it was his duty as a director to write plays and not merely advertise for them. He learned his trade as a dramatist quickly, and on May 31, 1937, he had an unusual little piece, *In the Train*, produced at the Abbey. It was not by any means a good play, but it had a spark of originality that hinted at O'Connor's future as a dramatist. He felt that the Abbey Theatre must keep intimately in touch with the Ireland of the day and could remain vital only if it was the direct voice of the people. The poetic play had its place, but the emphasis must be on realism, tragedy, and satire. *Katie Roche* by Teresa Deevy (March 16, 1936) was an indication of the kind of poetic play which was needed, and it was fairly successful.

O'Connor did not believe in offering prizes for plays. In his view, that practice argued a weak attitude. His policy was to approach a writer of genius, whether he was novelist or storyteller, and offer to produce any play he would care to write. Experience, he believed, was not necessary. From such an offer as this came

She Had to Do Something by Sean O'Faolain (December 27, 1937). O'Faolain's play was far from being a masterpiece, but it represented something of the new Ireland. It presented more than the old familar faces and attitudes, of which the audience was becoming tired.

In 1937 it was decided to send the company to America again. This time the only motive for the tour was to act as "ambassadors of the intellect and imagination of Ireland," as Dr. Starkie put it. The directors wanted to inform America that even though Yeats was no longer active in the theatre, there were others who were worthy of carrying the Abbey along in an equally brilliant manner. The plays might not be exactly the kind to flatter the country superficially, but even De Valera had come to realize they were important as propaganda. He even proposed to give the company his blessing, and at the farewell dinner given for the company before it sailed, various government ministers were present to add their morsel of approval and encouragement. It would only be a matter of a few years, De Valera thought, when by skillful maneuvering he would have complete control of the Abbey and would have it express the Ireland of his own imagination.

O'Connor, in his speech at this farewell luncheon, said he thought that some of the Abbey's recent work proved that the theatre was coming more and more into touch with the spirit of modern Ireland.

There had been two phases in the history of the Abbey Theatre [O'Connor continued]. The first was when Yeats discovered his country in the slough of sentiment, into which subject nations ever sink, and in which Wales and Scotland were today. In that period, the Abbey, in producing plays like *Kathleen Ni Houlihan*, had given with great power and imagination, the sentiment of street ballad raised to a literary level. The next phase was one which was rather harshly called the realistic phase. I use the word "harshly" because to my mind the most important and significant plays of that period were the realistic comedies. These gave back to the people the power to laugh at themselves, a power which was lost by all sentimental subject nations. Now we are passing out of that phase, and, having learned to laugh at ourselves, we are approaching a phase when we have to take ourselves seriously. We believe that the new phase would find tragedy predominant. The drift is now towards tragedy, and with it comes satire. We already had the first appearance of this movement in *Shadow and Substance*. The Abbey wants its young dramatists to express for the theatre the emotions and development going on all around us, to interpret the Ireland of today with its problems and tendencies.

F. R. Higgins also agreed with O'Connor's views and pointed out that the theatre "must grow in unity with the life of the nation."

O'Connor was grappling as well as he knew how with the challenge set before him, now that Yeats had passed from the scene. He was striving to take the place of Yeats as the dominant force in the Abbey Theatre. Indeed, O'Connor was the only man whose genius might hold out against the ever-present deteriorating influences on the Abbey's integrity.

In the coming season Higgins promised to have some plays produced expressive of that new development, plays essentially in the national spirit.

The Abbey company, led by Higgins, opened its season in New York on September 30, 1937. Until May of the following year it toured America as far as the West Coast. The plays gladdened audiences everywhere. On previous tours there always had been some opposition; now, even those who had criticized the players earlier were anxious to fête them. "We represent the new Ireland, revitalized and reorganized, expressing her own social consciousness without fear of misrepresentation," wrote Higgins in the *New York Times*.

While the first company was in America, O'Connor was busy at the Abbey Theatre. He had written a new play, *The Invincibles* (October 18, 1937), in collaboration with Hugh Hunt, and it was well received. The combination of Hunt's technical skill and O'Connor's creative ability blended well, and the result was a play of some power.

O'Connor was clearly progressing. The following February he and Hunt wrote and staged *Moses' Rock*, which, whatever its drawbacks, had original quality. The industry of Hunt and O'Connor was stimulating others to write. Even a dentist friend of O'Connor's, Andrew Ganley, was inspired to try his hand at a play, *The Dear Queen* (April 4, 1939). O'Connor was certainly revitalizing the Abbey; he was accomplishing more with the second company than had been done for years with the first.

In May, 1938, Higgins arrived home from America with the first company. Everyone looked happy and prosperous. Not long after the usual welcoming parties, Lennox Robinson, who was gradually moving into the background, dreamed up the idea of a festival of drama. It would take place from August 8 to 20, following immediately on the Dublin Horse Show, the fashionable event of the year. There would be a morning lecture at the Gresham Hotel on some facet of Irish drama, and evening performances of plays which would represent the progress of the Abbey Theatre from its earliest days. Neither Higgins nor O'Connor objected: even though they disliked looking backward, the festival would give them a chance to voice their views on the future.

The Abbey Festival was, generally speaking, a success, though the English newspaper critics, who had come over especially for the occasion, treated it rather roughly. The festival also caused much controversy in the Irish papers as to the actual achievement of the Abbey Theatre. Typical of the letters was the following:

The Irish people feel that the leaders of the Abbey Theatre group have not been all at one with them, and their philosophy has not sprung from the traditional creeds of the people—in fact they believe that the movement rests solely on the veneration of an artificial and unreal Ireland and on a mixture of AE's reveries and W. B. Yeats's philosophy.

What caused most comment was Yeats's new play, *Purgatory*, which had its first performance during the festival. The very title, with its implications of a Catholic doctrine, caused annoyance. In a short speech at the end of the play, Yeats said he had put into the play his notions about this world and the next. No one had understood what the play was about and Yeats's statement only added to the mystification. The critic for *The Irish Times* sarcastically commented, "It was a small container for such a large message; rather like pouring a vat of philosophy into a half-pint bottle of time."

The controversy over *Purgatory* really started after a lecture on Yeats by F. R. Higgins on August 11, when a Jesuit priest from Boston asked the lecturer to explain for the benefit of the audience what *Purgatory* meant. Higgins was completely unable to reply, and Robinson, who was chairman of the meeting, saved the situation by interjecting that Dr. Yeats was the only person who could answer that question. The Jesuit, who admitted he had read the manuscript of the play surreptitiously the previous night, then said:

Everyone spoke of the great spiritual quality of Dr. Yeats's work, and, unless the poet meant to pervert the meaning of words and use them as mere notes of music, it seemed to me that he must mean something when he spoke. I have read Purgatory and on the previous night I followed it carefully on the stage. The plot was clear, but I have to admit that I could not discover what it symbolised.

Many intellectuals took the Jesuit's part and stated that Higgins had no business lecturing on Yeats if he was unable to answer a question of this kind. Yeats, who was not present at the lecture, on being interviewed later by the press was asked to explain what he meant to state in his play, and this was his explanation:

My plot is my meaning. I think the dead suffer remorse and recreate their old lives just as I have described. There are mediaeval Japanese plays about it and much in the folklore of all countries. In my play a spirit suffers because of its share, when alive, in the destruction of an honoured house. That destruction is taking place all over Ireland today.[3]

The Jesuit had many defenders in the controversy which followed. A Mr. John Lucy, for instance, argued in a letter why Catholics were entitled to find out what *Purgatory* was about:

Catholics in particular would like to know what Dr. Yeats means by his *Purgatory* because, in the manner (rather illegal, I think) of many modern poets with a message, the doctor has taken and twisted the meanings of some of the words and symbols of Catholicism to express his particular views, and indeed, in a way, his grim play has a definite Catholic flavor, which to one quietly thinking about it smacks of perversion. In this perversion the Catholic priest probably sees some danger to frail-minded Catholics or to those not familiar with the previous works of Yeats.[4]

Then Frank O'Connor sought to close the debate with a letter to *The Irish Times:*

When will Irish people learn that impassioned airing of sectarian prejudice is the worst form of vulgarity? It is important to point out that when this gentleman demanded Mr. Higgins's views on Mr. Yeats's play, he admitted to having read it. I need hardly say that, however he secured the manuscript, it was not with the consent of the author or theatre directors, and his attempts to bully Mr. Higgins into discussing a play which he came primed to discuss and which Mr. Higgins and the members of the audience knew comparatively little of, was on the same plane with his questions.[5]

After some further public discussion the controversy subsided, the visitors returned to their own countries, and the temper of the Dublin public returned to normal.

Mr. Hunt left the Abbey at this time. He went to New York to produce Paul Vincent Carroll's *The White Steed* and did not return.

Immediately after the festival, Higgins was made managing director, a very powerful position which Lady Gregory would not allow to be created as long as she lived. The appointment was a bad move: Higgins, though outwardly friendly to O'Connor, was slightly jealous of his ability to move in where Yeats had been. From now on, O'Connor's enthusiasms would be curbed—by Higgins and the other directors. On December 26, 1938, he had his last play, *Time's Pocket,* produced at the Abbey. O'Connor was living with his head in the clouds, unaware of any opposition from within the theatre. He felt there was nothing anyone could do to him, and if he did suspect intrigue it would be from Higgins, the flamboyant, swaggering, very "Anglo" poet.

The newspaper critics ridiculed *Time's Pocket,* and it was sneered at by minor literary figures. It was said that O'Connor knew nothing about how a play should be constructed and that he himself was an egotistical nobody. O'Connor retorted: "Literary movements begin in a conspiracy between an author and a small section of his audience. The critics have no part in the conspiracy; they think only of 'construction' and 'action' and 'development' and 'psychology'—all of which have about as much to do with the theatre as the man in the moon."

It could hardly be expected that such a statement would soothe his enemies. It was the kind of infuriating statement that Yeats would have made, and indeed it endeared O'Connor to him. To his fellow directors, O'Connor seemed to be a bumptious Corkman who, finding himself by accident on the Abbey board of directors, was attempting to dominate it. He was receiving all the publicity, and it would seem to an outsider as if no one else mattered in the Abbey Theatre. Higgins, the managing director, tried to claim some attention by issuing exaggerated statements. The theatre, he said, would in future perform only new plays. But it was no use attempting to compete with O'Connor, on whom the cloak of Yeats seemed to be settling. It fitted awkwardly on his rough-hewn broad shoulders, but he would be satisfied with nothing less. With the exception of Robinson, the other directors had even less opportunity for their emotions than had Higgins. Dr. Hayes sat in, censoring films for the people of Ireland in the morning, and in the evening engaging in his medical practice. Starkie was away in Spain, and the Abbey might burn for all he cared. Yet he disliked having any of the board members usurp powers which might be his. Ernest Blythe had turned himself into a journalist in the Gaelic language, and from this he derived little emotional satisfaction. Blythe was as frustrated as Dr. Hayes, but there was nothing either man could do about it as long as Yeats was alive. His word was law, and they thought it prudent to keep quiet until time removed Yeats from the scene completely.

Yeats was in the South of France. He was a very sick man and had little energy to spend thinking of the theatre. He was satisfied the reorganized board of directors was a success; it had produced O'Connor, and the Abbey again had a leader. This was a happy thought for Yeats as he was wheeled around the sunny gardens in southern France.

Suddenly he had a premonition that something dreadful was about to befall the Abbey. He wrote at once to O'Connor advising him of his premonition and asking him to wire immediately if anything was wrong or if O'Connor needed his help. O'Connor was puzzled by Yeats's letter: nothing unusual was in the wind. No one had challenged his authority, and all seemed serene. He sat down to his desk and wrote to Yeats, telling him that everything was well and there was no need to worry. On his way to the post office to mail the letter he bought a newspaper. Across the top was the headline DEATH OF W. B. YEATS. The date was January 29,

1939. Yeats had died the day before at Mentone on the French Riviera.

When O'Connor recovered from the shock, a strange fear came over him. Could it be that Yeats had even seen into the farther future—that he had seen disaster awaiting the Abbey? As O'Connor looked about him, he could see only success for the theatre everywhere. New playwrights were coming forward, and he had great confidence in his own future as a dramatist. Still he could not be sure; if Yeats's warning were to be prophetic, no effort of his would avail to forestall disaster. He could only watch and be prepared. The guiding light of past years had gone out, and O'Connor was on his own.

Betrayal

Upon the death of Yeats everyone even remotely connected with the Abbey Theatre began to assert himself and explain publicly what the theatre's policies should properly be. It should be a people's theatre, said some. According to others it must be a Gaelic theatre; to others still, a government theatre. It was to be everything except the poetic theatre Yeats had visualized. Every possible degrading influence from within and from without was exerted on the Abbey. Every little society, from the Catholic Truth Society and the Children of Mary to the government's Fianna Fail party pushed and shoved that they might be in on the spoils. Nothing was left unsaid or undone to make certain the Abbey would never again be in a position to defame the holy name of Ireland.

The first move was to dislodge O'Connor from the directorate. He was the real obstacle. Higgins, the innocuous managing director, could easily be persuaded by the other directors to agree to the removal of O'Connor. Higgins, having no real interest in the theatre, soon was maneuvered into the camp opposite to O'Connor. The next step would be to make Richard Hayes a full director, and this was duly accomplished on March 24, 1939. Lennox Robinson alone of the directors was no part of the intrigue. He was neutral.

It was assumed from the start that O'Connor could be forced out if the conspiring directors contradicted him at every stage and so made themselves obnoxious to him. Accordingly, Hayes started dictating the kind of plays to be produced, and when communicating with playwrights he insisted on giving official advice on how plays should be written. O'Connor was, of course, unmoved by this show of vulgarity and would not be removed so easily; his fellow directors could hardly make themselves more obnoxious than they already were.

It was finally concluded that the only possible way to rid themselves of O'Connor was to alter the Articles of Association to empower them to dismiss a director. This was carried out on August 18 by special resolution, and O'Connor was promptly dismissed. The reason given for his removal was ironic: he had accepted the principle of divorce which Yeats had so eloquently defended in the senate in 1925.

O'Connor still refused to be defeated. He rejected the directors' demand that he hand over to them his shares in the theatre, and they found themselves in the embarrassing position of holding the annual shareholders' meetings in O'Connor's presence and being compelled to listen as he berated them for their ignorance. To waylay further annoying interference from O'Connor, they again amended the Articles of Association by special resolution on January 25, 1940, so that "no member shall have any right of inspecting any accounts or books or documents of the Company except as conferred by Statute or authorized by the Directors." Now O'Connor was effectively muzzled, and the degradation of the Abbey Theatre was almost complete.

Richard Hayes had won. Ernest Blythe, whose idea had been

to turn the Abbey over to the Gaelic League and its affiliated organizations, was willing for the moment to make no demands. Government efforts to force the Gaelic language on the country as its spoken language were failing, and Blythe regarded the Abbey Theatre as an excellent weapon for Gaelic-speaking propaganda. Further, Gaelic enthusiasts had not succeeded in producing one play of merit in that language, and Blythe believed that the technical abilities of the Abbey actors and producers might make up for the lack of genius among the playwriting members. Blythe, being a politician, believed in moving slowly and with care; he therefore confined his activities on the board of directors to making a knowledge of Gaelic a necessary qualification for every new actor. In appreciation of his work for the language, De Valera, his political opponent, appointed him to an important position in a government-sponsored factory. Things were working smoothly, and concessions were being made to everyone and to everything except to the ideals of Yeats and his associates.

Even the public would be catered to, and on August 5, 1940, *The Rugged Path*, a new play by George Shiels, was allowed to run for the unprecedented period of twelve weeks. This was very different from the early Abbey policy of changing the program twice a week. The audience, not the poet, was in control now, and it demanded to be flattered. The theatre was packed every night with people demanding, and receiving, soft sentiment and superficialities. Even the standard of acting had to be lowered to suit the tastes of the public. An audience can bully the actors by refusing to be moved at the right moments, and the actors were compelled to broaden their style after the manner of the commercial theatre and even to introduce gags. It was against this base kind of show that the Abbey Theatre had protested in the days of its glory. Now sensitive acting was a thing of the past, and the showman had come into his own again.

In 1947 O'Connor explained in *The Sunday Independent* of November 16 what had happened after the death of Yeats:

The death of the one man of whom everyone stood in awe meant that men whose intentions were good but whose technical knowledge of literature and acting were small felt themselves bound to do all the things which Yeats had done, and a number of things he would never have dreamed of doing. They interfered too much in the working of the theatre instead of merely directing it, people were appointed more for a knowledge of Irish than for other essential qualities; writers who knew infinitely more of literature than they did resented the treatment they received and gave up in despair. . . . Once after an impudent rejection note had been sent to a famous dramatist I said to the medical member of the Board: "If I laid down the law about medicine, as you laid down the law about literature, you'd tell me to shut up." He replied: "there is no analogy whatever." Too many people are inclined to forget that literature requires education and hard training. He had written articles himself and another director had translated "The Beautiful Isle of Capri" into Irish. What more was there to it? . . . I have no hope that the theatre will be saved. . . .

On January 7, 1941, F. R. Higgins died. This came as a surprise, for he was still a young man. An American theatre manager who once asked him if he, too, was in the "show business" must be forgiven, for Higgins had more of the showman in his character than of the poet. He was effusive rather than enthusiastic in his handling of Abbey Theatre affairs, and it must be remembered that his refusal to support O'Connor against the machinations of his fellow directors was one of the main reasons for the theatre's being swamped by the rabble.

Many genuine sympathizers of the Abbey hoped that even at this late moment the directors would see the light and return to the road pointed out by Yeats. It was hoped that Robinson would be made managing director even if they did not recall O'Connor. But Robinson was merely presented with his painted portrait and the position given with most indecent haste to Ernest Blythe. Further, the directors raised the salary which went with the post. Higgins had been content with £300 a year; now Blythe was to receive £600. The Abbey was to be a commercial theatre. To assure themselves of even greater control, a gentleman named Roibeard O'Fearrachain (Robert Farren), a Gaelic-language enthusiast, was appointed to fill the vacancy on the directorate.

The Abbey Theatre board of directors was now packed against the forces of intellect, taste, imagination, and poetry. The Gaelic League, which had attempted from the very beginning to wreck the Abbey, found itself in complete control of its policy. De Valera, now the Abbey's virtual leader, had a powerful weapon for political propaganda. He did not hesitate to use it against those who differed from him. For example, Dr. Starkie, who was one of the oldest of the directors, supported England during World War II. De Valera decided that a man of such heretical views was not worthy to be a director of Ireland's national theatre. At his insistence the Articles of Association of the Theatre Society were once more changed, to allow the elimination of Starkie from the board of directors. Starkie was director of the British Institute in Madrid and could not be present at all meetings of the Abbey board. By special resolution on September 30, 1943, Article 10A was altered to read: "If any director without the express consent of his colleagues absents himself from all meetings of the Board held during any period of six calendar months, and if the number of such meetings has been not less than six, he shall at the end of the said period cease to be a member of the board." Starkie had not fulfilled these conditions and therefore ceased to be a director. Taking his lead from O'Connor, he also refused to relinquish his shares.

One of Blythe's first decrees when he became managing director stated that no actor, whatever his capabilities, would be allowed to remain at the Abbey Theatre unless he learned the Gaelic language. Many of the actors disliked having to leave the Abbey, which had been a home to them, and though they were past the age when learning a new language was easy, they bowed to the decision, bought Gaelic grammars and began to study the mysteries of the infixed pronoun. The real pathos of it was that there were no plays in the Gaelic language worth producing: no one would write in Gaelic unless he had failed as a writer of English. So, many very bad plays in Gaelic were produced. This policy reached what must have been its lowest point when a pantomime in Gaelic, *Muireann agus an Prionnsa,* was performed during the Christmas season of 1945. This performance included a "leg show," and its highest point of distinction was the excellent translation of the popular hit "I Got a Gal in Kalamazoo." *Faustus Kelly* by Myles na gCopaleen (January 25, 1943) was the only play of any consequence produced during these years.

One might imagine that the insolence of the directors could not have been pushed further, that they would have retained some sentimental regard for the Abbey of past years. That was not so. In 1947 they refused to produce a new play by Lennox Robinson, *The Lucky Finger,* and only reversed that decision after he had it performed in America, on January 19, at Bowling Green College, Ohio.

The most popular play produced at the Abbey in the late 1940s was *The Righteous Are Bold* by Frank Carney (July 29, 1946). This was a melodrama of an extremely religious nature describing how a pious Catholic girl goes to work in England and becomes possessed of the devil. The bedeviled girl breaks so many statues and crucifixes on the stage while the priest is attempting to exorcise the spirit, that a well-known wit in Dublin, asked why he did not go to see the play, replied that a friend of his had gone and had got a splinter in his eye.

At the moment, the Abbey Theatre has become little more than a training school for Hollywood and English film companies.

One might have wished the Abbey Theatre had continued as a vital theatre after the death of Yeats. Yet it is some comfort to know that its swift collapse entitles one to the conclusion that the Abbey Theatre did indeed die with Yeats. It was his creation and he took it with him. The Abbey Theatre Festival, an Irish journalist wrote some years ago, was really the Abbey Theatre's funeral—a brilliant funeral, perhaps, but still a funeral. One might be forgiven for continuing the simile with the observation that the wake has been prolonged and the debauch is not yet over. It should be remembered that the Abbey Theatre did not consist of the Abbey Theatre building. When the directors, with the consent and the blessing of Mr. de Valera's government, planned recently to tear it down and replace it with a building of more modernistic design, they were being more honest than they realized. The Abbey Theatre was a dream in the mind of Yeats. He had made it a reality during his life, but when he died the reality returned to the dream and passed away with its creator.

Appendices

Appendix A

FIRST PRODUCTIONS OF THE IRISH LITERARY THEATRE AND THE IRISH NATIONAL THEATRE SOCIETY

Date	Name of Play	Author
1899		
May 8	The Countess Cathleen	W. B. Yeats
	The Heather Field	Edward Martyn
1900		
Feb. 20	The Bending of the Bough	George Moore
Feb. 21	The Last Feast of the Fianna	Alice Milligan
	Maeve	Edward Martyn
1901		
Oct. 21	Casadh an t-Sugain	Douglas Hyde
	Diarmuid and Grainne	Moore and Yeats

	1902		
April 2		Deirdre	George Russell
		Cathleen Ni Houlihan	W. B. Yeats
Oct. 29		The Sleep of the King	Seumas O'Cuisin
		The Laying of the Foundations	Fred Ryan
Oct. 30		A Pot of Broth	W. B. Yeats
Oct. 31		The Racing Lug	Seumas O'Cuisin
		Eilis agus an Bhean Déirce	Peadar Mag Fhionnloic

	1903		
March 14		The Hour Glass	W. B. Yeats
		Twenty-Five	Lady Gregory
April 20		The Sword of Dermot	Seumas O'Cuisin
June 3		The Land of Heart's Desire	W. B. Yeats
Oct. 8		On the King's Threshold	W. B. Yeats
		In the Shadow of the Glen	J. M. Synge
Dec. 3		Broken Soil	Padraic Colum

	1904		
Jan. 14		The Shadowy Waters	W. B. Yeats
		The Townland of Tamney	Seumas MacManus
Feb. 25		Riders to the Sea	J. M. Synge

AT THE ABBEY THEATRE

Dec. 27		On Baile's Strand	W. B. Yeats
		Spreading the News	Lady Gregory

	1905		
Feb. 4		The Well of the Saints	J. M. Synge
March 25		Kincora	Lady Gregory
April 25		The Building Fund	William Boyle
June 9		The Land	Padraic Colum
Dec. 9		The White Cockade	Lady Gregory

	1906		
Feb. 19		Hyacinth Halvey	Lady Gregory
April 16		The Doctor in Spite of Himself	Molière-Gregory
June 20		The Eloquent Dempsey	William Boyle
Oct. 20		The Gaol Gate	Lady Gregory
		The Mineral Workers	William Boyle
Nov. 24		Deirdre	W. B. Yeats
Dec. 8		The Canavans	Lady Gregory
		The Shadowy Waters (revised)	W. B. Yeats

	1907		
Jan. 26		The Playboy of the Western World	J. M. Synge
Feb. 23		The Jackdaw	Lady Gregory

188

March 9	The Rising of the Moon	Lady Gregory
March 16	The Interior	M. Maeterlinck
April 1	The Eyes of the Blind	W. M. Letts
April 3	The Poorhouse	Lady Gregory
April 27	Fand	W. S. Blunt
Oct. 3	The Country Dressmaker	George Fitzmaurice
Oct. 31	Dervorgilla	Lady Gregory
Nov. 21	The Unicorn From the Stars	Yeats-Gregory

1908

Feb. 3	The Man Who Missed the Tide	W. F. Casey
Feb. 13	The Piper	Conal O'Riordan
March 10	The Pie-dish	George Fitzmaurice
March 19	The Golden Helmet	W. B. Yeats
	Teja	H. Sudermann
April 4	The Rogueries of Scapin	Molière-Gregory
April 20	The Workhouse Ward	Lady Gregory
May 29	The Scheming Lieutenant	R. B. Sheridan
Oct. 1	The Suburban Grove	W. F. Casey
Oct. 8	The Clancy Name	Lennox Robinson
Oct. 15	When the Dawn Is Come	Thomas MacDonagh

1909

Jan. 21	The Miser	Molière-Gregory
March 11	Stephen Gray	D. L. Kelleher
April 1	The Cross Roads	Lennox Robinson
	Time	Conal O'Riordan
April 29	The Glittering Gate	Lord Dunsany
May 27	Imaginary Conversation	Conal O'Riordan
Aug. 25	The Shewing-up of Blanco Posnet	Bernard Shaw
Sept. 16	The White Feather	R. J. Ray
Oct. 14	The Challenge	W. M. Letts
Nov. 11	The Image	Lady Gregory

1910

Jan. 13	Deirdre of the Sorrows	J. M. Synge
Feb. 10	The Green Helmet	W. B. Yeats
Feb. 24	Mirandolina	Goldoni-Gregory
March 2	The Travelling Man	Lady Gregory
May 12	Thomas Muskerry	Padraic Colum
May 26	Harvest	Lennox Robinson
Sept. 28	The Casting-out of Martin Wheland	R. J. Ray
Oct. 27	Birthright	T. C. Murray
Nov. 10	The Full Moon	Lady Gregory
Nov. 24	The Suiler's Child	Seumas O'Kelly
Dec. 1	Coats	Lady Gregory

	1911		
Jan. 5		The Nativity Play	Douglas Hyde
Jan. 12		The Deliverers	Lady Gregory
Jan. 26		King Argimenes and the Unknown Warrior	Lord Dunsany
		The Land of Heart's Desire	W. B. Yeats
March 30		Mixed Marriage	St. John Ervine
Nov. 23		The Interlude of Youth	Anon.
		The Second Shepherd's Play	Anon.
Nov. 30		The Marriage	Douglas Hyde
Dec. 7		Red Turf	Rutherford Mayne
Dec. 14		The Countess Cathleen (revival)	W. B. Yeats

	1912		
Jan. 4		The Annunciation	Anon.
		The Flight into Egypt	Anon.
Jan. 11		MacDonough's Wife (later changed to MacDarragh's Wife)	Lady Gregory
Feb. 15		The Tinker and the Fairy (in Gaelic)	Douglas Hyde
Feb. 29		The Worlde and the Chylde	Anon.
March 28		Family Failing	William Boyle
April 11		Patriots	Lennox Robinson
April 15		Judgment	Joseph Campbell
June 20		Maurice Harte (Court Theatre, London)	T. C. Murray
July 4		The Bogie Man (Court Theatre, London)	Lady Gregory
Oct. 17		The Magnanimous Lover	St. John Ervine
Nov. 21		Damer's Gold	Lady Gregory
		The Hour Glass (revised)	W. B. Yeats
Dec. 26		A Little Christmas Miracle	E. H. Moore

	1913		
Jan. 23		The Dean of St. Patrick's	S. Paternoster
Feb. 20		Hannele	G. Hauptmann
March 6		There Are Crimes and Crimes	A. Strindberg
March 13		The Cuckoo's Nest	John Guinan
April 10		The Homecoming	Gertrude Robins
April 17		The Stronger	A. Strindberg
April 24		The Magic Glasses	George Fitzmaurice
		Broken Faith	S. R. Day & G. D. Cummins
May 17		The Post Office	R. Tagore
June 30		The Gombeen Man	R. J. Ray
Sept. 11		Sovereign Love	T. C. Murray
Oct. 2		The Mine Land	Joseph Connolly
Oct. 16		My Lord	Mrs. Bart Kennedy
Nov. 16		Duty	Seumas O'Brien
Nov. 18		The Bribe	Seumas O'Kelly
Nov. 20		The Critics	St. John Ervine

190

1914

Jan. 29	David Mahony	V. O'D. Power
March 13	The Orangemen	St. John Ervine
	The Lord Mayor	Edward McNulty
April 2	Kinship	J. B. MacCarthy
April 15	The Cobbler	A. P. Wilson
Aug. 27	A Minute's Wait	M. J. MacHugh
Sept. 3	The Supplanter	J. B. MacCarthy
Sept. 9	The Dark Hour	R. A. Christie
Sept. 23	The Crossing	Con O'Leary
Sept. 30	The Prodigal	Walter Riddall
Oct. 13	The Cobweb	F. Jay
Oct. 20	The Jug of Sorrow	W. P. Ryan
Nov. 3	The Slough	A. P. Wilson
Dec. 26	The Critic	R. B. Sheridan

1915

Jan. 27	By Word of Mouth	Moore & Flanagan
Feb. 2	The Dreamers	Lennox Robinson
April 5	The Bargain	William Crone
April 5	The Philosopher	M. J. MacHugh
April 8	Shanwalla	Lady Gregory
Nov. 30	John Ferguson	St. John Ervine

1916

Jan. 4	The Fraternity	Bernard Duffy
Feb. 8	The Coiner	Bernard Duffy
March 28	The Plough Lifters	John Guinan
Sept. 25	John Bull's Other Island	Bernard Shaw
Oct. 9	Widowers' Houses	Bernard Shaw
Oct. 16	Arms and the Man	Bernard Shaw
Oct. 25	Nic	William Boyle
Nov. 15	Partition	D. C. Maher
Dec. 11	The Counter Charm	Bernard Duffy
Dec. 13	The Whiteheaded Boy	Lennox Robinson

1917

Jan. 8	Tommy-Tom-Tom	M. J. MacHugh
Jan. 19	The Crusaders	J. B. MacCarthy
Feb. 2	Fox and Geese	S. R. Day & G. D. Cummins
Feb. 26	Man and Superman	Bernard Shaw
March 12	The Inca of Perusalem	Bernard Shaw
April 25	The Strong Hand	R. J. Day
May 26	The Doctor's Dilemma	Bernard Shaw
Sept. 24	The Parnellite	Seumas O'Kelly
Oct. 30	The Bacac	J. Barnewell
Nov. 13	The Spoiling of Wilson	R. J. Purcell

Nov. 20	Friends	H. Farjeon
Dec. 11	Blight	Alpha and Omega

1918

Jan. 8	Spring	T. C. Murray
Jan. 22	When Love Came Over the Hills	Fearon & Nesbit
Jan. 29	Hanrahan's Oath	Lady Gregory
Feb. 9	The Lost Leader	Lennox Robinson
March 12	Aliens	Rose McKenna
May 28	A Little Bit of Youth	C. Callister
Sept. 16	Sable and Gold	Maurice Dalton
Nov. 12	The Grabber	E. F. Barrett
Dec. 17	Atonement	Dorothy Macardle

1919

March 11	The Rebellion in Ballycullen	Brinsley Macnamara
April 21	The Dragon	Lady Gregory
Aug. 4	Brady	Sadie Casey
Aug. 19	The Fiddler's House (a revision of The Land)	Padraic Colum
	A Serious Thing	G. Ousley
Sept. 2	The Saint	Desmond Fitzgerald
	A Night at an Inn	Lord Dunsany
Sept. 30	The Labour Leader	Daniel Corkery
Oct. 7	Meadowsweet	Seumas O'Kelly
Oct. 14	Queer Ones	Con O'Leary
Nov. 4	Androcles and the Lion	Bernard Shaw
Nov. 25	The Enchanted Trousers	G. Ousley
Dec. 9	The Player Queen	W. B. Yeats

1920

Jan. 6	The Golden Apple	Lady Gregory
Feb. 10	The Devil's Disciple	Bernard Shaw
Feb. 17	The Daemon in the House	F. Barrington
April 27	The Good-Natured Man	Oliver Goldsmith
May 4	The Yellow Bittern	Daniel Corkery
May 24	The Tents of the Arabs	Lord Dunsany
Aug. 9	The Wooing of Julia Elizabeth	James Stephens
Sept. 7	The Drifters	F. J. H. O'Donnell
Sept. 21	A Royal Alliance	Fergus O'Nolan
Oct. 5	The Serf	Stephen Morgan
Oct. 12	The Island of Saints	St. John Ervine
Nov. 30	The Land for the People	Brinsley Macnamara
Dec. 27	Candle and Crib	K. F. Purdon

1921

Jan. 6	Bedmates	George Shiels
Feb. 24	The Revolutionist	Terence MacSwiney
March 17	Aristotle's Bellows	Lady Gregory

192

Oct. 18		The Perfect Day	Emile Mazaud
		A Merry Death	Nicholas Evreinov
Nov. 8		The Courting of Mary Doyle	Edward MacNulty
Nov. 15		The Piper of Tavran	Bernard Duffy
Dec. 13		Insurance Money	George Shiels
	1922		
Jan. 10		Aftermath	T. C. Murray
Jan. 31		The Round Table	Lennox Robinson
March 9		The Man of Destiny	Bernard Shaw
April 6		The Young Man from Rathmines	M. M. Brennan
		Ann Kavanagh	Dorothy Macardle
Aug. 29		The Moral Law	R. J. Ray
Sept. 5		A Lepracaun in the Tenement	M. M. Brennan
Oct. 3		Paul Twyning	George Shiels
Oct. 24		The Grasshopper (adapted)	Padraic Colum
Nov. 14		Crabbed Youth and Age	Lennox Robinson
	1923		
Jan. 9		The Long Road to Garranbraher	J. B. MacCarthy
March 8		'Twixt the Giltenans and the Carmodys	George Fitzmaurice
March 22		A Doll's House	Henrik Ibsen
April 9		The Shadow of a Gunman	Sean O'Casey
April 22		She Stoops to Conquer	Oliver Goldsmith
Sept. 3		Apartments	Fand O'Grady
Oct. 1		Cathleen Listens-in	Sean O'Casey
Nov. 27		The Glorious Uncertainty	Brinsley Macnamara
Dec. 26		First Aid	George Shiels
Dec. 31		The Old Woman Remembers	Lady Gregory
	1924		
Feb. 12		The Two Shepherds	G. M. Sierra
March 3		Juno and the Paycock	Sean O'Casey
April 8		Never the Time and the Place	Lennox Robinson
April 14		The Story Brought by Brigit	Lady Gregory
May 12		The Retrievers	George Shiels
Sept. 8		Autumn Fire	T. C. Murray
Sept. 29		Nannie's Night Out	Sean O'Casey
Nov. 3		The Kingdom of God	G. M. Sierra
Dec. 16		The Passing	Kenneth Sarr
Dec. 22		Old Mag	Kenneth Sarr
	1925		
Feb. 24		The Old Man	Dorothy Macardle
March 17		Anti-Christ	F. J. H. O'Donnell
March 31		Portrait	Lennox Robinson
April 21		Fanny's First Play	Bernard Shaw
April 28		The Proposal	Anton Chekhov
Sept. 14		Professor Tim	George Shiels
Oct. 12		The White Blackbird	Lennox Robinson

	1926		
Jan. 4		The Would-be Gentleman	Molière-Gregory
Feb. 8		The Plough and the Stars	Sean O'Casey
Feb. 16		Doctor Knock	Jules Romains
April 12		Look at the Heffernans	Brinsley Macnamara
Aug. 16		Mr. Murphy's Island	Elizabeth Harte
Sept. 6		The Big House	Lennox Robinson
Nov. 6		The Importance of Being Ernest	Oscar Wilde
Dec. 6		Oedipus the King	Sophocles-Yeats

	1927		
Jan. 24		The Emperor Jones	Eugene O'Neill
		Trifles	Susan Glaspell
March 14		Sancho's Master	Lady Gregory
April 5		Parted	M. C. Madden
May 9		Dave	Lady Gregory
May 16		Black Oliver	John Guinan
July 8		The Round Table (revised)	Lennox Robinson
Aug. 22		Drapier Letters	Arthur Power
Sept. 12		Oedipus at Colonnus	Sophocles-Yeats
Oct. 3		The Pipe in the Fields	T. C. Murray
Oct. 24		Caesar and Cleopatra	Bernard Shaw
Nov. 29		Cartney and Kevney	George Shiels

	1928		
March 6		The Master	Brinsley Macnamara
April 3		John Gabriel Borkman	Henrik Ibsen
April 30		The Blind Wolf	T. C. Murray
July 16		Before Midnight	Gerald Brosnan
Aug. 27		Full Measure	Kathleen O'Brennan
Oct. 22		The Far Off Hills	Lennox Robinson
Nov. 12		The Women Have Their Way	Quintero brothers
		(by the School of Acting)	
Nov. 26		King Lear	Shakespeare

	1929		
March 5		Mountain Dew	George Shiels
Aug. 13		Fighting the Waves (ballet)	W. B. Yeats
Sept. 10		The Woman	Margaret O'Leary
Oct. 8		Ever the Twain	Lennox Robinson
Oct. 29		Gods of the Mountain	Lord Dunsany
Dec. 31		Dark Isle	Gerald Brosnan

	1930		
Jan. 28		Peter	Rutherford Mayne
Jan. 18		The Reaper	Teresa Deevy
April 19		The New Gossoon	George Shiels
Sept. 15		Let the Credit Go	Bryan Cooper
Nov. 17		The Words Upon the Window Pane	W. B. Yeats

194

	1931		
Jan. 6	The Critic (revised by Lennox Robinson)	R. B. Sheridan
Feb. 9	The Rune of Healing	John Guinan
Feb. 23	Peter the Liar	André Leprovost
March 9	Money	Hugh P. Quinn
April 27	The Moon in the Yellow River	Denis Johnson
June 8	The Admirable Bashville	Bernard Shaw
July 7	Scrap	J. A. O'Brennan
Aug. 24	A Disciple	Teresa Deevy
Sept. 21	The Cat and the Moon	W. B. Yeats
Dec. 6	The Dreaming of the Bones	W. B. Yeats
	1932	
June 27	Michaelmas Eve	T. C. Murray
July 25	All's Over Then?	Lennox Robinson
Aug. 15	Things That Are Caesar's	Paul V. Carroll
Sept. 12	Temporal Powers	Teresa Deevy
Oct. 17	The Mating of Sean McGhie	T. H. Stafford
Oct. 24	Vigil	A. P. Fanning
Oct. 31	The Wild Duck	Henrik Ibsen
Nov. 7	The Big Sweep	M. M. Brennan
Nov. 14	Sheridan's Mills	Norman Webb
Nov. 21	Wrack	Peadar O'Donnell
	1933	
Feb. 16	Drama at Inis	Lennox Robinson
March 13	Men Crowd Me Round	Francis Stuart
July 17	Margaret Gillan	Brinsley Macnamara
July 25	The Drinking Horn (ballet)	Arthur Duff
Aug. 21	The Jezebel	J. K. Montgomery
Sept. 25	"1920"	F. X. O'Leary
Nov. 13	Grogan and the Ferret	George Shiels
Dec. 26	You Never Can Tell	Bernard Shaw
	1934	
Feb. 5	The Marriage Packet	Arthur Power
April 16	Days Without End	Eugene O'Neill
May 21	Church Street	Lennox Robinson
June 18	Bridgehead	Rutherford Mayne
July 9	On the Rocks	Bernard Shaw
July 30	The Resurrection	W. B. Yeats
	The King of the Great Clock Tower	W. B. Yeats
Oct. 1	Parnell of Avondale	W. R. Fearon
Oct. 25	Macbeth	Shakespeare
Nov. 12	The Gallant Cassian	Schnitzler
	The School for Wives	Molière
Dec. 3	Six Characters in Search of an Author	L. Pirandello
Dec. 26	At Mrs. Beam's	C. K. Munro

196

Dec. 12	Bantiarna an Ghorta	Seumas De Bhilmot
Dec. 26	Time's Pocket	Frank O'Connor

1939

Feb. 6	Caesar's Image	E. F. Carey
March 13	To-Morrow Never Comes	Louis D'Alton
April 8	The Heritage	J. K. Montgomery
May 15	Donnchadh Ruadh	Seumas O h-Aodha
July 31	Illumination	T. C. Murray
Aug. 28	Fonham the Sculptor	Daniel Corkery
Sept. 25	Kindred	Paul V. Carroll
Oct. 30	Give Him a House	George Shiels
Dec. 4	They Went by Bus	Frank Carney

1940

Jan. 29	The Spanish Soldier	Louis D'Alton
March 23	William John Mawhinney	St. John Ervine
April 23	Mount Prospect	Elizabeth Connor
May 13	Birth of a Giant	Nora MacAdam
July 15	To-day and Yesterday	W. D. Hepenstall
Aug. 5	The Rugged Path	George Shiels
Nov. 4	Three to Go	Olga Fielden
Nov. 25	Peeping Tom	Frank Carney
Dec. 9	Strange Guest	Francis Stuart

1941

Jan. 6	Trial at Greenstreet Courthouse	Roger McHugh
Feb. 10	The Summit	George Shiels
March 10	The Money Doesn't Matter	Louis D'Alton
May 19	The Lady in the Twilight	Mervyn Wall
June 30	Friends and Relations	St. John Ervine
Aug. 18	Remembered Forever	Bernard McGinn
Sept. 1	The Fire Burns Late	P. J. Fitzgibbon
Sept. 22	Swans and Geese	Elizabeth Connor
Oct. 20	Lover's Meeting	Louis D'Alton
Nov. 24	The Three Thimbles	Brinsley Macnamara
Dec. 26	Forget-Me-Not	Lennox Robinson
Dec. 28	Black Fast	Austin Clarke

1942

March 9	The Cursing Fields	Andrew Ganley
April 6	The Singer	Padraic Pearse
April 13	The Fort Field	George Shiels
May 3	La La Noo	Jack Yeats
July 6	The Whip Hand	B. G. MacCarthy
Sept. 7	An Apple a Day	Elizabeth Connor

1943

Jan. 25	Faustus Kelly	Myles na gCopaleen
Jan. 31	An Bhean Chrodha	Piaras Beaslai
March 8	The O'Cuddy	Anthony Wharton

March 21	The Assembly at Druim Ceat	Roibeard O'Fearrachain
April 4	An Coimisinéar (produced for An Comhar Dramiochta)	Tomas O'Suilleabhain
April 24	The Old Road	Michael J. Molloy
April 26	Lost Light	Roibeard O'Fearrachain
May 30	An Traona san Mhóinfhéir	Seumas De Faoite
Aug. 30	Thy Dear Father	Gerard Healy
Oct. 24	Órdóg an Bháis	Michael Ó h-Aodha
Dec. 27	Poor Man's Miracle (translation from Polish by F. Czarnomski)	Marian Hemar

1944

Jan. 30	Lastiar den Éadan	Eibhlin Ni Suilleabhain
Feb. 7	The Wise Have Not Spoken	Paul V. Carroll
March 6	The New Regime	George Shiels
March 26	Stiana	Peadar Ó'h-Annrachain
May 8	The Coloured Balloon	Margaret O'Leary
May 21	Sodar i ndiaidh na nUasal (Le Bourgeois Gentilhomme)	Molière
Aug. 28	The End House	Joseph Tomelty
Nov. 20	Railway House	Ralf Kennedy

1945

Jan. 7	An t-Ubhall Or (translation of Lady Gregory's The Golden Apple)	L. O'Briain
March 18	Giolla an tSoluis	Maire Ni Grada
March 31	Rossa	Roger McHugh
May 13	An t-Udar i nGleic	Labhras Mac Bradaigh
Aug. 6	Marks and Mabel	Brinsley Macnamara
Sept. 10	Tenants at Will	George Shiels
Dec. 20	Muireann agus an Prionnsa (a pantomime)	Anon.

1946

Feb. 11	Mungo's Mansion	Walter Macken
March 25	The Old Broom	George Shiels
July 29	The Righteous Are Bold	Frank Carney
Nov. 18	The Visiting House	M. J. Molloy
Dec. 29	Fernando agus an Dragon (a pantomime)	Anon.

1947

Feb. 18	They Got What They Wanted	Louis D'Alton
May 12	The Dark Road	Elizabeth Connor
Aug. 25	The Great Pacificator	Sigerson Clifford

198

1948		
Jan. 1	Realt Dhiarmuda (a pantomime)	Anon.
Feb. 16	The Caretakers	George Shiels
July 12	The Drums Are Out	George Coulter
Aug. 23	The Lucky Finger	Lennox Robinson
Sept. 13	Aris (a translation into Gaelic by Liam O'Brian of Henri Ghéon's La Joyeuse Farce Des "Encore")	
Oct. 11	Na Cloigini (a translation into Gaelic by Maighread Nic Mhaicin of The Bells by Erckmann-Chatrian), produced for An Comhar Dramiochta	
Oct. 18	The King of Friday's Men	M. J. Molloy
Dec. 27	Brian agus an Claidheamh Solais (a pantomime with music, fun, dance, and romance), produced for An Comhar Dramiochta	
1949		
March 14	The Bugle in the Blood	Bryan MacMahon
March 22	Oiche Bhealtaine	Micheál MacLiammhóir

199

Appendix B

EXTRACTS FROM FILE No. 3660
FROM THE REGISTER OF COMPANIES AND BUSINESS
NAMES, DUBLIN CASTLE.

Early in 1911 The National Theatre Society Limited was registered under the Companies Consolidated Act of 1908. The capital was fixed at £1,000, consisting of £1 shares— of which 390 were issued. Lady Gregory and Yeats held 376 of the shares between them. The original records were destroyed in the Four Courts fire, but the shares were probably held in 1911 as they were in 1921 (March 30), for which year we have the first record:

Lady Gregory	188 shares
Yeats	188 "
Wright, Udolpho	2 "
Allgood, Sara	4 "
Bourke, Edmund	2 "
Bailey, Rt. Hon. Wm. F.	2 "
Hanson, Philip	2 "
Robinson, Lennox	2 "
	390

COMPANIES CONSOLIDATED (ACT) 1908. Company Limited by Shares. ARTICLES OF ASSOCIATION of THE NATIONAL THEATRE SOCIETY, Limited.

4. The income and property of the Company, wheresoever derived, shall be applied solely towards the promotion of the objects of the Company as set forth in this Memorandum of Association, and no portion thereof shall be paid or transferred directly or indirectly, by way of dividends, bonus or otherwise, by way of profits to the members of the Company.

PROVIDED that nothing herein contained shall prevent the payment in good faith of remuneration to any officer or servant of the Company or to any member of the Company in return for any service rendered to the company or the payment to any such person or persons of royalties or fees at current rates in respect of any play or plays written by any such person or persons and performed or made use of by the Company.

5. The number of Directors shall be two, but the Directors may from time to time increase such numbers by appointing an additional Director or Directors, but so that the total number shall never exceed three. Two Directors shall form a quorum. The first Directors shall be Dame Isabella Augusta Gregory and William Butler Yeats.

7. If upon the winding-up or dissolution of the Company there remains after satisfaction of all its debts and liabilities any property whatsoever the same shall not be paid to or distributed among the members of the Company, but if and so far as effect can be given to the next provision, shall be employed in the furtherance in Ireland of Irish dramatic Art (whether the medium employed be the English or Irish language) or of some educational or artistic object to be determined by the members of the Company at or before its dissolution. . . .

10. The qualifications of a Director shall be the holding in his own right of 100 shares of the Company and the office of a Director shall be vacated:—

(a) if he becomes bankrupt

(b) if he becomes lunatic or becomes of unsound mind.

(c) if he ceases to hold at least 100 shares in the Company

(d) if he sends in his resignation in writing to the Board.

47. Every member shall have one vote for every share held by him.

55. The Books of Accounts shall be kept at the Registered Office of the Company, or such other place or places as the Directors think fit, and subject to any reasonable restrictions as to time and manner of inspecting the same that may be imposed by the Company in general Meeting shall be open to the inspection of the members during the hours of business.

60. Any notice required to be, or which may be, given by advertisement, shall be advertised once in the "Irish Times."

67. Any invitation to the public to subscribe for any shares or Debenture Stock in the Company is hereby prohibited.

SPECIAL RESOLUTIONS ALTERING THE ARTICLES OF ASSOCIATION.

(October 26, 1925)

At an Extraordinary General Meeting of the said Company duly convened and held at the Abbey Theatre, Marlborough Street, in the City of Dublin on the Twenty sixth day of October, 1925, the following special resolution was duly passed.

That the Articles of Association of the Company be altered in manner following:—

By the insertion after Article 5 of the following new Article to be numbered 5a.

5a. In the event of the Government of Saorstat Eireann giving financial assistance to the Company for the furtherance of its objects, and requiring a Director to represent them on the Board of Directors of the Company then, notwithstanding anything contained in Clause 5 hereof, the Directors may from time to time further increase the maximum number of three provided for in Clause 5, and such additional Director if expressly appointed to represent the Government with the consent in writing of the responsible Minister, shall notwithstanding Clause 10 hereof not require any qualifications.

(March 22, 1935)

At an Extraordinary General Meeting on 22nd March 1935 the following Special Resolution was duly passed.

That the Articles of Association of the Company be altered in manner following:—

202

By the insertion after Article 5a of the following new Article to be numbered 5b.

5b. Notwithstanding anything in Clause 5 the Directors may from time to time further increase the number of Directors in addition to the maximum number of four provided for in Clause 5 as amended by Clause 5a. such additional Directors not to exceed four and such additional Director or Directors shall notwithstanding Clause 10 hereof not require any qualification.

SPECIAL RESOLUTION
Passed August 18, 1939: confirmed September 8, 1939.

That the Articles of Association be altered in manner following:—
(a)   By the insertion after Article 10 of the following new Article to be numbered 10a.

10a. The Company may by extraordinary resolution remove any Director except any Director expressly appointed to represent the Government under the provisions of Clause 5a, and may (subject to the provisions of Clause 5, 5a and 5b.) by any ordinary resolution appoint another person in his stead. The person so appointed shall be subject to retirement at the same time as if he had become a Director on the day on which the Director in whose place he is appointed was last elected a Director. The Directors shall have power to fill a casual vacancy in the Directorate.

(b) By the insertion after Article 4 the following new Article to be numbered 4a.

4a. Notwithstanding anything contained in Clause 4 or Clause 5 no share in the Company shall be issued or allotted unless not less than 14 days' nor more than 21 days' notice in writing of the proposal to issue or allot such shares shall have been sent by post to each Director and unless at the meeting at which such share is issued or allotted there shall not be less than four Directors present and voting in favour of such an issue or allotment.

(c) By the insertion after Article 5b of the following new Article to be numbered 5c:—

5c. Notwithstanding anything contained in Clause 5, 5b, 8 and 10a the Directors shall not appoint any person to be a Director unless
(a) Not less than 14 days' or more than 28 days' notice of the proposal to appoint such person shall have been sent by post to each Director and unless
(b) At the meeting at which such person is appointed there shall be at least four Directors present and voting in favour of the appointment and unless
(c) Such appointment is either unanimous or is not opposed by more than one Director.

(d) By the insertion after Article 6 of the following new Article to be numbered 6a:—

6a. Notwithstanding anything contained in Clause 6 or Clause 7 any Director who has not the holding of shares in the Company specified in Clause 10 shall, if he is not a Director appointed under Clause 5a to represent the Government, cease to be a Director immediately after the conclusion of an ordinary meeting of the Company at which his appointment is not confirmed or reconfirmed by the Company, but such Director shall not be one of the Directors required to retire in rotation under the provision of Clause 6 and 7.

SPECIAL RESOLUTION
Passed January 25, 1940: confirmed February 9, 1940.

The following new Article shall be inserted after Article 55:
55a. . . . and no member shall have any right of inspecting any accounts or books or documents of the Company except as conferred by Statute or authorised by the Directors.

SPECIAL RESOLUTION
Passed September 30, 1943: confirmed October 21, 1943.

That the following Article be inserted after Article 10a:
10b. If any Director without the express consent of his colleagues absents himself from all meetings of the Board held during any period of six calendar months, and if the number of such meetings has been not less than six, he shall at the end of the said period cease to be a member of the Board.
(Two minor amendments were made in the Articles on this same occasion.)

(June 17, 1924)

DIRECTORS
Lady Gregory
W. B. Yeats
Lennox Robinson

SHAREHOLDERS
Gregory, Lady	139
Yeats, W. B.	139
Wright, Udolpho	2
Allgood, Sara	4
Bourke, Edmund	2
Executors of Wm. F. Bailey	2
Hanson, Philip	2
Robinson, Lennox	100
	390

(July 20, 1925) George O'Brien appointed Director. Resigned on January 27, 1927, and was replaced by Walter Fitzwilliam Starkie.

(May 21, 1926)

SHAREHOLDERS

Gregory, Lady	139
Yeats, W. B.	139
Wright, Udolpho	2
Allgood, Sara	4
Bourke, Edmund	(transferred to Robinson December 25, 1925

Dowdall, Annie, Exec. of Ed.
Dowdall dcd. exec. of Rt.
Hon. Wm. F. Bailey (transferred to Robinson December 25, 1925

Hanson, Philip	2
Robinson, Lennox	104
	___
	390

(September 12, 1934)

DIRECTORS
Yeats, W. B.
Robinson, Lennox
Starkie, Walter Fitzwilliam (new full director)

SHAREHOLDERS
Gough, Margaret & Kiernan, T. J.
exec. of Lady Gregory (139 shares transferred June 21, 1934)

Yeats, W. B.   159   (purchased 70 shares June 21, 1934 and transferred 50 shares June 21, 1934)

Wright, Udolpho	2
Allgood, Sara	4
Hanson, Philip	2
Robinson, Lennox	123

(purchased 69 shares June 21, 1934 and transferred 50 shares on same date)

Starkie, Walter F.   100
                            ___
                            390

(April 17, 1935)

DIRECTORS
Yeats, W. B.
Robinson, Lennox
Starkie, Walter Fitzwilliam
Hayes, Richard (appointed as Government Director February 19, 1934)

205

(May 6, 1935)

DIRECTORS
Yeats, W. B.
Robinson, Lennox
Starkie, Walter F.
Hayes, Richard
Weldon, John (pseudonym: Brinsley Macnamara). Appointed April 8, 1935
Blythe, Ernest. Appointed April 8, 1935
Higgins, F. R. Appointed April 8, 1935

(November 28, 1935)

DIRECTORS
Yeats, W. B.
Robinson, Lennox
Starkie, Walter F.
Hayes, Richard
Blythe, Ernest
Higgins, F. R.
Weldon, John (resigned)
O'Donovan, Michael (pseudonym: Frank O'Connor). Appointed October 11, 1935

(June 24, 1936)

Three hundred further shares were allotted for services rendered to the Company:

O'Donovan, Michael	100 ordinary shares
Blythe, Ernest	100 ordinary shares
Higgins, F. R.	100 ordinary shares

(August 23, 1936)

SHAREHOLDERS

Yeats, W. B.	159
Wright, Udolpho	2
Allgood, Sara	4
Hanson, Philip	2
Robinson, Lennox	123
Starkie, Walter F.	100
O'Donovan, Michael	100
Blythe, Ernest	100
Higgins, F. R.	100
	———
	690

(March 24, 1939)
To Richard Hayes was given 100 one-pound shares ordinary.

(August 23, 1939)

DIRECTORS
Robinson, Lennox
Starkie, Walter F.
Hayes, Richard
Blythe, Ernest
Higgins, F. R.
O'Donovan, Michael (resigned May 12, 1939. O'Donovan denies he
   resigned.)

SHAREHOLDERS

Wright, Udolpho	2
Allgood, Sara	4
Hanson, Philip	2
Robinson, Lennox	123
Starkie, Walter F.	100
O'Donovan, Michael	100
Blythe, Ernest	100
Higgins, F. R.	100
Hayes, Richard	100
Yeats, W. B.	159

Yeats, W. B. — * (deceased, but probate not then taken)

790

(August 23, 1940)

SHAREHOLDERS

Wright, Udolpho	2
Allgood, Sara	4
Hanson, Philip	2
Yeats, Bertha G. (exec. of W. B. Yeats)	

(159 shares transferred October 27, 1939)

Robinson, Lennox	123
Starkie, Walter F.	100
O'Donovan, Michael	100
Blythe, Ernest	100
Higgins, F. R.	100
Hayes, Richard	100
Blythe, Ernest & Starkie, Walter F.	159

790

(August 23, 1941)

SHAREHOLDERS

Wright, Udolpho	2
Allgood, Sara	4

Hanson, Philip	2
Robinson, Lennox	138
Starkie, Walter F.	136
O'Donovan, Michael	100
Blythe, Ernest	136
Hayes, Richard	136
Blythe & Starkie	(159 shares transferred September 6, 1940, to Hayes, Starkie, Higgins, Robinson, and Blythe)
O'Fearrachain, Roibeard	136
Executor of F. R. Higgins	(136 shares transferred May 22, 1941, to Blythe and Hayes)
Blythe & Hayes	(136 shares transferred May 22, 1941, to O'Fearrachain)

790

(March 10, 1942)

DIRECTORS
Robinson, Lennox
Starkie, Walter F.
Hayes, Richard
Blythe, Ernest
Higgins, F. R. (died January 8, 1941)
O'Fearrachain, Roibeard

(April 3, 1943)

DIRECTORS
Robinson, Lennox
Hayes, Richard
Blythe, Ernest
O'Fearrachain, Roibeard
Starkie, Walter F. (resigned; no date given on records)

(December 26, 1946)

DIRECTORS
Robinson, Lennox	Author
Hayes, Richard	Film Censor and Doctor
Blythe, Ernest	Journalist
O'Fearrachain, Roibeard	Talks Director, Radio Eireann

SHAREHOLDERS	OCCUPATION	SHARES HELD
Wright, Udolpho Garden House, Howth Road Dublin	Electrician	2
Allgood, Sara 28 Claude Road, Drumcondra Dublin	Actress	4
Hanson, Philip 1 Waterloo Road Dublin	Retired Civil Servant	2
Robinson, Stuart Lennox 20 Longford Terrace Monkstown, Dublin	Author	138
Starkie, Walter Fitzwilliam Botanic House, Lansdown Road Dublin	Professor	136
Blythe, Ernest 50 Kenilworth Square Dublin	Journalist	136
O'Donovan, Michael 53 Strand Road, Sandymount Dublin	Author	100
Hayes, Richard 26 Herbert Park, Ballsbridge Dublin	Medical Doctor and Film Censor	136
O'Fearrachain, Roibeard 31 Greenfield Road Mountmerrion, Blackrock Dublin	Talks Director, Radio Eireann	136
		790

Appendix C

THE GOVERNMENT SUBSIDY

SAORSTAT EIREANN
ESTIMATE FOR PUBLIC SERVICES

National Theatre Society, Limited (Grants in Aid)

1925-1926:	£850	1937-1938:	£1,000
1926-1927:	£1,000	1938-1939:	£1,000
1927-1928:	£1,000	1939-1940:	£1,000
1928-1929:	£1,000	1940-1941:	£1,000
1929-1930:	£1,000	1941-1942:	£1,500*
1930-1931:	£1,000	1942-1943:	£1,000
1931-1932:	£1,000	1943-1944:	£1,000
1932-1933:	£1,000	1944-1945:	£1,000
1933-1934:	£750	1945-1946:	£1,000
1934-1935:	£750	1946-1947:	£1,000
1935-1936:	£1,000	1947-1948:	£3,000
1936-1937:	£1,000	1948-1949:	£3,000

* The additional grant of £500 for the year 1941-1942, was for the acquisition of additional premises.

In 1937-1938 the sum of £2,800 was voted to the Abbey toward the cost of structural alterations necessitated by the bye-laws relating to public safety. The money was not spent.

The Estimate for 1948-1949 makes provision for a grant of a similar kind. It reads:

Provision to meet part of the cost of the National Theatre Society, Limited, of carrying out certain structural alterations in the Abbey Theatre necessitated by the bye-laws relating to public safety. Subject to a maximum payment of £2,800, a contribution of 80% of the cost will be made.

PUBLIC ESTIMATES

PLAYS IN IRISH (Grants in Aid)

(From the year 1925-1926 up to the year 1944-1945, An Comhar Dramiochta, the principal organization for the promotion of Gaelic drama, received an annual grant of £600. In 1944-1945 the grant was raised to £1,000; in 1946-1947 to £2,000; in 1947-1948 to £3,000, and in 1948-1949 to £2,500. Up to the year 1938-1939 the Estimates do not show where exactly the grant goes, but give the sum total of all the grants toward the promotion of Gaelic drama.)

GRANTS IN AID OF PLAYS IN IRISH:

1925-1926:	£600	1933-1934:	£1,200 [£10] *
1927-1928:	£3,000	1934-1935:	£1,200
1928-1929:	£1,200	1935-1936:	£1,400 [£55/17/8]
1929-1930:	£1,000	1936-1937:	£2,000
1930-1931:	£1,000	1937-1938:	£1,800 [£9]
1931-1932:	£1,200	1938-1939:	£2,025 [£16]
1932-1933:	£1,200	1939-1940:	£2,040 [£100/10/0]

THE PARTICULAR SOCIETIES WHICH BENEFITED BY THE GOVERNMENT GRANT FOR PLAYS IN IRISH FOR THE YEARS 1938-1939 TO 1948-1949:

	1938-1939	1939-1940	1940-1941	1941-1942
Taidhbhearc na Gaillimhe (The Galway Gaelic Theatre)	£1,000	£1,000	£1,000	£1,000
An Comhar Dramiochta (The Gaelic Drama Society)	£600	£600	£600	£600
Cumann Dramíocht na Sgol (The Schools Drama Society)	£325	£240	£320	£337
Drama sa Ghaedhealtacht (Drama in districts exclusively Gaelic)	£100	£100	£100	£100
	£2,025	£1,940	£2,020	£2,037

* [The figures in brackets represent the amount of the grant not spent. Where no such figures are given, the indication seems to be that all the grant was used.]

211

	1942-1943	1943-1944	1944-1945	1945-1946
Taidhbhearc na Gaillimhe	£1,000	£1,000	£1,000	£1,000
An Comhar Dramiochta	£600	£600	£1,000	£1,000
Cumann Dramíocht na Sgol	£118	£106	£61	£81
Drama sa Ghaedhealtacht	£100	£100	£50	£75
Cumann eile				£300
(Other societies)				
	£1,818	£1,806	£2,111	£2,456

	1946-1947	1947-1948	1948-1949
Taidhbhearc na Gaillimhe	£1,000	£1,000	£1,000
An Comhar Dramiochta	£2,000	£3,000	£2,500
Cumann Dramíocht na Sgol	£315	£370	£100
Drama sa Ghaedhealtacht	£75	£75	£75
Compantas Amharclainne na Gaedhailge		£800	£800
(The Gaelic Theatre Company)			
Ilgneitheacha			£200
(Other societies)			
	£3,390	£5,245	£4,675

Appendix D

WARRANT FOR LETTERS PATENT for a new Theatre in the City of Dublin

(Signed) Edward R & I.

Right Trusty and Well-Beloved Cousin and Councillor we greet you well!

Our Will and Pleasure is that you forthwith cause effectual Letters to be passed under the Great Seal of that part of Our United Kingdom of Great Britain and Ireland in the form and to the effect following.

EDWARD THE SEVENTH, by the Grace of God, of the United Kingdom of Great Britain and Ireland and of the British Dominions beyond the Seas KING, Defender of the Faith, to all to whom these Presents shall come

213

GREETING!

WHEREAS by a certain Act of Parliament of Ireland passed in the Twenty-sixth year of the reign of His late Majesty King George III entitled: "An Act for regulating the stage in the City and County of Dublin" it is among other things enacted that it should and might be lawful to and for his Majesty His Heirs and Successors to grant under the Great Seal of Ireland for such term not exceeding Twenty-one years and under such restrictions, conditions and limitations as to him or them should seem meet from time to time and when and so often as he or they should think fit one or more Letters Patent to one or more persons for establishing or keeping one or more well-regulated Theatre or Theatres, Play-house or Play-houses in the City of Dublin and in the liberties, suburbs and County thereof and in the County of Dublin.

AND WHEREAS Annie Elizabeth Fredericka Horniman of H-1, Montague Mansions, Portman Square, in the County of London, Spinster, by her Memorial represented unto you Our Lieutenant General and General Governor of that part of Our United Kingdom of Great Britain and Ireland called Ireland.

That by the Act of Parliament passed in the Twenty-sixth year of His late Majesty King George III, Chapter 57, entitled "An Act for regulating the stage in the City and County of Dublin" it was amongst other things enacted that it should be lawful for His said Majesty and His Successors to grant under the Great Seal of that part of the United Kingdom called Ireland for any term not exceeding Twenty-one years as therein mentioned from time to time Letters Patent for establishing one or more Theatre or Theatres, Play-house or Play-houses in the City of Dublin and in the suburbs and County thereof and in the County of Dublin.

That Memorialist was an English woman residing in London but being a patron of good dramatic art was very anxious to assist the Society known as the Irish National Theatre Society registered under the Friendly Societies Act, 1896. That the Society was formed to continue on a more permanent basis the work begun by the Irish Literary Theatre. Its objects were to endeavour to create an Irish National Theatre by producing plays written in Irish or English by Irish writers or on Irish subjects or such dramatic works of foreign authors as would tend to educate and interest the Irish public in the higher aspects of dramatic art. That it was not a Society having profit as its basis but the encouragement of dramatic art in Ireland. That the Society had already produced several plays both in Dublin and in London and had from all quarters met with great praise and encouragement. Memorialist referred to certain extracts from newspapers showing the opinions of some of the leading critics in England. That many of these critics had pointed out that Ireland had evidenced by the plays the beginnings of a distinct dramatic school growing out of the life of the Country and inspired by a high intellectual idea. That however successful this school of writers might

214

become it was not likely that the performance would ever attain so great a degree of popularity as to become a serious rival to the existing theatres. That such movements no matter how deeply they might affect the more thinking people could never under modern conditions reach a popularity which would make them of commercial importance:

That Memorialist recognised the fact that the Irish National Theatre laboured under the great disadvantage of not having any suitable premises in which to produce its plays:

That Memorialist being possessed of some means and very anxious to encourage the Irish National Theatre had agreed to take a lease for ninety-nine years from the First day of May one thousand nine hundred and four of the Theatre belonging to the Dublin Mechanics Institute, Lower Abbey Street, in the City of Dublin, and a lease for a similar term of adjoining premises in Marlborough Street now known as the old Morgue so as to afford better access to the Theatre and the necessary accommodation for dressing rooms, etc.:

That the Theatre of the Mechanics Institute was firstly known as the Theatre Royal (there being in Dublin another theatre of the same name) and subsequently as the Princess Theatre and had attached to it a Patent for theatrical representations:

That this Patent appeared to have expired about the year 1850 and never to have been renewed:

That the object of Memorialist in taking the premises was solely to benefit the Irish National Theatre. That her intention was to allow this theatre to have the use of the premises free of charge whenever required: at other times that Memorialist would desire to let the premises for concerts, lectures, amateur performances and such dramatic performances as those of the Elizabethan Stage Society. That she would, however, seek a general Patent:

That Memorialist did not contemplate letting to ordinary travelling companies. For this reason and as the premises would only seat some six hundred people Memorialist submitted that the premises of which she had agreed to take a lease could never rival those of the existing Theatres:

And Memorialist prayed that a Patent under the Great Seal of Ireland under the provisions of the said Act of the 26th. George III, Chapter 57, entitled "An Act for regulating the stage in the City and County of Dublin" might be granted to Memorialist for a term of twenty-one years to enable Memorialist to establish and keep a well-regulated Theatre within the said City of Dublin and County of Dublin and therein at all lawful times publicly to act represent or perform or cause to be acted represented or performed all Interludes, Tragedies, Comedies, Preludes, Operas, Burlettas, Plays, Farces, Panto-mimes or any part or parts thereof and of what kind or nature whatsoever:

And whereas Our Lord Justices General and General Governors of that part of Our said United Kingdom of Great Britain and Ireland called Ireland aforesaid in the absence of our said Lieutenant General and General Governor of Ireland did on the eleventh day of July

One thousand nine hundred and four, refer the said Memorial to Our Attorney-General and Solicitor-General for Ireland to consider thereof and to report unto Us what might be proper to be done thereon:

And Whereas Our said Attorney-General and Solicitor General duly considered the said Memorial and heard the statements of Counsel on the part of the said Memorialist and Counsel on behalf of patentees of the Theatre Royal, Dublin, the Gaiety Theatre, Dublin and the Queen's Theatre, Dublin, and what was offered on behalf of the said theatres and having received the consent of the said Annie Elizabeth Fredericka Horniman that any Patent that might be granted should be granted to Dame Isabella Augusta Gregory, of Coole Park, Gort, in the County of Galway, widow of the late Right Honourable Sir William Henry Gregory, K.C.M.G., as trustee for the said Annie Elizabeth Fredericka Horniman her executors, or administrators were of the opinion that We might if We should be pleased so to do, grant Letters Patent under the Great Seal of Ireland unto the said Dame Isabella Augusta Gregory for establishing and keeping a well-regulated Theatre or Play-house at the premises in Lower Abbey Street and Marlborough Street in the City of Dublin which were formerly known as the Dublin Mechanics Institute and the Morgue respectively for the term of six years under such conditions, restrictions and limitations as are herein set forth and We are graciously pleased to condescend thereto:

KNOW YE THEREFORE that We of Our special grace, certain knowledge and mere motion by and with the advice and consent of Our Right Trusty and Right Well-beloved Cousin and Councillor, William Humbel Dudley, Knight Grand Cross of Our Royal Victorian Order, Our Lieutenant General and General Governor of that part of Our said United Kingdom of Great Britain and Ireland called Ireland, DO HEREBY grant unto the said Dame Isabella Augusta Gregory, her executors, administrators and such assigns as are hereinafter mentioned in trust for the said Annie Elizabeth Fredericka Horniman her executors or administrators, under the restrictions, conditions and limitations hereinafter mentioned, full power and authority to establish and keep in the building formerly known as the Dublin Mechanics Institute and the Morgue in the City of Dublin and indicated in the plans deposited in Our Privy Seal Office in Our Castle of Dublin a well-regulated Theatre or Play-house and therein at all lawful times (except when We or Our Chief Governor or Governors of that part of Our said United Kingdom of Great Britain and Ireland for the time being shall see cause to forbid the acting or performance of any species of plays or theatrical amusements) publicly to act represent or perform or cause to be acted represented or performed all Interludes, Tragedies, Comedies, Plays in the Irish or English language written by Irish writers or on Irish subjects and such dramatic works of foreign authors as would tend to educate and interest the Irish public in the higher works of dramatic art and as may be selected by the Irish National Theatre Society under the provisions contained in

216

part six of the Rules of the Irish National Theatre Society that is to say:—

(a) The Reading Committee shall be selected at the annual General Meeting of the Society. The members shall be eligible for re-election on the expiry of their term of Office.

(b) The Reading Committee shall be six in number and they shall first consider all plays proposed for performance by the Society. No play shall be performed until it has been recommended by the Reading Committee. The final acceptance or rejection of any play thus recommended shall rest with the members of the Society to whom such plays shall be read at meetings summoned for the purpose when a three-quarters majority of those present shall decide. The author shall not be allowed to be present when a vote is taken.

(c) No official of the Society shall have power to accept a play on behalf of the Society or to reject one which shall have been accepted and passed in accordance with the foregoing rules.

(d) No play shall be accepted or rejected on political grounds solely and the literary dramatic and acting merits of the play shall primarily be considered and no objections raised to a play on the grounds that its performance would antagonise any political party shall be valid unless that it should be considered that there is any degradation of National ideals in the work submitted PROVIDED that all such Interludes, tragedies, comedies and plays shall be decent and becoming and not profane or obnoxious TO HAVE AND TO HOLD THE PREMISES unto the said Dame Isabella Augusta Gregory her executors administrators and such assigns as are hereinafter mentioned in trust for the said Annie Elizabeth Fredericka Horniman her executors or administrators and for them to act represent and perform all such hereinbefore mentioned interludes, tragedies, comedies, plays or any part or parts thereof of the said nature or kind decent and becoming and not profane or obnoxious for and during the term time and space of six years from the first day of December one thousand nine hundred and four fully to be completed and ended:

AND WE DO HEREBY for Us Our Heirs and Successors strictly prohibit and forbid all persons whatsoever for and during the term time and space hereinbefore limited from presuming to erect build or keep open in any manner whatsoever or howsoever any theatre or theatres, stage or stages whatsoever within Our said City of Dublin or County of Dublin or therein to act represent or perform any interlude, tragedy or comedy, prelude, opera, burletta, play, farce, pantomime or other exhibition such as shall be authorised by these Our Letters Patent or any part or parts thereof unless they have been or shall be thereunto duly authorised and appointed by Us Our Heirs and Successors grant unto the said Dame Isabella Augusta Gregory her executors and administrators and such assigns as are hereinafter mentioned full power and license and authority from time to time to gather, entertain, govern, privilege and keep such and so many players and persons to exercise and act represent and perform all such interludes, tragedies, comedies and plays as aforesaid or any part or parts thereof as the said Dame Isabella Augusta Gregory her executors administrators or such assigns as are hereinafter mentioned shall think fit and requisite for that purpose which said Company shall be servants of Us Our Heirs and Successors and shall consist of such number of players and persons as the said Dame Isabella Augusta Gregory her executors administrators and such assigns as are hereinafter mentioned shall from time to time think fit and such persons to continue during the pleasure of the said Dame Isabella Augusta Gregory her executors and administrators and such assigns as are hereinafter mentioned for the performance of the entertainments stated therein peaceably and quietly without any impediment or interruption of any person or persons whomsoever for the honest recreation of all such as shall desire to see the same. AND it shall and may be lawful to and for the said Dame Isabella Augusta Gregory her executors and administrators and such assigns as are hereinafter mentioned to take and receive of such persons as shall resort to hear or see any such plays and entertainment of the stage as aforesaid such sum or sums of money as have customarily been taken in the like kind or shall be thought reasonable by the said Dame Isabella Augusta Gregory her executors administrators and such assigns as are hereinafter mentioned in regard to the great expense in the erection of the said theatre and for scenes, music, decorations and other requisites:

AND FURTHER FOR US Our Heirs and Successors we do give and grant unto the said Dame Isabella Augusta Gregory her executors administrators and such assigns as are hereinafter mentioned full power from time to time and at all times for and during the term time and space hereinbefore mentioned to make such allowances out of the moneys which they shall so receive by such performances and entertainments as aforesaid to the performers and other persons employed in acting or representing or in any quality whatsoever about the said Theatre or so as they shall think fit.

AND WE ALSO empower and appoint the said Dame Isabella Augusta Gregory that she her executors administrators and such assigns as are hereinafter mentioned do and shall from time to time and at all times eject out of the said Company all scandalous disorderly or other persons as they shall think meet and that all and every person so by them ejected and discharged shall be disabled from playing or acting with the said Company in the said Theatre and shall from the time of such their ejectment or discharge stop and altogether cease from receiving any part proportion or salary out of the profits of the representations in the said Theatre or from the said Dame Isabella Augusta Gregory her executors administrators and such assigns as are hereinafter mentioned and for the better obtaining Our Royal purpose in this behalf We have thought fit hereby to declare that henceforth no representations shall be admitted on the stage by virtue or under cover of these Presents whereby the Christian Religion may in any manner suffer reproach. And we hereby strictly prohibit all and any degree of abuse or misrepresentation of Sacred characters which may in any degree tend to expose Religion or bring it into contempt and that no such characters be introduced or played in any other light than such as may increase the just esteem of those who answer the end of those sacred functions. And we further enjoin the strictest regard to such representations as anywise concern the civil policy or the Constitution of Our Government that these may contribute to support Our Sacred Authority and to the preservation of order and good Government. And it being Our Royal Will and pleasure that for the future the said Theatre may be instrumental in the promotion of virtue and instruction of human life WE DO HEREBY enjoin and command that no entertainment or exhibition whatsoever be acted or produced under the authority hereby granted which does or may contain any expression or passage or gesture offensive to piety or good manners until the same shall be corrected or purged by the Manager or Managers for the time being by expunging all such offensive expressions, passages and gestures. AND if the said Dame Isabella Augusta Gregory her executors administrators and such assigns as are hereinafter mentioned shall permit to be brought forward any representations at such theatre hereby authorized which shall be deemed or construed to be immoral and shall not forthwith discontinue and cease representing playing or acting the same on receiving notice for or in the name and by the authority of Our Lieutenant General and General Governor or other Chief Governor or Governors of that part of Our United Kingdom of Great Britain and Ireland called Ireland for the time being by any person or persons lawfully authorised by him or them in such cases these Presents and every grant privilege and immunity hereby given or granted shall become null and void to all intents and purposes whatsoever: PROVIDED ALWAYS that the said Dame Isabella Augusta Gregory her executors or administrators shall not assign or transfer her rights under these Presents to any person or persons residing in Ireland who shall be nominated in writing by the said Annie Elizabeth Fredericka Horniman her executors or administrators as Trustee or Trustees for her or them, and in the event of any breach or attempted breach of this provision or in the event of the said Irish National Theatre Society being dissolved during the term of these Presents then on the happening of these events these Presents and every grant privilege and immunity hereby given or granted shall become null and void to all intents and purposes whatsoever: PROVIDED ALWAYS and We do hereby declare and command that these Presents shall be and remain upon the conditions that if at any time during the said term hereby granted it shall be made to appear to Our Lieutenant General and General Governor of that part of Our said United Kingdom of Great Britain and Ireland called Ireland or other Our Chief Governor or Governors thereof that the said Theatre is not duly ventilated or kept in due or proper repair and in accordance with the said plans or that fit and proper commodious means of ingress and egress are not maintained and provided for those who frequent the same or that owing to the character of the performance carried on therein or the class or conduct of the audience or persons frequenting the said theatre or from any other cause whatsoever the said theatre shall not be or shall cease to be an orderly well conducted and respectable place of public entertainment then and in such case upon signification in that behalf made by Us under the hand of one of Our Principal Secretaries of State or made by Our Lieutenant General and General Governor of that part of Our said United Kingdom of Great Britain and Ireland called Ireland or Our Chief Governor or Governors thereof for the time being under his or their hand or hands or hand of the Chief Secretary for Ireland and which signification shall be published in the Dublin Gazette these Presents shall forthwith cease and determine and be utterly void to all intents and purposes anything herein contained to the contrary whereof in anywise notwithstanding AND WE DO FURTHER HEREBY declare command that these Our Letters Patent are upon the further condition that the said theatre shall be constructed, maintained and conducted subject to and in accordance with the rules and regulations following that is to say:—

(1) The said Theatre shall not be enlarged so as to be capable of accommodating more persons than the number which the said theatre can accommodate at the date of these Presents and which amounts to five hundred and sixty two persons.

(2) All doors and barriers to open outwards or to be fixed back during the time when the public are within the Theatre.

(3) All gangways passages and staircases intended to be used for the exit of the audience to be kept entirely free from chairs or any other obstruction whether permanent or temporary.

(4) All chairs or seats intended for the use of persons listening to the representations or performances in the said Theatre to be fixed and immovable.

(5) An ample water supply with hose and pipes to be available to all parts of the house where possible on the high pressure main.

(6) All fixed and ordinary gas burners to be furnished with efficient guards moveable and occasional lights to be where possible protected in the same manner or put under charge of persons responsible for lighting watching and extinguishing them, a separate and independent supply of light for the stage and auditorium no white metal gas pipes to be used in the building.

(7) The foot-lights or floats to be protected by a wire guard, the first ground line to be always without and unconnected with gas whether at the wings or elsewhere sufficient space to be left between each ground line so as to lessen risk from accident to all persons standing or moving amongst such lines.

(8) The rows of lines or gas burners at wings to commence four feet at least from level of the stage wet blankets or rugs with filled buckets or water pots to be always kept in the wings and attention directed to them by placards legibly printed or painted and fixed near

220

them, some person to be responsible for keeping the blankets buckets and so forth ready for immediate use.

(9) A fire proof curtain to be always in use in the said Theatre and to be lowered at least once during every performance to test its efficiency and condition.

(10) Hatchets hacks or other means to cut down scenery in case of fire to be always in readiness. The regulations as to fire to be always posted in some conspicuous place so that all persons belonging to the theatre may be acquainted with their contents.

(11) Counter weights where possible to be carried to the walls of the building and cased in and the ropes attached to them to be constantly tested. No structural alterations to be made in the Theatre without the sanction of the Commissioner of Public Works in Ireland or such person as Our Lieutenant General and General Governor of that part of Our United Kingdom of Great Britain and Ireland called Ireland or other Chief Governor or Governors thereof for the time being may afterwards appoint for that purpose, plans for such alterations to be sent to the Privy Seal Office Dublin Castle.

(12) Admission to be given at all times to authorized Officers of the Police.

(13) Permission to the Gallery in the interior of the Theatre to be given to so many persons as there shall be seating accommodation for.

(14) No profanity or impropriety of language to be permitted on the stage.

(15) No indecency of dress or gesture to be permitted on the stage.

(16) No offensive personalities or representation of living persons to be permitted on the stage nor anything calculated to produce riot or breach of the peace.

(17) No exhibitions of wild beasts or dangerous performances to be permitted on the stage, no women or children to be hung from the flies nor fixed in positions from which they cannot release themselves.

(18) No public masquerade to be permitted in the Theatre.

(19) No encouragement to be given to improper characters to assemble or apply their calling in the Theatre.

(20) No wines, spirits or beer or any other intoxicating or spirituous liquor to be sold in the Theatre or in any part of the Theatre premises.

(21) All refreshments to be sold in the Theatre to be sold only in such positions as do not interfere with the convenience and safety of the audience.

(22) All suitable and proper dressing rooms and accommodation to be provided for male and female performers in the said theatre premises.

(23) No smoking to be permitted in the Auditorium and if at any time there shall be a breach or breaches of any of the said rules and regulations or of any rules or regulations to be substituted therefor as hereinafter provided then and in such case upon signification in that behalf made by Us under the hand of one of Our Principal Secretaries of State or made by Our Lieutenant General and General

Governor of that part of Our United Kingdom of Great Britain and Ireland called Ireland or other Chief Governor or Governors thereof for the time being under his or their hand or hands or hand of the Chief Secretary for Ireland and which signification shall be published in the Dublin Gazette these Presents shall forthwith cease determine and be utterly void to all intents and purposes anything hereinbefore contained to the contrary thereof in anything notwithstanding.

PROVIDED ALWAYS that if the said Dame Isabella Augusta Gregory her executors administrators or such assigns as are hereinbefore mentioned shall at any time apply to Our Lord Lieutenant or other Chief Governor or Governors of Ireland to alter or modify any of the rules or regulations numbered 1 to 23 above and such alteration or modification shall be permitted then and in such case the said rules and regulations shall be deemed to be altered and modified accordingly: And further Our Will and Pleasure is AND WE DO HEREBY DECLARE that these Our Letters Patent or the enrollment or exemplification thereof shall be in all things good sufficient valid and effectual in the law according to the true intent and meaning of the same unto them the said Dame Isabella Augusta Gregory her executors administrators or such assigns as are hereinbefore mentioned and shall be taken construed and adjudged in the most favourable and beneficial sense for the best advantage of the said Dame Isabella Augusta Gregory her executors administrators or such assigns as aforesaid as well within all Our Courts of Record within that part of Our said United Kingdom of Great Britain and Ireland called Ireland or elsewhere as amongst all and singular the subjects of Us Our Heirs and Successors whatsoever and wheresoever:

PROVIDED ALWAYS that these Our Letters Patent be enrolled in the Record and Writ Office of Our High Court of Justice, Chancery Division, in that part of Our said United Kingdom of Great Britain and Ireland called Ireland within the space of six months next ensuing the date of these Presents:

AND We do hereby direct and require that you cause to be inserted in the said Letters Patent all such other powers and clauses as are usual in like cases or necessary or proper for rendering the same firm valid and effectual as Patents or Grants of the like nature:

And for so doing this shall be as well unto you as to all other Our Officers and Ministers a sufficient Warrant.

And so We bid you heartily farewell!

Given at Our Court at Saint James's
the twenty-second day of December 1904;
in the Fourth year of Our Reign.

By His Majesty's Command

[Signed] Lansdowne.

222

Notes

Notes

THE IRISH LITERARY THEATRE

[1] *Our Irish Theatre,* Lady Gregory, pp. 8, 9.
[2] *Dramatis Personae,* p. 35.
[3] *Our Irish Theatre,* pp. 21, 22.
[4] *Ideals in Ireland,* edited by Lady Gregory, 1901, p. 87.
[5] Holloway's *Diary,* Feb. 22, 1900.
[6] Feb. 24, 1900.
[7] *Dramatis Personae,* p. 69.
[8] *Ideals in Ireland,* pp. 45, 46.
[9] Nov. 2, 1901.
[10] Nov. 13, 1901.

IDEALS

[1] *Samhain,* 1901.

[2] *Two Essays*, Dublin, 1901.
[3] *The Cutting of an Agate*, 1912, p. 64.
[4] *Ibid.*, p. 135.
[5] *Idem.*
[6] 1903.
[7] *Collected Works*, Yeats, London, 1908, iv, pp. 121, 122.
[8] *Ibid.*
[9] *Dramatis Personae*, p. 196.
[10] *Samhain*, 1904.
[11] *Samhain*, 1902.
[12] *The Cutting of an Agate*, p. 29.
[13] *Samhain*, 1903.

THE IRISH NATIONAL THEATRE SOCIETY

[1] Nov. 9, 1901.
[2] *Diary*, April 3, 1902.
[3] *Letters of AE to W. B. Yeats*, 1936, pp. 29, 30.
[4] April 12, 1902.
[5] *Letters of AE to W. B. Yeats*, p. 30.
[6] *Salve*, George Moore, p. 138.
[7] *Letters of AE to W. B. Yeats*, pp. 42, 43.
[8] *My Diaries*, Wilfrid Scawen Blunt, 1919-1920, ii, p. 53.
[9] *Diary*, Aug. 22, 1903.
[10] *Diary*, Oct. 8, 1903.
[11] *United Irishman*, Oct. 17, 1903.
[12] Oct. 24, 1903.
[13] P. 202.
[14] *Diary*, Mar. 2, 1904.
[15] *Letters of AE to W. B. Yeats*, pp. 47, 48.
[16] *Ibid.*, pp. 49, 50.

THE ABBEY THEATRE

[1] *Diary*, April 11, 1904.
[2] For an account of the court proceedings see *The Freeman's Journal*, Aug. 5 and 9, 1904.
[3] "Lady Gregory . . . insisted . . . that I should sign a deed indemnifying her up to £200 if thereby she incurred any pecuniary loss." Letter from Miss Horniman to *John O'London's Weekly*, Aug. 20, 1932.
[4] *Dana*, Dec. 1904, p. 256.
[5] *Diary*, Dec. 16, 1904.
[6] *Our Irish Theatre*, Lady Gregory, p. 44.
[7] *United Irishman*, Feb. 11, 1905.
[8] *The Leader*, Mar. 5, 1904.
[9] *Ibid.*, Jan. 7 and Feb. 11, 1905.
[10] *Vale*, Moore, p. 203.
[11] *Diary*, Feb. 15, 1907.

[12] *W. B. Yeats*, Joseph Hone, 1943, p. 221.
[13] *Diary*, Nov. 10, 1905.

FIGHTING THE AUDIENCE

[1] Jan. 7, 1905.
[2] *The Report of the Registrar of Friendly Societies for the Year Ending December 31st, 1906*, Part A, Appendix O, p. 208. The File of the Irish National Theatre Society, Limited, stating its profits and losses from 1905 to 1911, was handed over by the Irish Department of Industry and Commerce in 1941 to the Clondalkin Paper Mills to be pulped and later possibly made into sweepstakes tickets.
[3] *The Fays of the Abbey Theatre*, W. G. Fay and Catherine Carswell, p. 211.
[4] *Vale*, p. 205.
[5] *Diary*, Feb. 1, 1907.
[6] *The Irish Independent*, Feb. 5, 1907.
[7] *Diary*, Feb. 1, 1907.
[8] *Ibid.*, 1907, p. 704.
[9] *Idem.*
[10] *Ibid.*, Feb. 15, 1907.

CHASTISING THE ACTOR

[1] *W. B. Yeats*, Hone, p. 226.
[2] *My Diaries*, ii, p. 172.
[3] *Diary*, Oct. 3, 1907.
[4] P. 333.
[5] *W. B. Yeats*, Hone, p. 234.
[6] *Idem.*
[7] *Vale*, p. 208.

TOWARD FREEDOM

[1] *Diary*, Feb. 13, 1908.
[2] *The Irish Independent*, Feb. 15, 1908.
[3] *Diary*, Feb. 28, 1908.
[4] *Dramatis Personae*, p. 142.
[5] *Diary*, 1909, p. 363.
[6] *Dramatis Personae*, pp. 109, 110.
[7] *Our Irish Theatre*, Lady Gregory, pp. 277, 278.
[8] *Ibid.*, p. 152.
[9] *Diary*, Aug. 28, 1909.
[10] *Vale*, p. 218.
[11] *Diaries*, Blunt, ii, p. 310.
[12] *W. B. Yeats*, Hone, p. 254.
[13] File No. 3660 in the Office of the Registry of Companies and Business Names in Dublin Castle.

A POETIC THEATRE

[1] *Diary*, Jan, 13, 1911.
[2] *Ibid.*
[3] *W. B. Yeats*, Hone, p. 274.
[4] *Diaries*, Blunt, ii, p. 351.
[5] *Irish Times*, Nov. 24, 1911.

TOURING AMERICA

[1] *Diary*, Oct. 24, 1912.
[2] *Ibid.*, April 26, 1914.
[3] Feb. 1913.
[4] *The Irish Review*, Feb. 1913.
[5] *Ibid.*, April 1914.

INTERMISSION

[1] Nov. 29 and Dec. 6, 1919.

THE ABBEY DURING THE CIVIL WAR

[1] *Diary*, July 21, 1935.

SEAN O'CASEY

[1] *Lady Gregory's Journals*, edited by Lennox Robinson, p. 99.
[2] Thursday, Feb. 11, 1926.
[3] Feb. 15, 1926.

AMERICAN SOJOURN

[1] Jan. 27, 1933.
[2] Jan. 31, 1933.
[3] May 9, 1934.
[4] *New York Times*, Aug. 14, 1934.

NEW DIRECTORS

[1] *The Irish Independent*, Aug. 28, 1935.
[2] His real name is Michael O'Donovan.
[3] *The Irish Times*, Aug. 13.
[4] *Ibid.*, Aug. 15.
[5] *Ibid.*, Aug. 16.

228

Index

Index

231

232

234

236

238

240

241